THE GENEALOGICAL IMAGINATION

THE GENEALOGICAL IMAGINATION

TWO STUDIES OF LIFE OVER TIME

Michael Jackson

DUKE UNIVERSITY PRESS · DURHAM AND LONDON · 2021

Designed by Matthew Tauch

Typeset in Arno Pro by Westchester Publishing Services

Library of Congress Cataloging-in-Publication Data

Names: Jackson, Michael, [date] author.

Title: The genealogical imagination : two studies of life over time / Michael Jackson.

Description: Durham : Duke University Press, 2021. | Includes index.

Identifiers: LCCN 2020030898 (print)

LCCN 2020030899 (ebook)

ISBN 9781478011934 (hardcover)

ISBN 9781478014072 (paperback)

ISBN 9781478021384 (ebook)

Subjects: LCSH: Jackson, Michael, 1940—Travel—Sierra Leone. | Anthropology—Sierra Leone. | Ethnology—Sierra Leone. | Kuranko (African people)—Social life and customs. | Philosophical anthropology.

Classification: LCC GN655.S5 J335 2021 (print) | LCC GN655.S5 (ebook) | DDC 306.09664—dc23

LC record available at https://lccn.loc.gov/2020030898

LC ebook record available at https://lccn.loc.gov/2020030899

Cover art: Nature Picture Library / Alamy Stock Photo.

My personal existence must be the resumption of a prepersonal tradition. There is, therefore, another subject beneath me, for whom a world exists before I am here, and who marks out my place in it.

MAURICE MERLEAU-PONTY, *Phenomenology of Perception*

If something comes down in time . . . it comes down from one person to another. There are lots of metaphors for it—ancestry, genealogy, or whatever—it doesn't make any difference. Something does descend from generation to generation. In time.

JAMES BALDWIN, *A Rap on Race* (in conversation with Margaret Mead)

Contents

FATHERS AND SONS

PREAMBLE

This book is an exploration of genealogy as a relational model or metaphor for understanding our experience of being-in-time. This existential perspective departs from the traditional anthropological view of genealogy as a framework for social organization and a moral charter for social life more typical of tribal than of modern societies. When W. H. R. Rivers published his seminal essay on the genealogical method in 1910, his focus on "systems" of thought, succession, and inheritance led him to claim that a "great difference" lay "between the systems of relationship of savage and civilized peoples."[1] Emphasizing different modes of reckoning descent (cognatic, agnatic, or uterine), Rivers inadvertently perpetuated the popular prejudices of his day, as well as a culturalogical bias toward inferring experience from ideology rather than quotidian contexts of action and interaction. By contrast, I hope to show that underlying different cultural idioms for conceptualizing human relationships there exist universal experiences of birth, begetting, and belonging, and that, contrary to the ideal order suggested by genealogical charts, lived relationships involve oedipal and sibling rivalries, psychological complexes, knots, and double binds. I argue, moreover, that relations with ancestors always implicate, to some degree, relations with the natural environment, history, the gods, and material objects, and, like kinship, these relationships are vexed and subject to continual negotiation. While I am mindful of the deep differences between what we call tradition and modernity, my chronicles of a Kuranko family over a period of almost 150 years suggests that individual preoccupations with personal well-being, wealth, and mobility never completely occlude kinship relations and the gravitational pull of the past. Individual lives are always embedded in sociohistorical contexts, and while biographies are never completely reducible to histories, the intelligibility of both oral and written history derives from their likeness to life stories.

My interest in intersubjectivity over time and space inevitably implicates my own relationships with the people I write about. Phenomenologically, one imagines "the situation of the other from the inside out" and, reciprocally, reimagines one's own life from the standpoint of another, as described by Pablo Neruda in his *Memoirs*, when he confesses, "Perhaps I didn't live just in myself, perhaps I lived the lives of others. . . . My life is a life put together from all those lives."[2]

Here, however, we encounter the phenomenological impasse of how it is possible to know what's going on in another person's mind. During my initial fieldwork in Sierra Leone, my Kuranko interlocutors would repeatedly caution me against second guessing what others were thinking or feeling. "Morgo te do ka ban" (A person can never be fully understood), I would be told. "N'de ma konto lon" (I don't know the inside story). "N'de sa bu'ro" (I don't know what's in the belly). It wasn't that Kuranko did not have complex inner lives; rather, making one's idiosyncratic experiences public risked compromising the appearance of consensus and unanimity on which communitas depends. Thus, Kuranko insisted that what really mattered was a person's behavior: whether he did his duty, performed her role, was a good friend, neighbor, parent, or chief. This emphasis on exteriority runs counter to the European bourgeois focus on fathoming a person's deep subjectivity or plumbing the depths of the unconscious. How, therefore, could I at once respect this objectivist bias in Kuranko thought and satisfy my own desire, reinforced by a literary sensibility and an interest in psychoanalysis, to write about people's inner experiences? How could I do justice to intrapsychic as well as intersubjective life? My dilemma was compounded by the discursive split between the social sciences, which tend to infer subjective reality from external behavior or collective representations, and literature, where the focus is on interior motivations, compulsions, complexes, and drives. If Kuranko were correct, and it was impossible to accurately read the minds of others, then anything I wrote about their subjectivity or, reflexively, about my own experiences in the field would be conjectural and unverifiable. Since I did not want to reduce the human condition to either exteriority or interiority, would it be possible to reconcile these opposing perspectives by invoking Heisenberg's uncertainty principle? Although one must accept that the world will appear differently to us depending on the theoretical lens through which we see it, we are not obliged to make a choice between one perspective or the other. Rather, it behooves us to recognize both perspectives for the different insights they yield, though it is important to deploy them successively (juxtaposing them) rather than simultaneously (conflating them). When I wrote my "ethnographic novel," *Barawa*, almost forty years ago, I made the mistake of mixing the factual with the fictional.[3] *The Genealogical Imagination* avoids this category error by drawing a line between "Chronicles of the Barawa Marah," which is an ethnographic documentary, and "Fathers and Sons," which is largely a work of the imagination. The latter therefore bears comparison with Robert Desjarlais's *The Blind Man*, which he describes as a phantasmography.[4]

This, then, is my rationale for juxtaposing ethnography and phantasmography in a single book. By writing in an ethnographic vein, I satisfy the "reality hunger" that drew me to social science, while exploring the deep intersubjectivity that characterizes both phenomenology and literature.[5] But beyond my ambition to overcome the traditional dissociation of science and art, I hope to show the value of seeing the world from different points of view, using different methodologies and different styles of writing. Rethinking genre and disciplinary categories, or seeing the world through the eyes of others, real or invented, may prove more edifying than persisting in the view that there is only one measure for deciding whether we have spoken truth to reality.

Considering my itinerant life, it is not surprising that I have transgressed disciplinary as well as geographical boundaries and that my writing has intermittently switched among ethnography, poetry, fiction, and memoir. Although this shape-shifting has often drawn the criticism that a jack-of-all-trades is the master of none and that such literary promiscuity risks blurring the line between art and science, I continue to believe that a human life is never a seamless whole or reducible to a single story. We lead many lives in the course of one, and there is no necessary connection between the stories we tell ourselves and the stories we create with others. That we sometimes claim to possess singular identities or pay lip service to conventional genre distinctions is not because they mirror reality but because we would find it difficult to relate to one another without them. Accordingly, a recurring problem for any writer is how to articulate personal thoughts and feelings without abandoning the social and discursive frameworks that would make this experience intelligible to others. Nevertheless, it is inevitable that scholarly and literary conventions become shopworn and outmoded, ceasing to satisfy our desire to be edified or entertained. Accordingly, scientific paradigms shift, and even the novel that emerged in the early eighteenth century is no longer novel.

In a recent review of these stylistic and paradigmatic changes in the history of anthropology, Anand Pandian and Stuart McLean refer to a "heterogeneous corpus of writings marginal to the established canons of the discipline: memoirs, life histories and ethnographic novels, sometimes pseudonymously published, often the work of women, or people of color" that constitutes a "little tradition" that is nowadays inspiring increasing numbers of ethnographers to experiment with craft and technique (montage, graphic images, prose narrative) and rethink the practice of fieldwork (collaboration, reflexivity, engagement).[6] Rather than presaging a transformation of ethnography into literature, these developments suggest a renewed interest in the philosophical question of verisimilitude—how we can best speak truth to life—and a deep questioning of all truth claims, not in order to finally arrive at the truth once and for all but in order to more deeply appreciate the nuanced complexity of what is at play for any person, in any moment, or in any one society. This spirit of open-mindedness echoes Michel Serres's view that what really matters is not determining the line that divides documentary from fiction but making our ethnographies press "closer to the turbulence preceding the emergence of an intelligible, discursively knowable world."[7] To this end, the imagination may complement our empirical observations, and ethnography take its place among the expressive arts of fiction, poetry, painting, and cinema, giving us insights into other lifeworlds as well as other lives. This psychological displacement also finds expression in the act of writing, which goes beyond immediate experience, either by interpreting it or reimagining it. In either case, trying to put the world into words may be impossible.[8] It is a leap of faith that bears comparison to the mystic's dark night of the soul, unrequited love, nostalgic or utopian longing, or an ethnographer's attempt to know the world from the standpoint of others. Yet it remains true that every writer—whether of ethnography or fiction—presumes that his or her own experiences echo the experiences of others and that his or her work may consummate a vital relationship with them.

CHRONICLES
OF THE
BARAWA MARAH

To the descendants of Tina Komé Marah
and Sanfan Aisetta Mansaray

....

KILE KA MA FAGA

THAT THE PATH NOT DIE

Being-in-Time

Chances are that I may never return to the village that figured so centrally in my life, my thinking, and my dreams for almost fifty years. It isn't only impaired vision and lack of funds that hold me back, but the deaths of all my Kuranko peers. In writing about Noah, Sewa, Ali, and Abdul, I bring them back to life, much as reciting the names of one's ancestors at a rice-flour sacrifice resuscitates the bonds between the living and the dead. And so, in retracing my steps in memory along a winding laterite path, with brakes of elephant grass burning and charred stalks like commas punctuating my way, I begin not a journey to another place but a journey through genealogical time.

Such a journey inevitably leads one to broach age-old questions of fate and free will.

For Homer, human beings are swayed and swept away by demonic or divine forces they can neither fully explain nor completely control. Our lives are spun by the gods as wool is handspun on a spindle. Though modern thought argues that we are determined by biogenetic or sociocultural forces, we continue to ask how much free will we possess and where lie the limits of our humanity and our lot. Are we doomed to repeat the mistakes of the past and cursed by our inheritance—a view that finds expression in the Christian notion of original sin, karmic eschatologies, and Karl Marx's chilling comment, "The tradition of all the dead generations weighs like a nightmare on the brains of the living"?[1] Or do we prefer Walter Benjamin's messianic emphasis on the infinite possibilities for redeeming the past in the here and now? Or might we heed George Eliot's remarks at the end of *Middlemarch* where she reflects on Dorothea's life: "a mixed result of young and noble impulse struggling amidst the conditions of an imperfect social state, in which great feelings will often take the aspect of error, and great faith the aspect of illusion. For there is no creature whose inward being is so strong that it is not greatly determined by what lies outside it."[2]

In this book, I leave open the question as to whether the past is irrevocable and irredeemable, preferring to remark discontinuities without seeing them as the result of individual agency and to reveal continuities without explaining them in terms of compulsive repetitions or implacable fate. In the spirit of Eliot, my interest is in the imperceptible and incalculable effects that "unhistorical acts" may have on our destinies.

This perspective suggests a particular approach to understanding being-in-time.

While biographical time unfolds between the bookends of an individual's birth and death, and historical time is marked by definitive events and epochs, genealogical time suggests a succession, if not a cycle, of generations in which the critical issue is the generation and regeneration of life.[3] A lineage is not simply a corporation, inheriting and holding resources and entitlements. It holds and redistributes the wherewithal of life itself, and encompasses relations between ancestors and successors, as well as close and distant kin. The focus of a genealogical imaginary is, therefore, not autonomous individuals or finite events but constellations of elements that have no one center or determinate beginning, and whose combinations and permutations cannot be explained by cause and effect.[4]

While one may, for analytical purposes, draw distinctions between different modes of being-in-time, it will become apparent in this work that human consciousness is continually and often unpredictably shifting between genealogical, historical, biographical, theological, mythological, and even biogenetic temporalities, and it is doubtful whether we can characterize individuals, let alone entire societies, in terms of a single dominant mode of time reckoning. What is true of time is also true of human existence. Our consciousness is continually shifting between the face we turn to the world and the face we keep in the shadows, and our allegiances, affections, and attention are constantly moving between different places, people, and possibilities. To do justice to this oscillation between contending forms of consciousness and behavior in everyday life, William James developed his method of radical empiricism. Rather than emphasize intransitive states of mind or settled points of view, James drew attention to the transitive, transitory, and transitional aspects of human life, and he used the homely image of the life of a bird, alternatively resting and moving, nesting and flying, to make his point. In theorizing personhood, James adopted the same approach. We sometimes act and experience ourselves as singular and unique beings, sometimes as if we were identical with others, birds of a feather flocking together. Our sense of self is seldom settled for very long. We constantly shape-shift in relation to the situation in which we find ourselves and the person or persons we are with. It isn't that we are divided selves, or even possess multiple personalities; rather, we have a remarkable capacity for transitivity, and without this capacity sociality would be impossible, for to be social one has to not so much be oneself as to become the person who, in a given situation, can relate to others and to whom others can relate.

My interest in genealogical time was first sparked by the Māori notion of *whakapapa* (genealogy), in which an implicit comparison is made between human generations and sedimentary layers of earth. Even before I embarked on fieldwork in West Africa and Aboriginal Australia, I was aware that among preliterate peoples precise chronologies and individual identities are less important than the life blood of one's lineage, flowing continually between mythical and contemporary realms. Although my fieldwork among the Kuranko of Sierra Leone and the Warlpiri and Kuku-Yalanji of Australia brought me to consider genealogy as both a principle of social organization and a mode of imagining one's being-in-the-world, the beginnings of this book date to my conversations with René Devisch, who came to Harvard in 2006 to participate in a symposium titled Sites of Memory in Africa. René stayed with me and my wife in Lexington, and in the course of a conversation that seemed to flow on unbroken from where we had left it in Copenhagen almost two years before, I told René that a Sierra Leone friend now living in London had recently piqued my interest in the ways that the past continually reappears in our present lives while remaining largely beyond our ken, so that we glimpse it as we might glimpse a specter, fitfully and in fragments. When Sewa described the history of factional fighting in his lineage, I had the impression that migrating to the United Kingdom had made him feel guilty about abandoning his father's chiefly legacy and that he was torn between his fealty to the past and his present aspirations.[5] I told René that I was reminded of my own identification with my maternal grandparents, who migrated to New Zealand from England in 1906. Their loss of the old country, which for my grandmother proved traumatic, was a theme to which I had returned many times in my writing, as if my own sense of not belonging echoed their struggle to feel at home in the country in which they had sought a better life.

I was curious to know what René had to say about this systole and diastole of history in which certain traits are reincarnated or reappear after having been seemingly forgotten or lost, and I mentioned my wife's frequent comments on the uncanny ways in which our son Joshua seemed to embody her father's mannerisms, though Frank had died many years before Joshua was born. I was also mindful of the recurrence in every generation of my own family of a maverick who turns his or her back on home and settles elsewhere, and I told René that whenever I sought to explain this kind of phenomenon, I sometimes had recourse to the Kuranko notion of *sabu nyuma* or "good cause," which alludes to the ways in which a significant predecessor clears a path for us, enabling us to realize certain possibilities in life that were hitherto closed. Or I would fall back on the Warlpiri dialectic of presence (*palka*) and absence (*lawa*)—the mysterious way that experiences, events, and even personality traits lie dormant for a generation only to reemerge in a dream and are then drawn out and reanimated in dance, replayed in the telling of a myth, or reincarnated in a newborn child. Was this what Michel Serres speaks of as topological or "folded time," in which chronologically or geographically distant events come into conjunction within consciousness?[6] Or similar to the relatively unexplored "space between" events that produces the phenomenon Friedrich Nietzsche called "eternal recurrence"? Could one address these questions without the kind of moral bias that sees the past as a shadow, our parents' unresolved struggles left for us to address, or the iniquities of the fathers visited on the children to the third and fourth generations? And could one also avoid the reductionism in science that argues that the phylogenetic imperatives of selfish genes or selfless memes outweigh the imperatives of individual existence? Could one simply affirm and celebrate, without any moral or epistemological judgment, that the life that flows through us is always more than the life we identify as ours?

My spate of questions happened to resonate with issues René had been reflecting on for many years, and he recounted how his initial experiences of fieldwork among the Yaka of southwest Congo in 1971 evoked memories of his childhood on a farm near the border between Belgium and France and only a few miles from the coast. René's awareness of occupying a borderland space of indeterminacy and transgression was intensified by the everyday switching between Flemish and French and the regional traffic in contraband that embroiled his family.

In the Congo he again experienced the confusion of being on a seashore, fearing the submergence of his identity in "an indefinable and massive otherness." And yet, René was also enthralled by the prospect of being swept away and immersed in something completely new, "like high tide washing over you as you lie on the beach."

Then a strange thing happened. Only ten days after arriving in the village of Yitaanda, the maternal uncle of the ailing Taanda chief begged René, on behalf of the chief, for medicine. His intervention was to no avail, and when the chief died the community was plunged into mourning and plagued by fears that with no ruler to hold together the fabric of the social world it would be torn apart by thunderbolts and predatory leopards. Yet people were mindful of having seen René at the bedside of the dying chief soon after a lightning bolt burned the house of his successor to the ground, and a delegate from one of the highest-ranking lineages argued that René was the reincarnation of the late chief's predecessor, who had been ostracized by the colonial authorities in 1939 for having been active in a millenarian cult and died in exile in the Lake Region to the northeast of Bandundu. René now found himself received into the Taanda community as an ancestor reborn and regarded as possessing the powers to settle dynastic disputes and divert evil or danger. The irony of his bearing the name René, literally "the reborn," had not, it seemed, entered into his hosts' thinking.

René went on to speak of how the Yaka believe that a person's health (*-kola*) and well-being (*-syaamuna*) depend on his or her vital relationship with a web of forces (*mooyi*) that includes kin and community, as well as realms that are largely inaccessible and inexpressible—the world of witchcraft and sorcery, of strangers and spirits, and of the dead. In his recent writing, René had adopted Bracha Ettinger's concepts of the matrixial and borderlinking to theorize this intersubjective flow of emotions, thoughts, and intuitions between oneself and the world beyond oneself. The matrixial, Ettinger writes, "is an unconscious borderspace of simultaneous co-emergence and co-fading of the I and an unrecognized non-I," and this echoed the Yaka worldview, René said, since it assumed that the source of life is ultimately maternal, and the most critical relationships in a person's life are with his or her uterine kin.[7] Yaka regard ill health as a sign of blockage or confusion in the interplay of forces that link inside and outside, or self and other. Hence, healing was a matter of reweaving or re-sourcing this lost connection between the individual and the wider field of being of which he or she is vitally and necessarily a part.

That agnatic descent was also important for the Yaka, I knew from René's published ethnography, but this was not what René wanted to emphasize.[8]

Against the phallic principle of uprightness, straightness, dominance, containment, and order, René wanted to give full due to the uterine principle of sympathetic attunement, sensual openness, union, and flow.

"Yet it is always discursively difficult," I said to René, "to include in any account of a person's life all the connections that bear upon his or her destiny," and I broached the question of how our relations with grandparents complement our relations with parents, just as our relations with our fathers and their families complement our relations with our mothers and theirs. This led to a conversation about the mystery of why, in societies all over the world, three generations are central to a person's existence and how, in his ethnography of the Tallensi of northern Ghana, Meyer Fortes wrote of the "equivalence of alternate generations" in Africa, where grandparents and grandchildren not only share the same name but joke together as though they were familiars.[9] "I have always thought," I remarked to René, "that Lévi-Strauss's notion of the atom of kinship downplays relations between predecessors and successors in order to emphasize the significance of the affinal link between contemporaries, and this is a blind spot in his work." But as we talked on, it became clear that for René and me the inadequacy of structural analysis lay less in its attempt to correlate different kinds of relationship within the family (patrilineal and matrilineal descent, and siblingship[10]) with positive or negative emotions than with its failure to explore how relationships are played out over time—the oscillation, for instance, between the centrifugal forces within a generation (manifest in sibling rivalry and oedipal tensions) and the centripetal forces that bring nonadjacent generations together or renew old alliances through marriage—an oscillation that one may also observe among the first three generations of migrant families as well as other families, my own included, where my mother questioned her parents' values at great personal cost while I bonded with them so deeply that I felt greater kinship with my mother's father than with my own. By the same token, what one generation fails to accomplish another may realize, and what is thwarted in reality may be realized in fantasy and dream.

Being of Two Minds

In the weeks before going to Sierra Leone, my wife and I camped in the Bois de Boulogne in Paris, awaiting word from the shipping line that would take us from Le Havre to Freetown. It was an unseasonably balmy October, and I should have been grateful for this period of idleness, but the delay in our departure only intensified the anxiety that had oppressed me for some time as I tried to imagine myself in a remote village, learning an unwritten language, interacting with complete strangers, and gleaning the knowledge I would need to write a doctoral dissertation. To distract myself, I would go for long walks in Puteaux and Suresnes, often finding myself at the old Fort Mont-Valerien, where I would sit and contemplate the haze-blurred city where only the upper level of the Eiffel Tower was visible. Or I would lie in the grass outside our tent in the Bois reading Marc Chagall's first enraptured impressions of Paris. I knew I could work in this light and that my dreams would take shape in it. I was overwhelmed by it all. When I saw Seurat I was dazzled. When I saw Monet I could have wept. And yet, even in these luminous recollections, Chagall cautions that it is not art that inspires art but immersion in the world. "Theory and technique have not enabled me to advance one step. I owe everything to life."[1]

Our indolent days in Paris ended abruptly when Pauline fell ill. After consulting a specialist, we were advised to return to England, where she could receive free treatment from the National Health Service. Within twelve hours of flying back to London, Pauline underwent an operation in Middlesex Hospital for the removal of an ovarian cyst and was found to be pregnant. Yet within ten days of her discharge from the hospital, we were on our way to Sierra Leone, this time on a dilapidated DC8 that had a plaque on one of the bulkheads that read, "This Philippine Airlines DC8 flew non-stop from Tokyo, Japan to Miami, Florida, a distance of 8705 statute miles in 13 hours and 52 minutes, establishing a world distance record, Feb. 22, 1962." I was reminded of the way we deploy words magically to create semblances of order in a sea of chaos, and contrive the impression that we actually grasp the hidden meaning of the world in which we move, ships that pass each other in the night, or aircraft climbing above the pack ice of cloud into air so cold and rarefied that if we were exposed to it we would not survive. Would the language of anthropology prove any different, or would it also be little more than another form of sorcery, confusing words and things, an arcane technique for consoling lost souls that the world is indeed within their grasp?

About a year before we left England for Sierra Leone, a story broke in the *Sunday Times* about the fate of an English yachtsman called Donald Crowhurst. His trimaran ketch, *Teignmouth Electron*, had been found adrift in the mid-Atlantic. The life raft was lashed in place, the helm swung freely, and the sails lay folded on the deck ready to be raised. But Crowhurst had vanished.

Three blue-bound logbooks on the chart table revealed what had befallen him.

Crowhurst had set sail from Teignmouth, Devon, on October 31, 1968, in a bid to win the Golden Globe single-handed round-the-world race. His trimaran had been built and equipped in a hurry. There had been no time for intensive sea trials, and Crowhurst had sailed late with his course unplanned. To make matters worse, hatches leaked, steering gear malfunctioned, and the electrics failed. The reasonable course would have been to abort the voyage. But loath to admit defeat, Crowhurst began to work out an elaborate deception in which he would calculate and radio false positions, giving the impression that he had rounded the Horn in record time and was making excellent progress across the Pacific. In fact, he was sailing in circles in the South Atlantic, well away from shipping lanes, awaiting an opportune moment to announce that he had reached the Cape of Good Hope and was again in the Atlantic on the final leg of a circumnavigation of the globe.

What brought Crowhurst to the realization that he would never be able to pull off the hoax? Inconsistencies in his carefully forged logbooks? Guilt over having deceived those who loved him and had supported his enterprise? Doubt in his ability to remember every detail of his concocted story and remain consistent in everything he said on his return to a hero's welcome in England?

In the ineluctable silence and solitude of the sea, the yachtsman began to lose touch with reality. Entangled in the web of lies he had spun, he saw that his voyage was doomed. By the time he sailed into the Sargasso Sea, he had retreated into a wholly private world. Becalmed and having lost all track of time, he began to imagine that he could leave his body at will and make himself divine. Surrounded by a debris of dirty dishes and dismantled radios, he penned one of the last entries in his log:

> It is the end of my
> game the truth
> has been revealed

A few minutes later, he climbed the companion ladder to the deck and stepped off the *Teignmouth Electron* into the sea.

As Pauline and I stepped from our aircraft, the hot soup-sweet African night enveloped us.

My body felt swollen. My shirt stuck to my skin. Inside the airport terminal, African bodies pressed around us, pungent and impatient. It took two hours to get our passports stamped, reclaim our baggage, and clear Customs. We moved in a state of torpor, saying nothing, as if we had become strangers.

It was after midnight by the time we got away from the airport. Lightning flashed along the Bullom Shore, and the humid air was heavy with the stench of decomposing vegetation.

In the taxi, the sea breeze through the open windows revived me. But I was beginning to rue the promise I'd made to my friend Alex Guyan in London. Alex had insisted that when we arrived in Freetown we stay at the City Hotel. Graham Greene had killed a lot of time there during the war, and Alex was an avid fan of Greene's. It amused him to think of me sitting on the same balcony where Wilson sat at the beginning of *The Heart of the Matter*, his bald pink knees thrust against the ironwork . . . his face turned to the sea.

I asked the taxi driver if he knew the City Hotel. Sure, he knew it. He could take us there for only thirty leones. It sounded like a lot of money, but I didn't know the exchange rate, and besides, it was a bit late now to negotiate our fare.

Too tired to take anything in, we crossed the Sierra Leone River on a listing ferry and were driven through labyrinthine streets, lit by braziers and flickering oil lamps. By the time our taxi set us down outside the City Hotel, our minds were in a fug and we had lost track of time.

In the darkness, the wind thrashed at the palms in the hotel forecourt. Thunder rolled and caromed in the peninsular hills.

We found the main entrance to the hotel barred by a metal grille, and the shuttered windows showed no signs of life. Already we were wishing we had taken the airport bus with the other whites and gone to the Paramount Hotel, even though the cost of a room there would have been prohibitive. Anyway, hadn't we vowed to steer clear of tourists, to plunge straight into Africa and keep our promise to Alex?

I shouted up at the dark and decaying concrete facade. "Anybody there?"

A first-story window was wrenched open, and a woman called down to us in Krio. At the same moment the rain came bucketing out of the sky.

Pauline and I must have looked ridiculous, soaked to the skin, with our shoes awash in the floodwater sluicing down the street.

The woman at the window was joined by others. They laughed and shouted down at us.

"We don't speak Krio," Pauline shouted back.

"Wait," the first woman said, "I dae kam."

They all traipsed down, dressed in miniskirts, shrieking with laughter. They held beach umbrellas above their heads to protect their jet-black wigs from the downpour.

They wanted a dash (a tip).

I dug in my pockets and came up with some English coins. The women took them gleefully and ran around to the front of the hotel, beckoning us to follow.

The lobby was feebly lit. Off to the left was a deserted saloon bar. Ahead was a flight of wooden stairs. The prostitutes clattered up the stairs in their high heels and fishnet stockings, gales of laughter going into the darkness, the smell of cheap perfume lingering in the clammy air.

When the hotel porter emerged from the shadows, bleary-eyed from his interrupted sleep, I explained that we had come in on the London flight and wanted a room.

"Kam we go," he ordered. Dragging a bunch of ancient keys from his pocket, he started to climb the stairs, using the bannister to pull himself up. Pauline and I lugged our suitcases after him.

Our room was at the end of a dingy corridor on the first floor. It was furnished with a double bed under a torn mosquito net, two chairs, and a chest of drawers. The room stank of mildew and excrement.

I went into the bathroom. The toilet hadn't been flushed, nor would it flush. When I pulled the chain, there was an ugly gurgling in the pipes, and a mess of paper pulp and shit disgorged into the stained bowl.

We were too tired to care. I bolted the door and we stripped off our wet clothes, toweled ourselves dry, and crawled under the mosquito net onto the bed where we lay jarred and spent from our journey. I thought: We have done what Alex wanted us to do. I can write him tomorrow and say we have experienced Greeneland in all its seediness. Then we can find somewhere else to live.

We woke at first light to the jangle and blare of highlife music. I went to the louver window and looked down into the street. Several Toyota and Datsun taxis were parked at an angle to the curb, and the drivers were washing their cars with buckets of sudsy water. I was reminded of the way young men in the Congo used to wash their bodies, soaping themselves until they were all but invisible for lather.

Beyond the intersection, over laterite stonework and rusty roofs, I glimpsed the sea. Far out, a sunken freighter showed only its funnel and mastheads above the surface of the ocean. It must have gone down during the war, when Atlantic convoys used to assemble in the harbor. I made a mental note to mention this in my letter to Alex.

"What are you looking at?" Pauline asked.

I told her about the taxi drivers and the sunken freighter on the sandbar. Then I asked if she felt like getting up and going downstairs to find something to eat.

"Don't even talk about food," Pauline said. She was suffering from morning sickness. She felt as if she were going to throw up.

"We'll move out of here," I said.

"At least let's get a room with a toilet that flushes. I'm going to try to get some more sleep. If you go out, try not to make too much noise when you come back."

I lifted the mosquito net and kissed her on the mouth. "I'll see you in a while," I said.

I went out of the room thinking we should not have come to Africa. I felt sick to my stomach at the thought of Pauline pregnant and having our baby in such a place. I should have called it off, this year in Sierra Leone doing fieldwork for my PhD. I should have come alone or not at all.

In the downstairs dining room, some retired Krio clerks were eating breakfast. No one looked up as I walked in.

When the waiter asked if I wanted an English breakfast, I made the mistake of saying yes and was served braised Spam, glutinous eggs, and chips fried in rancid drippings. The cook had been with the hotel since colonial times. Like the ex-clerks in their English serge and bowlers, his menu parodied the world that Sierra Leoneans had once been encouraged to emulate.

I had no appetite for the food in front of me and was beginning to think that my dream of returning to Africa, which had sustained me for five years, had been as misguided as the idea of empire. I had worked as a volunteer for the United Nations in the Congo only to become disenchanted with community development and determined to find a way of living in Africa on African terms. But now, on the threshold of fulfilling this ambition, a terrible sense of despair came over me, such as Malcolm Lowry describes in his story "Through the Panama" as "the inenarrable inconceivably desolate sense of having no right to be where you are."

In the days that followed, I filled my notebooks with such misgivings, not knowing where I would do my fieldwork, what exactly I would research, and how I might proceed. Every night I was tormented by the same dream, in which I wandered disoriented in an immense building, looking for a room where I was supposed to enroll.

Pauline grew impatient with me and recollected the series of events that had brought us to Freetown together—the month we had spent in Copenhagen, where she did an intensive course in Danish, the modern language most akin to Old Icelandic, the weeks in Paris waiting for a cargo boat to West Africa, and finally the flight back to London and her hospitalization. "I want to be here," she assured me. "I want to have our baby here, in this climate, with you!"

Vultures wheeled high above the city. In the street markets, peddlers cried, "Biscuit dae! Five five cents." We tried out our Krio, "Omus for da wan dae? Omus for dis," buying pineapples, bunches of bananas, and scoops of groundnuts wrapped in funnels of brown paper. We went to Immigration to get our visas. In the piss-soaked alley outside the Immigration Department, a sign had been posted: Urinating Prohibited in This Area. We found a pharmacy with the improbable name of Vulga Thera.

Beggars crowded around us. Some leaned on staves, their legs like burned matchsticks. Paraplegics sat in little carts and shoved themselves along on their knuckles. Pauline pressed coins into the fingerless hands of a burnedout leper. In the street, a Toyota Coaster moved slowly through the traffic, a logo above the cab saying, Sweet Are the Uses of Adversity.

Now reconciled to remaining in our hotel, we sat on the hotel balcony in the cool of the evening, drinking tonic water and writing postcards home as the sad-eyed Swiss proprietor, who had run the hotel in Graham Greene's time, limped to and fro behind the bar.

Our waiter was a thickset man with a coarse-featured, morose face. He derived unending pleasure from prizing caps off bottles of Star beer with a grand sweeping gesture, then watching as kids scrambled around his feet, fighting for the bottle tops. If there was a blue star printed under the cork inlay, you won a lottery prize.

Fortunes are precarious here, I wrote to Alex. We met a deaf-mute boy on the street today who thrust a scrap of paper under our noses and urged us to read what was written on it: "Good morning I am no hable to spick and I can not find chob Please will you help me Tankyou God pless . . ."

I was going to add something about the inescapability of poverty when I became aware that a boy was standing close to me, watching me write.

"Kushe," I said, and hoped he would go away.

He said his name was James. He had been attending school but could not continue because his family did not have the money to pay his fees. He begged us to help him out.

"Wusai you dae?" I asked.

James said he lived in the East End. His expression wavered between shiftiness and shame.

"Can you come and see us in the morning?" Pauline said. "If you bring your school books, I can get some idea what you've been doing."

James said he would come early. Then he announced that he was going and disappeared into the street.

"Do you think he's on the level?" I asked.

"I've no idea. Does it really matter?" Pauline said.

A couple days later, I was lying on the bed in our hotel room reading Melville's *Typee*. Pauline was sitting at a desk near the window, turning the pages of a cheap notebook, correcting James's exercises. James stood stock-still beside her, chewing his fingernails.

"Do you prefer reading books or listening to stories?" Pauline asked.

"I like to read books," James replied.

"Why?"

"Because they're true."

"Do your mother and father tell you stories?"

"Yes."

"Do they tell you stories about Conny Rabbit?"

"I know those stories."

"Aren't those stories just as interesting as the ones you read in books?"

"No, people always tell them in different ways and change them, and you never know which one is true."

"Aren't they more exciting and interesting like that—when they're different every time?"

James shook his head.

"Why not?"

"Because you never know which one is true."

"Are all books true?"

"Yes."

My ears were ringing. I was bathed in perspiration. I pushed through the crowded streets, determined to finalize the business of getting our Land Rover released from customs. But no sooner was one obstacle overcome than another arose. Day after day, I trudged from one Port Authority office to another, collecting customs clearance certificates, import-duty exemption authorizations, set surcharge forms, insurance schedules, shipping notes, delivery and condition reports, certificates of importation and release. Then there were letters of affiliation to the university, residence permits, vehicle registration and insurance, a driver's license . . . more visits to dismal offices where clerks sat slumped over their desks and some taciturn minion would want his palm greased with a dash.

I began to think of abandoning my plans to do fieldwork. I imagined myself holed up in the City Hotel, drawing on my scholarship money to write an ethnography of an entirely fictitious society. The task did not seem too daunting. The Fourah Bay College library was well stocked with monographs from which I could glean the formulaic patterns of structural-functionalist ethnography. To invent a society, one had only to decide the nature of the economy, the mode of descent and inheritance, and the principles of legal and political life, and everything else could be deduced. Since conventional ethnographies were generally devoid of in-depth descriptions of actual individuals, I need not concern myself unduly with details of real lives. Stereotypes would suffice. And sweeping generalizations would gloss over the subtleties of lived experience and give my account an aura of objectivity. Even the language of my make-believe world could be constructed as a dialect of some actual West African language. Hadn't Jorge Luis Borges done something akin to this in his account of the world of Tlön?

The more I pondered my idea, the more it engrossed me. But when I confided my scheme to Pauline, she said I should not let myself be disheartened by the weeks we had been stuck in Freetown. It was hard not knowing where we were going or what we were going to do, but shouldn't we give ourselves time to get acclimatized and find our feet?

What brought me to my senses was a map. The map was stapled to the corridor wall in the Institute of African Studies at Fourah Bay College. It showed Sierra Leone divided into tribal areas. The research I had proposed at Cambridge for my PhD would have meant living among the Mende in the southeast, studying the impact of literacy on village life. I had never been enthusiastic about this plan—a continuation of research I had done for my master's degree on the impact of literacy in early nineteenth-century Māori New Zealand—but I had not been able to come up with anything else.

The map showed a region in the north, defined by a dotted line. Across this blank space was written, "Kuranko."

I do not know why I responded as I did to this map. All I knew was that this remote region was where I wanted to go. I told the director of the institute of my plans. He said that very little was known about the Kuranko. This was all I needed to make me absolutely sure of my path. A few days later, Pauline and I loaded our supplies into the Land Rover and headed north.

A warm wind flowed through the cab of the vehicle. Grasslands stretched away under an immense sky. The road behind us was lost in billows of red dust.

We were going to a town called Kabala. We were enamored of the name. It invoked the Hebrew kabbalah and its esoteric traditions of cosmic union. But we couldn't be sure where we would end up at the end of the day. Few roads were signposted, and north of Makeni the road degenerated into a tortuous and eroded track.

We passed through towns where people were celebrating the end of Ramadan. Women danced in tight circles, resplendent in voluminous gowns and silken kerchiefs. Men lounged in hammocks slung under the eaves of verandas.

We crossed turbid streams where butterflies danced in shafts of sunlight. In the lophira plains, the air was filled with the odor of burned elephant grass.

I reached for Pauline's hand, and we glanced at each other and smiled.

"It's hard to believe I seriously thought of staying on in Freetown and writing a fake ethnography," I said.

"The trouble with lying," Pauline said, "is that you always have to make a mental note of everything you say, so you won't be caught out in the future.

If you tell the truth, you don't have to remember anything. You are free to live."

"Do you have any regrets?" I said. "About Sierra Leone, I mean."

"I couldn't be happier."

It was then that I remembered the story of Donald Crowhurst and became aware that for as long as we had been in Freetown, this story had been at the back of my mind, casting its shadow over everything I thought and did.

Koinadugu

Arriving in Kabala after a long day negotiating degraded roads without a map was like coming to the threshold of a new life. Although darkness was falling before we located the district commissioner's bungalow on a hill overlooking the town, the DC welcomed us and suggested we park our Land Rover in his compound. After unrolling our mattress in the back, we instantly fell asleep.

I woke at dawn in a place I had first dreamed of in the Congo five years earlier. Everything enchanted me. The scattered acacia trees on the slopes of the hill, their wizened seedpods littering the ground. The dusty streets along which we picked our way. Women with basins of cassava leaf or bundles of firewood on their heads. Kids trundling hoops or toy trucks made of wire along the road. The insistent patter of distant drums. The thronged market where we bought bananas, oranges, bread, and Pickwick tea bags before following a path across a dry paddy field where three cows with white egrets at their feet grazed the stubble.

When I told the DC I was interested in studying the Kuranko, he assumed I meant the language, not the people, and suggested I get in touch with Noah Bockarie Marah, a teacher at the District Council School. When I met Noah that afternoon and explained that I was doing a PhD in anthropology at Cambridge and hoping to write a book about the Kuranko, his enthusiasm was immediate and overwhelming. He had often thought of writing something about his own society and was only too happy to assist me. Before the

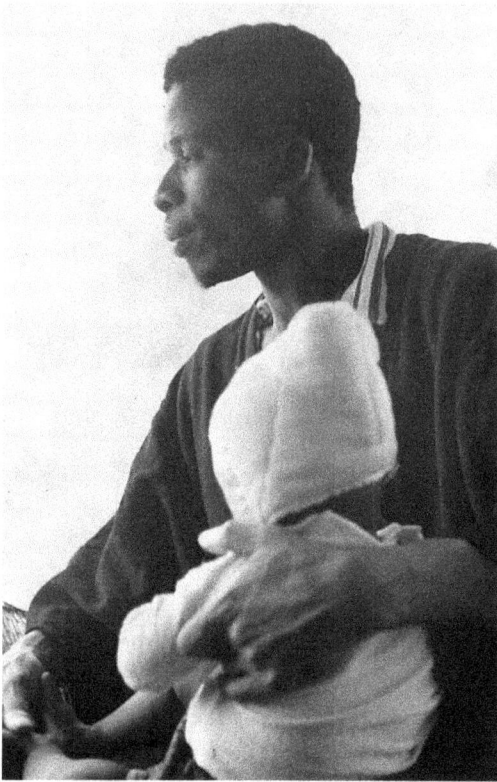

1 Noah in Kabala with his daughter Aisetta (N'Na), January 1970.

day was out, I found myself sitting on the porch of Noah's house, practicing Kuranko phrases of greeting and learning Kuranko kinship terms. As for actually using these greetings, this would prove as difficult as moving from a formal knowledge of the kinship system to knowing how to navigate everyday interactions. Collective representations are one thing; quotidian know-how is quite another. But for a moment I could not believe my luck. And though rumors would soon spread that Noah had a djinn working for him who would bring him luck, the truth was that he was my hope (*yigi*), the source of my good fortune.

Noah was not only fluent in English but eager to show off his knowledge of English law. Though I would soon tire of his long-winded legal disquisitions, his account of his heritage fired my imagination. He hailed from Barawa, a chiefdom over which the Marah clan had ruled for some three hundred years. According to a Kuranko adage, other clans might be older than the Marah, but it is under a cotton tree planted by the Marah that they were raised (morgo sikina yan mara kode, koni ma ku ta maran ku finyan bandan kore). Like most Marah, Noah said, he was *suniké*, a word he translated as *freethinker*, though it also connoted nobility.

Within days, Noah agreed to take a year's leave from his teaching job and work for me as a paid field assistant. He helped us find a place to live—a newly built three-room, mud-brick, pan-roofed bungalow on the edge of town—and introduced us to his wives, Yebu Bah and Yebu Bangura, and his mother, Sanfan Aisetta, a formidable woman who had borne eight children, all of whom were still alive. Aisetta immediately took Pauline under her wing, and in Yebu Bah Pauline found a kindred spirit. Soon we had worked out a modus operandi for my fieldwork. While Noah and I made forays to remote villages, Pauline would remain in Kabala, where she would have access to the local clinic in case of a medical emergency, and where she could devote her free time to translating the Icelandic family sagas she had brought with her from Cambridge—the basis of her own PhD. Noah's mother and wives would keep her company and attend to her needs.

That Christmas, Noah and I made our first trip to his natal village of Firawa. The first stage of our journey was by Land Rover—twenty-five miles along a potholed track to Koinadugu town, then on to the Seli River. From there we began the ten-mile trek to Firawa, skirting swamps and crossing plateaus where the fired elephant grass covered the path with filigrees of ash. Before us stood the great inselberg Senekonke—"gold mountain"—where the Marah rulers once offered sacrifices for the protection of the land. Sometimes, Noah said, the death of a ruler is presaged by the creaking of granite doors in the inselberg, and the music of xylophones carried on the wind. In retrospect, this may have been my first inkling of the idea that while genealogical time encompasses distant relationships and long-ago events, these relationships and events are made perpetually present in the physicality of the landscape and the layout of villages.

Though we entered Firawa in the heat of the day when most people were resting, praise singers quickly hurried out to greet us with xylophones and flattery.

"Nomor [Powerful One], nomor," they cried. And then, as Noah distributed coins, they declaimed with even greater enthusiasm, "Nomor, Marah, nomor!"

As we crossed the compound named for Noah's branch of the ruling lineage, two of his elder brother's wives approached and, bowing low, clasped his ankles. "In sene, in sene" (You are welcome, you are welcome), they cried, and they clapped their hands as we pressed on into the heart of the village.

In the chief's compound, a collapsible tin chair was brought out for me, and I was bidden to sit down. Then, elders began to appear, summoned by the chief's drum, and Noah moved among them, shaking hands, enviably in his element.

I felt conspicuous and awkward under the quizzical and sometimes suspicious scrutiny of the old men, and when chief Tala Sewa emerged from his house, his anxious face only increased my disquiet. Noah, however, had prepared his introduction carefully. As he explained that I was a pen pal who had come to visit him and see the place where he had spent his childhood, nods of approval were directed my way, and even Tala Sewa appeared reassured.

Finally, through the praise singer who relayed the chief's words to his audience, Tala Sewa let it be known that I was welcome, and that I would come to no harm while I remained in Firawa. This said, he signaled that gifts be brought forth. First was a winnowing tray piled high with unhusked rice. Then a young man pushed through the crowd and squatted in front of me with two russet hens compressed between his knees. Noah explained that such gifts were always offered to strangers—at once a tangible expression of goodwill, since food sustained life, and a subtle way of disarming a potential enemy.

I thanked the assembly, using the Kuranko phrases Noah had taught me. Several of the elders smiled, either in appreciation of my attempt to speak their language or in amusement at my ineptitude. I was then led to the house next to Tala Sewa's.

Anomalous among the circular, thatch-roofed, wattle-and-daub houses that enclosed the compound, the house in which I was to lodge was built of concrete blocks and roofed with corrugated iron. It had been built by a police sergeant from Firawa who had made a small fortune in the diamond districts of Kono, where he still lived. Inside I was surprised to find a spacious parlor with prayer mats on the floor, a low table, and several framed photographs of members of the sergeant's family on the walls. My bedroom was furnished with an iron-frame bed, wooden chairs, a table, and a kerosene lamp.

As it turned out, this show of hospitality was not entirely gratuitous, for among the freight I had reluctantly trucked from Kabala to the Seli river crossing during the previous weeks was the cement the sergeant needed to complete the steps of his house. "We have a saying," Noah explained. "Nyendan bin to kile, a wa ta an segi—when you walk through the nyendan grass we use for thatching, it bends before you; when you return, the grass bends the other way." Thus, greetings, goodwill, assistance, and gifts move to and fro within a community, keeping the paths open, keeping relationships alive, including relationships with one's ancestors. And Noah pointed out a solitary coconut palm in the center of the village, marking the place where his father was buried. There had been a second palm, Noah said, marking his father's brother's grave, but it had died.

Until that moment, I had not considered the possibility that reciprocity might extend through time, or that remembering one's forebears and making sacrifices to them might be as vital to one's well-being as exchanging greetings, rice, and kola with one's contemporaries. But for how long, and how far back in time, I wondered, did such connections remain vital?

When Noah returned to his elder brother Abdul's house, I unpacked my rucksack and scribbled some notes, relieved to be alone for a while.

My privacy was short-lived.

"Honk, honk!" It was Noah's nephew, Sewa, and though Sewa had never seen a motor vehicle, he knew how to mimic a horn.

In the parlor, two of Abdul's junior wives had left enamel dishes of parboiled rice, with a palm oil sauce of chicken and cassava leaf. Sewa made gestures and grinned, encouraging me to eat.

I took the food out to the front porch, only to be ambushed by a crowd of children. The older ones, having quickly overcome their trepidation, propelled their terror-stricken younger siblings toward the *tubabu* (white man). But I was glad of their company. I could practice my Kuranko with them without embarrassment.

That night I fell asleep not long after nightfall, hearing the shuffling of bare feet on a cement floor, and the ping and ticking of the iron roofing as it cooled.

During the next few days, I found myself so captivated by the things I heard and saw around me that it was all too easy to believe I intuitively understood them. But understanding is seldom born of enchantment, any more than initiation is consummated in newness alone. Understanding is born of suffering the eclipse of everything you know, all that you have, and all that you are. It is, as the Kuranko say, like the gown you put on when you are initiated. To don this gown, you must first be divested of your old garb, stripped clean, and reduced to nothingness.

I would begin my days at Abdul's house. The porch was of mud and dung, and as burnished as a river stone. Sitting with my back against the wall, I could observe the comings and goings in the compound and ply

Noah and Abdul with questions. Abdul was ensconced at a treadle sewing machine at the other end of the porch, putting the finishing touches to the white country-cloth gown his niece would wear for her initiation. He was a taciturn man at the best of times, and I suspected that the row of pins he held tightly between his lips was a pretext for ignoring me. So, it was Noah who bore the brunt of my incessant curiosity as groups of strangely attired women performed in front of the house before receiving a dash and moving on, or groups of pubescent girls, their hair braided, beaded, and decorated with snail-shell toggles, their waists encircled with strings of beads, danced out the last days of their childhood. But behind the drumming that lasted long into the night, and the air of festivity, there were ominous whispers. I was told of the neophytes' vulnerability to witches and of the dangers attending clitoridectomy. I heard of fearful encounters with bush spirits and arduous hazings. And I wondered how these young girls would feel, returning after weeks of sequestration in the bush, not to the security of their parental homes but to the uncertainties of life as newlyweds in the houses of strangers.

If I empathized with the neophytes, it was, I suppose, because I was also like a child. The shock of too many new experiences—a language I could barely understand, food I often found unpalatable, customs that mystified me, afflictions I could not cure—was beginning to erode my self-confidence and make me vaguely paranoid. This increasing sense of ignorance and incompetence came to a head one morning, when Noah arranged for me to meet a group of elders who would help me understand the origins of the Marah hegemony in Barawa. Interpreting my questions and the elders' responses to them, Noah gave me a thumbnail sketch of what anthropologists would call the Kuranko lineage system. Every individual belonged to a clan (*sie*, lit. many) whose origins could be traced back to the great fourteenth-century empire of Mande. All Kuranko clans "came from Mande, from up" (*teliboi*, lit. sun comes from, i.e., the east), and each was associated with a totem (*tane*, lit. prohibited thing), usually a bird or animal that had altruistically saved the life of a clan ancestor. While some clans, like the Marah, were rulers (*tontiginu*, lit. law owners), others were commoners, Muslims (*morenu*), or *nyemakale*—the lowest-ranked clans, including praise singers and genealogists. Every clan consisted of several subclans called *kebile* (lit. inheritance takers, i.e., people sharing a common patrimony), but because kebile included so many members and were widely dispersed, kinsmen living together constituted for most practical purposes the most important unit in everyday life. The relationship between these family groups and the wider subclan or kebile was sometimes compared to the relationship between the boles of a great silk cotton tree; its trunk, ascending to a canopy, was likened to the clan as a whole.

When Noah pressed the elders to speak more specifically about the Barawa Marah, matters became a little more complicated. According to tradition, a warrior called Yamisa first settled the country, descending from the forested foothills of the Loma range where his elder brother Borsingbi had already made his home. Legend had it that Yamisa declared, "M'bara wa"—I am going to my own place—and thenceforth this tract of country became known as Barawa. Subsequently, the Marah clan split into five subclans or houses, each named after one of the sons of a chief called Mamburu. Although the firstborn sons of these houses were all eligible to contest the chieftaincy, the Woldugu, renowned as warriors, had "owned Barawa" for the last one hundred years. In the early nineteenth century, however, the Woldugu house divided. Following the death of Marin Tamba, his sons Morowa and Balansama founded separate houses. Morowa, the eldest, became the eleventh chief of Barawa, and his younger brother Balansama succeeded him. The current chief, Tala Sewa, was a direct descendant of Balansama, while Noah, his brothers, their father, and their paternal grandfather were all Morowa's descendants.

As I scribbled down the names of the Barawa chiefs, it occurred to me to ask if the names of their mothers were also remembered. The question was impertinent, if not outrageous, and no sooner had Noah conveyed it to the elders than one man hitched the sleeve of his gown over his shoulder and walked out of the room in disgust. The dismay on the remaining faces was obvious. Even though I apologized for my gaffe, it was clear that my impropriety had cost me a lot of goodwill. Yet it also yielded a crucial insight, for I had glimpsed what I would later call the paradox of patriliny, namely, that while men vaunted their power by censoring genealogical references to women, the generation of life was literally inconceivable without women, and, as numerous adages made clear, a man's fate was in his mother's hands, since receiving his paternal ancestors' blessings was contingent on his mother's dutiful behavior toward her husband. Although men would tell me that a child is born of the seed of a man, and the mother simply provides a vessel in which the seed can germinate (sometimes breaking open a groundnut to show me the seed within the husk), I would come to see that it was women who raised the children and determined their destinies, and that men envied women's procreative power and sought to deny it. Moreover, personal names were almost always prefaced by the mother's name. Thus, chief Sewa Marah's mother's name was Tala, while Noah's father and father's brother both bore the name of their mother, Tina. It would also become clear to me that while men dismissed women as emotional and unreliable, kinship (*nakelinyorgoye*, lit. mother-one-relationship), was defined in terms of motherhood, while the ethic of forbearance and fortitude to which men paid lip service was, more often than not, actually exemplified by the behavior of women. According to a Kuranko adage, bearing a child is not hard, but raising a child is (dan soron ma gbele, koni a ma kole). Ironically, nothing would seem to be more difficult (*gbele* means hard, difficult, or problematic) than bringing a child into the world, especially when infant mortality is high and many women die in childbirth; but the fact remains that the labor of nursing a child through its earliest years, caring for a child through times of famine and illness, protecting a child from the pitfalls of a politically unstable world, and working hard for a hard-hearted or indifferent husband so that one's child is blessed by its patrilineal ancestors, amounts to greater hardship than the labor of giving birth. At the same time, this adage implies that although the bond between mother and child begins with birth, it is actually born of the intimate interactions and critical events that characterize primary intersubjectivity. Accordingly, one might argue that the progenitor of a lineage, from whom countless individuals derive their names and the substance of their being, does not wholly determine the life courses of his descendants, even though the mythos of genealogical time implies that this is so, since, in reality, genealogical ties are forged in the crucible of lived experience over time, and the meaning of genealogy as generation derives not from male potency but from the power of begetting, of giving birth, which is the prerogative of women.

Curiously enough, at the very moment that my meeting with the elders broke up, I became aware of a chorus of women's voices in the courtyard outside as they accompanied the neophytes on their rounds of the village, celebrating their unique power to bring new life into the world.

Over the following days, it became clear that my faux pas had been forgiven. I was undoubtedly not the first white man to prove insensitive to local protocols. Nor would I be the last. Perhaps what redeemed me in the elders' eyes and, for that matter, redeems the anthropological project itself, is one's preparedness to risk oneself in a foreign lifeworld, struggling to master its language and adapt to its customs, refusing to give up on the possibility of finding common ground.

For Noah, belonging to a dynasty of famous chiefs was both a source of pride and a bone of contention, for it was his dream that the Barawa

chieftaincy would one day return to his ruling house. That the preoccupations of nonrulers were very different took me some time to grasp, though
it was already clear to me that without the formidable memories of praise
singers and bards, the genealogical knowledge of chiefs would be as shallow
as anyone else's. Moreover, I became only gradually aware of the extent to
which Noah was determined to demonstrate his privileged position to me
by mediating disputes among villagers and showing me how skilled he was
in applying customary law. Yet without the respect he commanded in Firawa
I would never have been able to persuade the *jelibas* and *finabas* associated
with his branch of the family to share their knowledge with me. For this was
not common knowledge but reserved for occasions when chiefly ancestors
had to be recalled and extolled as a way of legitimating a current chief's right
to rule.[1] I was beginning to understand that these performances of power—
singing a ruler's praises and emphasizing his legitimacy—required a ritual
disparagement of underlings and outsiders. In celebrating the virtues of their
chiefs, praise singers often censored historical defeats in battle or played
down occasions when a ruler failed in his duties to protect and provide for
his people. Often, too, chiefs resented the power that jelibas had over them,
in rather the same way that men resented the influence of women. Thus,
while proverbial wisdom cautioned against placing one's trust in women,
chiefs would readily blame praise singers for emboldening and persuading
their ancestors to embark on campaigns that proved ruinous.

Something of this ambivalence of rulers toward women and jelibas was
also evident in their relationship with the Masters of the Djinn. In due
course, I would hear of great Marah chiefs who commanded occult powers
and could assume the form of leopards, or strike their enemies with thunderbolts. But secular and supernatural powers seldom coincided in the same
individual, which meant that chiefs were often at odds with men whose power
derived not from the moral domain of the town but from the wild and anti-
nomian realm of the bush. This was equally true of the Marah's relationship
with Islam.

During my daily strolls around the village, greeting people and trying to
get a sense of whether the various compounds (*luiye*) could be unambigu-
ously identified with different families, I came to realize that the clans clus-
tered around the compound at the farthest end of the village were Muslim.
Did this distance reflect a historical antipathy between the allegedly pagan
Marah and the Moris?

The more I explored this question, the more confused I became. I was
told repeatedly that "the first father" or "the first ancestor" of the Kuranko

was a certain Manse Yilkanani, whose son, Saramba, "came down" from Mande and occupied the West Guinea Highlands, apportioning fiefdoms among his fifteen sons. But not only was Yilkanani not Kuranko, he was not even African. The name by which Kuranko knew him derived from the Arabic Dhul-Quarnein (The Two-Horned), otherwise known as Alexander the Great. Moreover, according to Mandinka jelibas, Yilkanani was a contemporary of Muhammad and Suleiman (Solomon), and Allah appointed the prophet as Yilkanani's mentor.[2]

Nor, it turned out, had the Marah always resisted Islam. Abdul performed his daily prayers on the porch, seemingly oblivious to the people coming and going around him. And Tina Komé had embraced Islam when he married Sanfan Aisetta Mansaray, though Noah once confided that his father had become an unwilling slave to bamboo wine, and Islam's rule of abstinence offered him salvation.

If legend is to be believed, Marin Tamba Marah, the tenth ruler of Barawa, set the precedent when he was visited in the early nineteenth century by a Fula *karamorgo* (literate teacher) and *mori* (Muslim) called Karakome Alfa Ibrahim. The Alfa converted Marin Tamba to Islam, which so pleased the chief that he became known as Sewa, meaning "happy." A Fula clan— the Thoronka—was subsequently given the chieftaincy in the neighboring chiefdom of Kalian.

Some caution must be exercised, however, in how we interpret *conversion* in this context, for though the word roughly translates the Kuranko verb *yelama*, "to change or exchange," as in changing one's clothing, changing places with another person, or undergoing change from childhood to adulthood, it does not carry the Euro-Christian connotations of revelation or rebirth, suggesting a complete psychological transformation of a person's life and worldview. Indeed, "conversion" to Islam among the Kuranko may be a euphemism for military conquest followed by vassalage, or may simply mean that Islam disseminated downward from a ruler to his subjects. Marin Tamba's conversion to Islam may have also reflected a reciprocal arrangement, independently reached by his successors, to offer pastoral Fulani grazing rights for their herds in return for the cattle needed for chiefly sacrifices or as gifts to seal political alliances (often involving intermarriage and cattle bridewealth) with neighboring polities. But other oral histories suggest a different story. Not long after Marin Tamba's alleged conversion, he rebelled against submission to Fula military forces from Solima in the north. Barawa was invaded by Fula and their Solima allies, and the defeated Marin Tamba (alias Sewa) took his own life.

Jihad and Colonization

Integrating oral traditions and recorded histories is often as impossible as reconciling different witnesses' recollections of a single event, and this Rashomon effect is particularly irksome when European historians invoke objectivity to legitimize their interpretations of historical consciousness, disparaging oral traditions as inferior, unreliable, and mythical. I therefore trod carefully when, in the year following my first fieldwork, I consulted the writings of several European explorers who traversed Kuranko country in the course of searching for the source of the Niger, for though dates might help me establish a timeline for the traditions I had collected, my interest was in gaining insights into recurring existential and political quandaries rather than writing objective history.

In 1822, after a failed attempt to locate the headwaters of the Niger, the Scottish explorer Alexander Gordon Laing met the Marah chief Balansama at the town of Kamato. Having got wind of Laing's presence in his country, Balansama traveled from his village of Kolakonké (under the Kola tree) to Kamato, accompanied by three hundred armed men and an equipage of drummers, xylophonists, flautists, elephant-tusk horn players, and praise singers. The warriors wore burnt umber gowns covered with sachets of protective charms, and at a shout from their commanders they drew their swords from tasseled leather sheaths and brandished them, while bowmen shot arrows skyward. The ground shook from the rhythm of stamped feet as columns of men intoned in unison.

When Balansama emerged from the melee, Laing observed a large goiter on his neck, suggesting that salt was a scarce commodity in that region. Laing also noted that three of the drummers were decked out in brand-new uniforms of the Fourth West Indian Regiment and the Royal Africa Corps, and surmised that the outfits had been sold by regimental pensioners and had found their way upcountry with other merchandise.

As an overture to trade talks, Balansama gave Laing an earring of gold filigree to present to Governor MacCarthy as a token of the Barawa people's desire for friendship. To further demonstrate his eagerness to establish commerce between the interior and the coast, Balansama sent some of his entourage to Kolakonké to declare the road now open, allowing Sankaran and Kuranko gold, cloth, camwood, and ivory to be traded with the white men by the sea. To seal the alliance, his brother, his son, and one of the Kamato chiefs would accompany Laing to the coast. Balansama then ordered everyone to dance.

Had I known these details of Balansama's sphere of influence, and of the extensive trading networks that already connected coastal colonies with polities as far away as the Niger and Sankaran Rivers, I would not have entertained the illusion of isolated villages cut off from history and the outside world. Yet in the complaints of Abdul's wives, who were obliged to tote headloads of supplies from the riverside to stock his small store, I began to understand why villagers dreamed of the Seli being bridged, and of a road made to Firawa, for didn't these yearnings echo the hopes that Balansama had expressed to Laing 150 years before?

Opening oneself up to the outside world may be compared to venturing into the bush, because while one stands to gain material advantages and extraordinary powers thereby, one also stands to lose one's autonomy and even one's life. Not a day passed that I did not remark this tension between a moral ideal of openness (the very notion of personhood, *morgoye*, implies transparency and magnanimity) and a pragmatic wariness that found expression in a fear of the forces of the night, and a guarded attitude toward strangers. Hence the deployment of a host of protective devices, worn on the body, placed on the lintel or threshold of a house, or marking the boundary of a farm.

It may be, as Barawa's turbulent history suggests, that a successful balance between independence and dependence, like the balance between autocracy and democracy, has always proved elusive, and that Kuranko have suffered a succession of wild oscillations between these extremes. Balansama clearly saw that his country's well-being depended on forging trade deals and political alliances with the outside world, including the British, who had established their Freetown colony only thirty years before his meeting with Laing. But in his eagerness for imported goods, Balansama inadvertently abetted the erosion of Barawa's autonomy that began with the British declaration of the Protectorate in 1896, continued with the imposition of a hut tax and indirect rule, and culminated in the amalgamation of hitherto separate polities, including Barawa, which became a marginalized section of the chiefdom of Nieni. Though these losses may be attributed to colonial rule, the tension between isolationism and engagement has been a constant of human history. For how can one be open to novel possibilities without compromising one's identity, risking one's ontological security, and being borne into a future over which one has little or no control? International trade agreements and geopolitical alliances undermine one's sense of being at the center of the world and so, inevitably, the pendulum swings back toward insularity and the building of walls to keep foreigners out. Though Abdul's wives, Tilkolo and Ferema, complained about the isolation of their village, I would return to Firawa fifteen years later to find that the Seli River had been bridged and a road made to the village, only to hear complaints about the entrepreneurs who came after harvest time in their battered trucks and bought rice for a fraction of the price it would fetch on the Kabala and Freetown markets. Just as their grandparents had been powerless to resist the colonial administrators who interfered in the election of chiefs and replaced ancestral protocols with British law, so now farmers were too poor and powerless to control the market.

This existential struggle between being an actor and being acted upon would come to preoccupy me, not only as it played out in the politics of chieftaincy and in economic life, but as it found expression in the vexed relationship between ethnographers and their interlocutors. That this struggle informed my relationship with Noah was something it took me too long to appreciate and amend. Indeed, it would take a shocking experience in Freetown to bring me to my senses. But I am getting ahead of myself.

Albitaiya

An immense granite inselberg, known as Albitaiya (Under the Protection of Allah) overshadows the town of Kabala, and on my return from Firawa I began, with Noah's help, to understand the significance of this place for the people of Barawa, and add another chapter to my chronicle of the Barawa Marah.

In the mid-nineteenth century, Barawa was ruled by Bol' Tamba Marah, a tireless warrior who made frequent forays into the Kissi country to the east in search of slaves. He was also renowned for his power to conjure thunder and lightning at will, even in the dry season, and thereby strike fear into the hearts of his enemies. Such power can protect as well as destroy, and in the 1860s, mindful of the rise to power in the upper Niger of a Mandinka warlord called Almami Samori Turé, the Kuranko rulers of Diang, Kalian, Morfindugu, Neya, Mongo, and Sa Nieni elected to put their lands under the protection of Bol' Tamba. "This is what we can do in the name of Allah and Muhammad," declared Marama Sandi of Diang. "Let us take this country and give it to Bol' Tamba so that we may live without fear." In placing their countries in the hands of Bol' Tamba, the chiefs asked that he should keep *ferensola* (the Kuranko area as a whole) in his heart, to which Bol' Tamba replied that if he was to safeguard their collective lands and livelihoods, it was only proper that one of the other chiefs should keep vigil on the bird-scaring platform—an analogy for the upland rice fields, which, as the grain ripens, are prey to scavenging birds and are protected by a network of strings that can be activated by pulling on a lead string, or by boys with slingshots sitting on platforms high above the fields.

And so, Maran Lai Bockari, whose country Morfindugu lay to the east, became Bol' Tamba's lookout.

Although Samori would soon declare a jihad against the pagan Yalunka and Kuranko, and in the 1880s leave a trail of death and destruction throughout the Kuranko heartland, oral tradition gives one to understand that before this happened Samori heard of Bol' Tamba's reputation and sought an alliance with him. "Let us meet," he is alleged to have said, "and swear an oath that neither of us should threaten the other."

On his way to meet Samori, tragedy overwhelmed Bol' Tamba from an unexpected quarter.

According to Kuranko traditions, the people of Barawa were betrayed by their Sa Nieni neighbors, who informed the Kono to the south that Bol' Tamba had left his country unprotected. Seeking plunder, Kono warriors under Senkerifa traveled north through SaNieni and sacked and burned almost every village in Barawa. To this day, people remember the names of the fifteen destroyed towns that were never rebuilt.

Bol' Tamba was at a town called Kamaia when he heard that the lands under his protection had been invaded and laid waste. "Then accept my dead body now," he said. Entering the house where he had lodged that night, and without using either knife or gun, the then took his own life.

When Samori heard of Bol' Tamba's suicide, he said, "Ah, you have done a courageous thing. But before killing yourself you should have come to me and told me that war had entered your country." Samori then dispatched warriors to drive the Kono from Barawa.

For all its dramatic poignancy, the story of Bol' Tamba's suicide may be apocryphal or may arise from a confusion with Marin Tamba, who was also known as Sewa. It is also possible that this Sewa was confused with the Yalunka chief Sewa, who, with his family and several elders, killed himself rather submit to Islam or be enslaved by the Sofas besieging his capital, Falaba, in 1884. In any event, whether because of the loss of their lord and protector or the destruction of their villages and granaries, the people of Barawa trekked north as refugees. For a while they found refuge in Morfindugu, but the locals feared domination by the exiles, who dispersed again, some seeking distant kin, before settling around the Wara Wara Hills behind Kabala. Here, however, they quickly came into conflict with the local Limba. After an incident in which Aisetta Karifa was driven from Albitaiya when he went there to cut grass for thatching, the Barawa refugees took up arms and made Albitaiya their own. The cotton trees they planted for protection around the new settlement are still there today.

It was from Albitaiya that Noah's father's father, Manti Kamara Kulifa, went out to wage war against Samori's Sofas.

Though his given name was Yira, he had earned the nickname Kulifa' (Leopard Slayer) as a boy when he single-handedly fought off the attack of a leopard that, he was later told, was most likely an enemy who had assumed animal form. As it turned out, the shape-shifting facility of an enemy would prove less daunting than the fickleness of a woman.

In time of war it was the prerogative of a principal warrior to take his wives with him on his campaigns. So Kulifa took his first wife, Kumba (who hailed from the Sankaran country that Samori now dominated), and left his younger wives, Sirasie and Tina, to look after the children. Moving constantly from one strange place to another, and under threat of attack, Kumba yearned to return home and asked her husband if she might stay with her parents while the war lasted. Manti Kamara Kulifa refused to let her go, but one evening, on the pretext of collecting firewood in the bush, she ran away.

Her husband set out after her the next day, despite warnings from his men of the dangers of venturing further into Sofa-held country.

At Kumba's village, the girl's parents begged him to leave their daughter in their care. Kulifa said he would wait three days: this would be time enough for them to remind Kumba of her duty.

At midnight on the third day, alarmed by rumors of Sofa spies, Kulifa went into the bush beyond the village to reimmunize himself against swords and sorcery. Under the feeble light of a waning moon, he sprinkled herbs and gunpowder in two calabashes of water, then stripped naked and sat between them. The water began to stir and simmer and, without his aid, stream across his body from one vessel to another.

He was never to know that a Sofa spy, having overheard Kumba carelessly talking about her husband, bribed her to confide the secret place and time that Manti Kamara Kulifa was without his sword and war gown. Before the magical immunization could take effect, he was seized by the Sofas. The following day he was taken to Worekoro. There, with wrists bound and legs shackled, he was led out of the town to an outcrop of granite surrounded by bleached bones. The Sofa leader ordered Kulifa's head shaved in case his hair was imbued with the power to deflect sword blades, and he was executed.

Manti Kamara Kulifa's younger brother Sewa inherited the young widow, Tina. Tina's youngest son, Komé, was a small boy when his father was killed. But he would grow up hearing the story of his father's betrayal. Nor was Kulifa the only brother Fa Sewa lost in the war, and for as long as he lived he nursed two grievances—that the white men had supplied the Sofas with arms, and that the deceitfulness of women was more ruinous than war. In years to come, even though three wives would desert him, Tina's youngest son Komé would vow never to pursue an errant wife and would warn his sons to divine well the character of a woman before marrying her.

The Sankaran and Kuranko countries were devastated by the Sofas. In the ruins of Kolakonke, Firawa, Yamisaia, and Sanyala, courtyards became overgrown with grass and *combretum*, and the rafters of burned houses were strung with the nests of palm birds. The only sounds were the eternal piping of a suluku bird and the yelping of monkeys. Piles of bleached bones remained unburied on the outskirts of villages, and many of those who had survived the war now lived in the bush in makeshift houses of palm fronds. "Considering what they have undergone," wrote a European observer, "one can hardly be surprised that they regard strangers with a certain amount of reserve, and that they cannot credit them with any motive except to kill and plunder."[1] As people struggled to find seed rice and replant, they ate wild yams and fruits, and camouflaged small gardens of rice and cassava around swamps.

Over this ruined region, British and French diplomats wrangled, seeking treaties with Samori while negotiating their separate spheres of colonial control. When the Sofa wars finally ended, the two European governments ordered a joint commission to plot the course of the upper Niger and its tributaries in order to define the boundary between their domains. In December 1865 an expedition consisting of policemen, army engineers, interpreters, servants, hammock boys, and bearers passed through Kuranko country on its way to the headwaters of the Niger. Using plane tables, meridian and circummeridian observations of the stars, trigonometrical plotting, and lunar distances, the surveyors established the precise location of the Niger's source. An agreement signed in Paris on January 21, 1895, had already determined on paper the line of partition. The line ran through the heart of Kuranko.

When I came to read Colonel J. K. Trotter's account of the expedition he led to the source of the Niger in 1895, I was struck, not only by his indifference to indigenous boundaries and his mercenary allusions to the country's potential for exploitation, but by the plethora of quantitative data on every-thing from altitude, air temperature, latitude, and longitude to distance marched each day, all of which reflected a predilection for scientific objectivity, which, since the Enlightenment, had become Europe's magical means of giving legitimacy to its predatory expansion and its power. Where, I asked myself, did anthropology's claims to knowledge rest if not in the magic of number and the illusion of all-encompassing concepts?

Primus inter Pares

Although it is relatively easy to retrieve the data I recorded in Firawa from my red Guinea notebooks, bearing an image of Samori on their covers, it is a very different matter when I try to remember details of my life at One-Mile with Pauline. Even with such aide-mémoire as color transparencies, I struggle to recall the ambiance of those distant dry-season days. Noah would come by most mornings, and we would share a pot of tea before Pauline repaired to her room to work and Noah, ensconced in the hammock in our parlor with my cassette recorder on his lap, pressed the start and pause buttons again and again as he painstakingly translated a clan myth or folktale that I had recorded in Firawa. We would frequently digress, discussing how best to interpret an arcane phrase or reconcile alternative versions of the same myth, or for Noah to tutor me in Kuranko. Yet there were days when he was reluctant to work, preferring to play checkers with a friend or simply stroll around town and exchange small talk with whoever he chanced to meet. Perhaps, I told myself, he had not reckoned with the demands I would make on his time, or my relentless questioning. As for Pauline, she never doubted her decision to throw in her lot with me, or resented my return visits to Firawa, or the hours I spent with informants in and around Kabala. She would work on her sagas, drive to the market, or visit neighbors until around noon when, benumbed by the heat, we would collapse on the straw palliasse in our bedroom and watch the nesting palm birds through the barred window, or a mason bee diligently accreting another layer of clay to its conical nest on the plaster wall—mirror images of the labors in which we were separately engaged. Toward evening we would prepare a meal of rice, cabbage, and dal, and afterward stroll along the dusty path that wound among boulders, long grass, and palms toward the Wara Wara Hills. As night fell, we would read for a while by the light of a hurricane lantern—*Middlemarch, The Alexandria Quartet, Speak, Memory*—or play chess, or discuss intriguing parallels between the feuds and factions of thirteenth-century Iceland and nineteenth-century Barawa.

I must surely have also shared with Pauline my fascination with a recurring motif in the ancestral lore (*kuma kore,* lit. old words) that Noah was helping me transcribe.

Despite a hierarchical worldview that ranked men above women, rulers above praise singers, elders above juniors, and humans above animals, clan myths repeatedly called these distinctions into question. Birth, it was implied, was not an absolute guarantee of worth. Not only was hereditary power sometimes abused, but virtue might find its most consummate expression in the actions of an underling.

In one myth, to which I would return many times in the years to come, the half brothers of a legendary war chief called Saramba conspire to ambush and kill him. But Saramba's lowly *finaba,* Musa Kule, gets wind of the plot and persuades his master to change clothes and places with him. Journeying to a distant town, they come under attack, but Musa Kule, who is riding ahead, is killed, while his master, following on foot, survives. For Saramba, the self-sacrifice of Musa Kule nullifies the hierarchical relationship between lord and master, and he declares that a privileged relationship now exists between his descendants and those of Musa Kule.

The same motif recurred in an account of how the leopard became the totem of the Marah.

My informant was Bala Kondé, who lived in a ramshackle wattle-and-daub house behind the Kabala market. A country cloth tunic barely covered Bala's bony torso, and as Noah and I explained the reason for our visit, Bala bade us sit and, after shucking off his plastic sandals, leaned back in his hammock.

Long ago, Bala began, rapidly repeating the word *fiu* to suggest remoteness from present time, the ancestor of the Kondé and the ancestor of the Marah were close friends, though the Kondé were the more powerful. The Marah were anxious that in the event of the Kondé and Marah settling the same country, the descendants of the Kondé would look down on the descendants of the Marah. The Kondé ancestor assured the Marah that he wished only that their friendship (a relationship of equality) should endure, even if they settled the same country (and the Kondé ruled over the Marah). The Marah then proposed that they eat rice flour together to seal their friendship.

In the same year this oath was taken, the Marah died. But on his deathbed he had requested, in the name of friendship, that the Kondé take care of his two sons. A few years later, the Kondé also passed away, though not before asking his sons to honor the bond of friendship that existed with the Marah. Though they might quarrel, they should never come to blows.

One day, when the young men were clearing and burning underbrush on their farm, the elder of the Kondé brothers, whose name was Fadu, gave his gun to the elder of the Marah brothers and went to a nearby stream to slake his thirst. At the streamside, he came upon a female leopard in labor. As he made to retreat, the leopard beckoned him back, and as he approached in trepidation, the leopard said, "I know you are a hunter, but you find me here in labor. If you allow me to give birth to my cub in peace I will give you a spell that will help you find game." Fadu Kondé spared the life of the leopard, who gave birth to her cub before telling Fadu the magical words that would help him in the hunt. When Fadu asked the leopard why it attacked and killed people, the leopard replied, "Because you people attack and kill us. Had we not struck a bargain just now, you would surely have killed me, or I would have killed you."

The leopard now declared that none of its descendants would ever harm a Kondé, and Fadu Kondé declared that none of his descendants would ever harm a leopard.

When Fadu Kondé returned to the farm, the Marah demanded to know what he had found at the streamside, and what had kept him so long. Fadu refused to speak of what had happened, declaring that it was a secret he was not at liberty to divulge. The two men came to blows. Though Fadu Kondé struck first, he died seven days later from the injuries he had suffered at the hands of the Marah. But people did not blame the Marah. They blamed Fadu Kondé for breaking the oath of friendship his father had taken with the Marah.

The elder Marah brother now went to the streamside and met the leopard. He told the leopard what had happened, and that his "elder brother" (Fadu) was dead. The leopard now befriended the Marah, just as it had befriended the Kondé, and shared the secret words with the Marah that it had earlier shared with the Kondé. The leopard thus became the totem of the Marah.

My growing fascination with the conditions under which social hierarchies are subverted by altruistic actions led me to ponder the question of natural justice. If absolute power corrupts, is it sometimes also true that the privileged assign virtue to the underprivileged in order to allay their guilt over their superior status, or in an attempt to compensate the downtrodden for what they lack? In refusing to reduce life-as-lived to prescribed rights and obligations, I was departing radically from the paradigms of my Cambridge teachers, as well as from the structuralist models of Claude Lévi-Strauss that had inspired my initial interest in comparative analysis. I accepted Lévi-Strauss's argument that the intrinsic properties of a totem are less significant than its relationship with other totems in a comprehensive schema, and that the relationship between totemic species is compared with the relationship between social groups, implying that "natural species are chosen not because they are 'good to eat' [their 'subjective utility'] but because they are 'good to think' [their 'objective analogy']."[1] In the Kuranko case, the superior power of the Marah vis-à-vis nonruling clans is compared to the superior powers of the leopard vis-à-vis all other animals. But just as I rejected the structural-functionalist reduction of human experience to collective representations, I resisted the structuralist reduction of experience to unconscious structures of the mind. I wanted to explore the dynamic interplay between social givenness and individual creativity—and would, in due course, draw inspiration from a single illuminating phrase of Jean-Paul Sartre's: "We are not lumps of clay, and what is important is not what people make of us but what we ourselves make of what they have made us."[2] I could never hope to know how Manti Kamara Kulifa imagined or acted out his totemic identification with the leopard, but perhaps in learning more about Noah's elder brother Kulifa, who had inherited his grandfather's name but abandoned his birthright and gone to Liberia many years ago, I might satisfy my curiosity in how different individuals respond to the historical, cultural, and social circumstances that are visited upon them by the accident of their births and the inheritance of their names.

Lifelines and Lineages

One thing I struggled to get used to during my first months of fieldwork was the discrepancy between the villagers' sense of time and my own. I would sit on the porch at Abdul's house for hours at a time or stroll around the village in the hope that something would happen to alleviate my boredom. The heat only increased my lassitude, and though the village sprang to life after sundown, my social and linguistic ineptitude made it difficult for me to participate in the raillery, storytelling, and gossip that animated those moonlit dry-season nights. Part of the problem was, of course, that my fieldwork bore no relation to what Kuranko farmers regarded as work, and though people would politely respond to my childlike questioning or could be persuaded by Noah to help me understand why they made sacrifices to their ancestors or married their cross-cousins, I was aware that the women had rice to pound and children to care for, while the men wanted nothing more than to doze through the noonday hours and make the most of their respite from farmwork. In short, my time and their time were at complete odds. While I saw my sojourn in Sierra Leone as a race against time, an attempt to compress into a single year the tasks of learning a foreign language and amassing enough data to write a doctoral dissertation, not to mention the impact a child would have on my routines, it seemed that everyone in Firawa, including Noah, had all the time in the world. And while they went about their unhurried lives, I grew exasperated at the snail's pace at which my fieldwork was progressing. Court hearings would, to my mind, drag on far longer than necessary, villagers appeared to take a perverse delight in creating palaver over trivial issues, and I would be increasingly irritated by Noah's pedantic commentaries on neighborhood disputes. Even when it dawned on me that all this banter was not motivated by a search for doctrinal resolutions but by a social imperative to work at creating social harmony, even if that harmony was more performative than fully realized, I could not curb my impatience. Although I saw the truth of the adage "neighborliness is not sweet" and recognized the need to resolve land disputes, conjugal grievances, and in-law conflicts before they got out of hand, I found myself unable to overcome my ingrained cultural habit of drawing a line between personal goals and social obligations. When upbraided by a villager for not taking the time to recite a long-winded litany of greetings with her—something vital to the everyday affirmation and reaffirmation of communal solidarity—I hurried on my way as if her question, "Don't you know who I am?" did not merit an apology or reply.

The derogatory expression "African time" is not so much a reflection on African reality as an oblique expression of a Protestant ethic of personal industriousness and self-making. The term fails to capture the positive value traditional Africa places on social cohesion and communitas as the foundations of a viable economic and political order. While the European Enlightenment extolled agency over patiency and elevated end-gaining to the level of a moral imperative, traditional lifeworlds remind us of what we lose in dismissing the past as synonymous with superstition, forgetting our indebtedness to our forebears, and setting our own welfare above the well-being of others. Though these insights were born of my experiences of village life, they continued to come up against ingrained habits I could not break. In not wanting to reproduce the past, recapitulate the worldview of my grandparents, or reiterate the paradigm of structural-functional anthropology, I was echoing the frustrations of young Kuranko, increasingly resistant to becoming farmers by seeking their fortunes in the diamond districts of Kono or the cities to the south, and opening themselves up to the future rather than slavishly repeating the past.

My growing awareness that lived experience never mirrors collective representations, and that personal realities are seldom congruent with social ideologies, began to erode my confidence in the normative tenets of the anthropology I had been taught, particularly the assumption that human beings are culturally conditioned. That I found myself dissenting from this view, or saw that individual Kuranko often paid lip service to values they no longer regarded as relevant, made me wonder whether all human beings are driven, to some extent, by a need to unmake the world into which they are born in order to make something of themselves. I suppose I was beginning to ask whether the distinction between premodern genealogical societies and modern societies consisting of "autological subjects" was not definitive, but relative.[1] A matter of context and emphasis, rather than fixed identity. The image of a genealogical society depends as much on the imaginations and interests of particular individuals as the image of autological subjects depends on an ideology that values capital accumulation and competition over collective well-being.

Although I saw the fallacy of deriving an understanding of human experience from the dominant discourse of a society or, for that matter, an academic discipline, I struggled with the question as to how else one might gain access to subjective life. I had made some headway in seeing how Kuranko thought about genealogical relations with predecessors, contemporaries, and successors, but I was handicapped by a visualist bias that reflected not only a long-standing conflation in European philosophy of thought with clear seeing (insight, perception, perspective, and similarly optical terms), but with literacy as the dominant technology of communication. This might explain why I had tended to fall back on received anthropological wisdom by translating intersubjective experience into genealogical diagrams in which social relations were reduced to Euclidean lines connecting individual dots. This abstract model would then be described as a network or web, giving the impression that the system of lineal connections remained constant over time, and as one individual died another simply took his place, performing the same role in the social order as his predecessor.

My interest in the affective and psychophysical aspects of living in genealogical time was further piqued by Noah's intriguing comments on the phenomenon of *fo' koe* (lit. dead thing, or the action of the dead). According to Noah, your ancestors are ever-present, observing you, aware of what is happening in your life, and potentially a source of benefit to you. He spoke of his own father in these terms, giving me the impression that the presence of the dead is not a function of memory but of intersubjectivity, since one remains neurologically and socially connected to the dead, although they have ceased to exist as fully embodied beings. Perhaps, I told myself, life stories would help me better describe the world, not as it is in essence but as it appears, in all its confusing and often contradictory detail, with extant understandings and instant experiences of past and present times always copresent but never fully reconciled. In developing this phenomenological approach to lived reality, metaphor and image would become increasingly significant as I began to compare the Kuranko with other West African peoples and to question the anthropological fetishization of lineages and lineal descent. I would discover that even when one found an indigenous word that was nearly identical to the English word *lineage*, there was an indeterminate relationship between the word and what it appeared to designate. For example, among the Tiv of Nigeria, the word *nongo* means literally line or queue, though it "refers primarily to the living representatives of a lineage," a grouping without any real genealogical depth.[2] A more inclusive term, *ityo* (patrilineage), which one might expect to suggest a descent line, conjures up for the Tiv an image of "the father's path" or way of doing things rather than a line of succession and ancestry.[3] This is reminiscent of the way the Kuranko speak of their relationships with both contemporary kin and forebears as networks of paths or ropes.[4] When ancestors are named at a sacrifice, they are called at random as they come to mind and asked to "pass on the sacrifice to everybody, named and unnamed," including God.[5] Moreover, remembering the names of ancestors more than three generations back was generally more important for rulers than commoners, since the legitimacy of a ruler depended entirely on demonstrable genealogical links to previous incumbents. When sharing genealogical information with me, Kuranko villagers would generally not list the names of forebears in strict lineal sequences but rather cluster them as belonging to the father's or mother's place (*fa ware* or *na ware*) or as "paternal ones" and "maternal ones" (*fa keli meenu* and *na keli meenu*), suggesting emotional relationships with place and parenthood, not abstract lines of descent.[6]

Meyer Fortes's Tallensi ethnography provides a telling example of how relationships are conceptualized spatially and expressed temporally in images of a house and a begetting. Yet, considering his pioneering work in lineage theory, Fortes notes somewhat surprisingly that "the Tallensi have no term for the lineage."[7] He then goes on to assimilate their metaphors to his own: "A lineage of any order is designated the 'house' (yir) or the children (biis) of the founding ancestor. . . . In contexts where the emphasis is on the lineage considered as a segment of a more inclusive lineage, it is commonly described as a 'room' (dug) of the more inclusive 'house' (yir). . . . As this nomenclature shows, the internal constitution of the lineage is modelled on that of the polygynous joint family." What Fortes calls a lineage is thus a house or household (*yidem*), a group of people who feel they share "one blood" or "one begetting." Rather than work with these vital and visceral images of shared substance and natality, Fortes elects to impose his concept of a lineage on this lived reality and to reinforce this conceptual imposition with lineal charts and diagrams.

In his ethnography of the Nuer, E. E. Evans-Pritchard shows a greater sensitivity to this problem of translation. "When illustrating on the ground a number of related lineages [the Nuer] do not present them the way we figure them . . . as a series of bifurcations of descent, as a tree of descent, or as a series of triangles of ascent, but as a number of lines running at angles from a common point." Nuer see the "lineage system," Evans-Pritchard says, "primarily as actual relations between groups of kinsmen within local communities rather than as a tree of descent, for the persons after whom the lineages are called do not all proceed from a single individual."[8]

The problem with the concept of lineage is not only its bias toward linear perspective; it gives rise to models of segmentary organization and social order that take on a life of their own. One consequence is that the lifeworld becomes eclipsed by an anthropological worldview, and entire societies are compared not in terms of empirical realities but in terms of reified models that conflate map with territory and confuse the structure of discourse with the structure of experience. A second consequence is that the jargon of anthropologists creates an illusion of radical cultural difference, masking what ethnographers may have in common with the people they study, namely, an analogical mode of thinking about the world, a sense of changing through time, yet begotten by someone and belonging to some place. Clearly, when we turn from abstract linearity to consider the lived reality of lifelines, we discover that lines are seldom straight for very long, nor symmetrical like branches of a family tree, nor wholly ruled by cultural determinations. "Life," as the Russian proverb says, "is not a walk across an open field."[9]

An existential perspective emerged from my immersion in village life, eavesdropping on conversations, participating in the ebullient and indefatigable routines of greeting, exchanging news and making palaver that had first exasperated but now enthralled me. This was the never-ending work (*wale*) of everyday life, the project of realizing the possibility of communitas despite the competing interests of individuals and the fickleness of their fortunes. John Berger compared this process to the composition of a group portrait, a process that is never-ending because "experience is indivisible and continuous, at least within a single lifetime and perhaps over many lifetimes," and a community's self-image is constructed not out of stone but "out of words, spoken and remembered: out of opinions, stories, eye-witness reports, legends, comments and hearsay."[10] This explains the diversity of oral

2 Village scene, Firawa, January 1970.

traditions that, despite their illusion of fixity, are, like human memory itself, undergoing perpetual revision.

As my sense of the tenor and complexity of village life deepened, I became increasingly mindful that anthropological models never mirror the life they purport to capture or encapsulate. Life simply does not admit closure and completeness. Consider the image in figure 2 of a young man in Firawa, patiently making a bamboo mat by threading carefully split canes through a grid of raffia strings that were tied to small stakes in the ground.

A second man has set up his weaving frame nearby, and as others sleep during the heat of the day, he adds to his long narrow strip of white country cloth, winding it into a tight ball. The work of both men mimics my own work in progress. Work that will not end with the country cloth being woven, or when it is dyed and stitched into a garment, or worn and finally worn out. Work that will not end with the making of the mat, which will in time also fray and fall apart. Work that is never done, but is like Penelope's web, always beginning anew.

Prospero and Caliban

Victor Turner characterized his relationship with Muchona, a Ndembu hermeneut, as "professional" rather than "personal," noting that they "maintained towards one another a certain reserve." Yet when they finally went their separate ways, Turner felt sure that Muchona would miss their lengthy conversations on ritual symbolism, and he regretted that "the philosophy don would have to return to a world that could only make a witchdoctor of the paramountly intellectual Muchona."[1]

Turner's distinctions between the professional and personal, and his reluctance to admit that he might miss his informant as much as Muchona might miss his friend, hardly does justice to my relationship with Noah, which began uneasily but evolved, over the years, into a close friendship.

One thing was clear to me from the outset: as long as Noah remained my hireling and I remained dependent on his help and resentful of his independence, true friendship was impossible, and even trivial differences in taste would be obstacles to mutuality.

Noah's favorite song was the 1960 Ray Peterson hit, "Tell Laura I Love Her." This melodramatic ballad tells of a teenage boy who is head over heels in love with a girl named Laura. Tommy wants to marry Laura and enters a stock car race in the hope that winning the prize money will enable him to buy her a wedding ring. His car overturns and bursts into flames, and as Tommy lies dying on the track his last words are, "Tell Laura I love her. . . . My love for her will never die." In the final verse, Laura is praying in a chapel, still hearing Tommy's fading voice as he repeats his dying words.

The only place in Kabala that Noah could hear his favorite record was Lansana Kamara's bar near the market, and we repaired there occasionally in the evening, where I would order two bottles of cold Fanta and Noah would badger L. K. into playing the scratchy 45 record on his turntable, filling the bar with Ray Peterson's maudlin strains and driving me quietly to distraction.

What did Noah hear in these lyrics? What did he respond to in this melancholy story of tragic teenage love? Married with two young wives and a young son, what possible emotional link could he have with this song? Was it the tone of lives lost—the same nostalgia that led him to work for me, salvaging a record of a vanishing lifeworld?

Three months into my fieldwork, Noah accompanied me on a trip to Freetown where I planned to buy various household supplies that Pauline and I needed.

When Pauline and I first arrived in Sierra Leone, we met an American student at Fourah Bay College who, like me, was embarking on his doctoral research. While I anticipated fieldwork in a remote village, Hal was hoping to interview various political figures in Freetown who would provide him with insights into the military coup and countercoup of 1967–68. When Pauline and I left for Kabala, Hal told us to let him know if we were ever in Freetown; he would be happy to have us stay with him. I reciprocated the offer of hospitality.

After explaining all this to Noah, I asked if he would be comfortable with me taking up Hal Tarrant on his offer. But Noah had very different ideas and had assumed we would stay with his sister Ai, who had a house in Brookfields. The truth is that I needed a complete break from fieldwork, and so I insisted we stay with Hal and spend as much time with Ai as time permitted.

The road to Kabala had been partially washed out by heavy rain, and it took us several hours to reach Makeni, where we bought bowls of Jolof rice from a street vendor. Though the road south was tar sealed, it was choked with battered *poda-podas*, lorries laden with firewood or charcoal, and cars belching blue smoke into the cloying air. By the time we reached Freetown and found our way to Hal's bungalow in the West End, night was falling, and both Noah and I were reeling from our hours on the road.

When Hal's cursory greeting was followed by an offhand invitation to make ourselves at home, but with no suggestion as to where we might sleep or whether a meal would be offered, I should have realized we were intruding.

Hal's abrupt announcement that he and his roommates were about to go out for the evening should have been enough for me to accept Noah's suggestion that we drive to his sister's house. But I ignored all the signs, and as soon as Hal and his friends had left I returned to the Land Rover, moved our bags into the house, and told Noah to use the couch in the living room as his bed; I would sleep on the floor.

It was then a question of finding something to eat. After telling the watchman we were going out for a meal, we headed downtown, with Noah making a last-ditch effort to make me see reason; Ai's house was very close; we could eat there, and even stay.

I can only explain my obduracy as a kind of vengeance for having become so dependent on Noah that my autonomy had been undermined. When the only place I could find to eat was a nightclub where two hamburgers and French fries cost as much as a Kuranko farmer would earn in a year, and Noah sat morosely in the semidarkness as perfumed prostitutes and their drunken clients shouted and shrieked around us, I remained determined to see the evening through. In ignoring Noah's protestations about the cost of the food and his discomfort, was I perhaps humbling him as I had felt humbled in Firawa?

I hardly slept that night. It wasn't only the tiled floor and the lack of a blanket to keep me warm as the night air cooled. It was my appalled awareness that I was as ill adapted to village life as I was contemptuous of the affluent enclave in which Hal had found refuge.

But my disquiet was about to become worse.

Noah and I woke to find Hal rushing about the house in tennis whites, racket in hand.

"What's going on?" I asked.

"Richard's had some money stolen from his room."

It didn't take long before the finger of suspicion fell on us. Or, rather, on Noah. But instead of accosting him directly, Hal and Richard took me into the kitchen and confided that the culprit could not have been anyone but Noah.

Outraged, I tried to explain how preposterous this was. Kuranko were known throughout Sierra Leone for being honest to a fault, even owning up to thefts in the diamond districts they had not committed, simply to clear the air. "What about your servants?" I asked. The gardener, the night watchman, the cook, the houseboy?

Now it was Hal's turn to take umbrage. He knew and trusted them all. It had to be Noah. The outsider. The intruder.

I told Noah to pack his bag, and I did the same. We walked out on Hal and his dismayed friends and drove to Noah's sister's house, where we shared the story of Noah's humiliation.

That afternoon we called on Noah's brother Sewa, known as S. B., who ran the Alitalia agency in Freetown. As I recounted details of our night at Hal's, I noticed that Noah had assumed a deferential, even self-abnegating, attitude, not participating in the conversation but edging toward the door as if he was intruding on something that was not his business. I would never get used to this strange formality between the brothers, any more than I would accept S. B.'s frequent denigration of Noah as a wastrel or, reciprocally, Noah's resentment of Sewa as someone who had always treated him like a slave.

The longer we remained in S. B.'s small office, the more aware I became of how cold it was by contrast with the stifling heat in the street outside, not only because S. B. had the air conditioner blasting glacial air into the room but because the various placards advertising the exotic places that Alitalia flew to were in such stark contrast with the run-down quarters of Freetown where I had been buying supplies that morning ahead of our journey back to Kabala.

Despite the coldness between S. B. and Noah, they were clearly in agreement about Hal Tarrant, and for the first time I saw the unforgiving side of Noah's brother. When he declared that he would neither help nor hinder Hal Tarrant in his research, I was guiltily aware that S. B. had, by contrast, bestowed his blessings on my endeavors, and this was confirmed when he slipped me his business card after writing on it a message to the effect that I should be given safe passage wherever I traveled in Sierra Leone.

Though I resented Hal for his inhospitality, I failed to see that I had exhibited the same arrogance that everyone in a position of power easily falls prey to, and that it would take more than a single generation for anthropologists to awaken from the nightmare that was colonialism.

In 2004, when my book based on the life of S. B. Marah was published, I received a letter from Hal. Addressing me as Dr. Jackson, as if we had never met, Hal informed me that he had been in Sierra Leone between 1969 and 1971 and "remembered S.B. well and indeed befriended him." He had "only the fondest of memories of S.B.," whom he described as "one of the kindest people I encountered during my stay in Freetown."

I wrote to Hal, expressing surprise that he did not remember me and reminding him of the episode involving Noah at his house in Brookfields in 1970.

Here is Hal's reply.

Michael,

I guess my memory has faded over time. I recall our paths crossing but I wasn't absolutely sure that they had so thanks for telling me. So much happened to me during my time in Freetown both good and bad. Now that you mention the incident with Noah that really jogs my memory. I can't believe that I accused Noah or anyone else of stealing money. I apologize, even if it is thirty-four years too late. I had quite a few people staying with me from time to time when I was at Brookfields—not all of them close friends—so perhaps one of them was behind this incident. By the way, I eventually had to move out of Brookfields. I had to let my night watchman go at one point and a few days later he returned with a panga gang and almost slashed to death the new guy on the job. I had to take him to Connaught Hospital bleeding from head to toe. I was sound asleep at the time. Had I been up and around who knows what might have happened. I then moved back up to Fourah Bay College where I felt a lot safer. Sometimes my stay there seems like a dream.

Tina Komé

When S. B. spoke of his father, Tina Komé Marah, he was often overcome by emotion. Hesitant, his voice almost a whisper, he once told me, "One of the greatest . . . things I have lost . . . in my life, or someone I have lost . . . is my father. I love him so much that even now . . . when I think of him . . . I shed tears. Just because of the simple fact that he was a man who wanted his children to do something that humanity would appreciate."

Noah's nostalgia was no less overwhelming. As the last born in a family of eight, his father had doted on him, and Noah would regale me with stories of how, as a small boy, he would accompany his father on his rounds as court messenger, carried on the shoulders of Tina Komé's fathful praise singer, Yeli Pore.

I became intrigued by this heroic figure whose lifetime coincided with the period of colonial rule in Sierra Leone, and the beginning of a gradual atrophy of traditional life that would culminate in Tina Komé's great-grandson's indifference to his ancestry, never visiting Firawa or learningKuranko.

Born in Albitaiya, the mountain refuge to which his people fled after the Kono war, Tina Komé was only a child when his father, Manti Kamara Kulifa, was betrayed to the Sofas and executed. Thus, before he was even conscious of his birthright, separation and loss cast their shadows over his life. The same violent impress of history marked his youth. Though his elder brother, Tina Kaima, argued against the changes being wrought by the British, Tina Komé saw them as presaging a future that they would be foolish to ignore.

For these reasons, my growing interest in Noah's father's life and times resonated with my reading of George Eliot's *Middlemarch*, where the great Victorian novelist has one character suggest that "our deeds are fetters that we forge ourselves," only to have another argue "that it is the world that brings the iron."[1] Though colonialism was the iron, neither Tina Komé nor Tina Kaima could be accused of becoming slaves to it, bound by fetters they themselves forged. On the contrary, each responded in his own way to the same external circumstances, Tina Komé choosing to make use of the new regime to improve the lot of his children, who would be bound to live in a radically changed world, and Tina Kaima choosing to turn his back on those same changes and take refuge in tradition. Thus, choice has no reality except in relationship to necessity. Freedom is never a matter of acting without constraint, but a question of finding what one can do within set limits. That these brothers, so emotionally close, should take such different paths also brought home to me the value of Ranajit Guha's insight that colonized peoples do not respond to domination in identical ways but rather develop a variety of responses, including resistance, acquiescence, and collaboration. Nor does domination assume a unitary and universal form, since it involves both persuasion and coercion, interest and indifference.[2]

Around the turn of the century, having married for the first time, Tina Komé made several journeys to Freetown, which people called Saralon, traveling for safety in caravans of about two hundred people, for there was a constant danger in those days of being captured and enslaved. The caravans would travel from Kabala to Bafodia, Bofodia to Kamakwie, Kamakwie to Batkanu, Batkanu to Gbinti, Gbinti to Port Loko, then across the Rokel by canoe before continuing south to the coast. The northerners carried beeswax, kola nuts, soda, songbirds, and leopard skins to sell to the white men and purchased beads, salt, tobacco, soap, and Manchester cotton to take back to their villages.

In 1904 the British made Kabala their administrative headquarters, and G. H. Warren was appointed district commissioner. Tina Komé and Tina Kaima were, at this time, farming together near the village of Belikoroia, some five miles from Kabala. Late in the dry season of 1906, their only sister, Tina Dondon, married a man from Sengbe and went to live in Koinadugu town. No one expected the marriage to last. The husband was an old man, indifferent to women and partial to bamboo wine. Before the rains were over that same year, Tina Dondon left her husband and eloped with her lover.

The old man's sons went to Kabala and filed a lawsuit against Tina Dondon's brothers for refund of bridewealth. For two days receipts were laboriously recalled and counted—the gifts the husband's family had given to Tina Dondon's family on this or that occasion: the mats, salt, palm oil, kola, soap, and rice during her initiation, the necklaces and trinkets when she married, the five days' hoeing done for her mother Tina, the *lapa* and head ties that had also been given to her, the lengths of country cloth and bunches of tobacco that Fa Sewa had received.

The brothers pleaded for time to make the repayment, but their in-laws were in no mood for leniency. "It is customary to refund on the same day of the accounting," they reportedly said. "We never wanted this divorce. It creates bad feeling all around. Your sister always seemed happy. But what is done is done. We cannot change it."

Tina Komé and Tina Kaima sought help from friends and distant kin, but the main rice crop had not been harvested, and they were unable to amass even half the amount required. They considered going to fetch their errant sister from Lengekoro, where she had gone with her lover, and demand that she return to her husband, but Fa Sewa, perhaps mindful of his brother Kulifa's tragic misadventure, advised against it.

The in-laws descended on Belikoroia like scavenging birds. They thronged into the house and brought out everything they could lay their hands on. Hoes, machetes, boxes of clothing, sandals, hearthstones, mats, baskets, rice, pots, mortars and pestles, and even a bunch of bananas were piled outside. As the women chased hens around the yard, trapping them against the fence, the men entered the plundered house and hoed up the clay floor, hacked at the walls with their machetes, tore the thatch from the roof, and made up bundles of poles to carry away. Enraged and humiliated, Tina Komé pulled off his gown and threw it down for the scavengers to claim. Fa Sewa was spared the spectacle, but Tina saw it all. The brothers were left with nothing but their trousers, their mother with only a single lapa. They returned to live with their mother and Fa Sewa, and over the following months worked from daylight to dark on neighbors' farms, repaying kindnesses and earning the right to call on help to make their own farms. Their mother wore herself out pounding rice for neighbors in return for a small pannier of grain, some groundnuts, and red peppers. Her three hearthstones, made of clay from an anthill, had been taken, but she refused to replace them. For cooking she made do with a hearth of river stones and a chipped country pot.

That same year the outside world imposed its own changes. Having discovered why the people of Barawa were living in and around Kabala, District Commissioner Warren ordered their return home. He had toured the country, he told Chief Belikoro, and found it exceedingly rich in palm kernels. Kuranko would remember Warensi for the cases of champagne he took with him, the tent he preferred to a house, and the elephant cow he shot and wounded near the inselberg of Senekonke. In his intelligence diary for September 14, 1907, Warren noted, "I have told the people that if they don't return there I shall have to hand over the country to some other chief."

Tina Kaima returned to a chiefdom he had never known. His grandfather and namesake had founded the village of Kurekoro when returning exhausted from a border skirmish.[3] Famished and thirsty, he and some other warriors rested in the shade of a *kure* tree. After eating ripe fruit and drinking cool water from a nearby stream, the replenished Kaima declared that they would return there to farm and build a town that would be called Kurekoro—Under the Kure Tree. His grandson, however, decided against returning there, and he and other men of the ruling lineage founded a new settlement, sited under a steep hill, where two streams flowed into a third. They called it Firawa—Place in the Bush—after one of the old towns. It was there that Tina Kaima died in 1942. The coconut palm that Tina Komé planted over his brother's grave is still there, capturing the setting sun in its fronds.

Tina Komé did not join the returnees. Earlier that year, a British recruitment officer with the West African Frontier Force had visited Belikoro in Kabala and demanded a levy of Kuranko men. On April 17, 1907, Tina Komé, along with thirty-five others, enlisted at the Wilberforce Barracks in Freetown and was assigned the name Bokarie Kabala. Many of his kinsmen and peers took the view that Tina Komé had thrown his life away to become a child of the white men. As he saw it, perhaps, his life had already been thrown to the four winds and he had nothing to lose.

When war broke out in June 1914, the Sierra Leone battalion of the West African Frontier Force was made ready to embark for the German colony of Neu Kamerun. Two companies of the Sierra Leone battalion and eight hundred carriers left Freetown on the first of September. The troopship was overcrowded. Cockroaches gnawed the soles of men's feet as they slept. Soldiers chewed lime and red peppers to suppress seasickness. In the hot and humid atmosphere, food become moldy.

On the twenty-seventh, after a furious naval bombardment, Duala was taken, and the troops disembarked. Tina Komé first saw action at Yabasi, a railroad town on the Wuri River, north of Duala. Advancing through head-high elephant grass and raked by bursts of machine-gun fire, the initial assault failed, though the town was taken the next day. The Sierra Leoneans then held it for over a month against a German counteroffensive, torrential rain, mud, trenches, and barbed wire entanglements presaging the nightmare of the Western Front. After a further eight months in the field, marching barefoot through abandoned banana, cocoa, rubber, and oil palm plantations, slogging along mountain trails turned into quagmires by the rains, enduring sickness, chigoe infection, and heavy casualties, the Sierra Leoneans were finally pulled back to Duala. Following a stint of garrison duty, they returned to the front and a succession of desperate skirmishes at Mbo, Mborokoh, Kayraybi, Mborowah, Sha, Bakan, Bamu, and Fakuundeh (the spellings are Tina Komé's own), in the course of which the Germans retreated, first to Yaounde in the south, then to the Spanish enclave of Rio Muni. As British and French diplomats busied themselves with partitioning another piece of Africa, the troops that had so courageously served imperial interests were shipped back to Freetown, where they arrived in April 1916, almost two years after they had left. This was not, however, the end of Tina Komé's war, as he would note thirty years later in a letter to the district commissioner, Northern Province (December 22, 1946), submitting his name as a candidate for the Barawa chieftaincy. In the letter, he describes how, in 1917, four companies of Sierra Leonean troops were dispatched to Nigeria where a French outpost at Zinder had been attacked by the Tuaregs under the urging of Sanusi chiefs from Tripolitania. The Sanusi were calling for a jihad in Niger and Nigeria, and the British believed that German advisers were fomenting the rebellion. As it turned out, the Tuareg rebellion was suppressed without the Sierra Leoneans being called upon, but during their four months in Nigeria they were not entirely inactive. "When the emir of Zaria refused to pay taxes," Tina Komé writes, "we were sent to arrest him and bring him to Lokojah. During the Cameroon war," he continues, "I was appointed Company Sergeant Major, and subsequently awarded some medals as follows: 1914 Star, British War Medal, Victory Medal, Long Service and Good Conduct Medal, and again awarded the Jubilee Medal, and again I received a Coronation Medal from His Majesty King George VI together with a compliment from the Colonial Secretary." During the war, he also taught himself to read and write. Proud of his war service, and having proven himself the equal of any of his warrior forebears, it is difficult to know whether Tina Komé ever questioned the new world order he had so loyally served, and which, after the war, continued to impact his life. In the light of the hut tax wars in Sierra Leone, what did he think when he was ordered to arrest the Nigerian emir? Was he ever aware of the thousands of Senegalese conscripts who went to their deaths on the Western Front in a war that would provide no possible amelioration of their own situation in West Africa? And did he ever reflect on the bitter irony that he had risked his life transferring the Cameroons from one colonial power to another? In any event, he returned to the town whose name he had carried as his own for ten years, to find that both his mother and father had died the year he went away to war.

Tina Komé broke his journey home to visit Mapema, where an army friend, Manga Sori Mansaray, asked his father to betroth Sori's infant sister Aisetta to his friend, an affirmation of the bond between them. So it was that Tina Kome tied four kola nuts in a leaf parcel and presented them to his friend's father, then tied the red thread of betrothal around the infant girl's wrist. But it would not be until 1929, when Sanfan Aisetta was sixteen, that she came to live with her husband, now a sergeant-major with the Court Messenger Force in Panguma.

Tina Komé also returned from the war to an imperiled birthright. A series of colonial ordinances enacted between 1901 and 1905 (and later, in the 1930s) dramatically reduced the powers of chiefs and even permitted the replacement of rulers unwilling to implement colonial decrees. At the same time, a series of amalgamations effectively undermined the autonomy of many chiefdoms, among them Barawa, which was absorbed into the expanded chiefdom of Nieni.

"We have passed through three ages," an old man once told me in Kabala. "The world began in Mande. We then left Mande and came to this country. Then began the time of the white man's rule. Yesterday and today are not the same, but whatever sun shines, that is the sun in which you must dry yourself."

For as long as he lived, Tina Komé was regarded with ambivalence by many of his countrymen. One year, when the British were short of district officers, Sergeant-Major—for this how people addressed Tina Komé after the war (his wives included)—was appointed acting district officer. S. B., then a small boy, would remember his father doing the rounds of the Bonthe district, collecting taxes. People would call him a black district commisioner, acknowledging his power but unsure if it was compatible with chieftaincy. "His children are white men," some said, meaning that they were receiving an English education. "His wives are not Kuranko. If we follow this man, our children will never succeed." When Tina Komé made his bid for the Barawa chieftaincy in 1946, following the death of Pore Bolo, the then district commissioner, Victor Ffennell-Smith, and the Sengbe Paramount chief, Denka Marah, both advocated his election. But the house of Balansama, which had ruled Barawa since the early nineteenth century, resented the return of chieftaincy to the house of Morowa. When the votes went against him, Tina

Komé rebuked them all. "Ah, you Barawa," he said. "I've worked for you and helped you, and you do not know it. But tomorrow you will."

"Our father was an honest man," S. B. told me in 2001. "Very friendly. Very fair. He wanted his children to succeed in life. That is why, when I was at Fourah Bay College in 1954 and received news that my father had died, I felt crushed. Three years later I became a member of Parliament. I wish my father could have lived to see that day, and to see me now, leader of government business in the House of Parliament. Whenever I think of him—and I think of him constantly—I thank him for having given me the little education I possess today. I know I would have stopped at nothing to get a good education, but nevertheless I appreciate what my father did for us as a family. I admired him. He was my mentor. Even today I still hear his voice saying, 'Carry on. Be a man. Be a Kuranko.' These words are always in my ears. Not to be afraid. Setting us on the right path. May his soul rest in perfect peace."

Abdul's Reminiscences

Life stories, like myths, are seldom recounted in their entirety. They are adduced piecemeal—an episode cited to make a moot point, or an edifying fragment brought to mind by some incident in the here and now. Literacy enables us to bring these shards together as a lineal narrative, with every element given its logical place in a foreordained sequence. This coherence masks the fact that the story's original context of use has been lost, and that every story is a retrospective collocation of disconnected elements.

That my chronicles of the Barawa Marah are, in these ways, artful if not artificial does not mean that they are fictions, for every detail is faithful to the individual who shared it with me. And while these snippets were gathered adventiously over a period of almost five decades, and from numerous interlocutors, they would hardly have made coherent reading unless they were chronologically ordered and converted into narrative form. Noah's story only came to me in 1979, when my interest in biography had developed to such an extent that I was reframing my anthropology as the exploration of intersubjective life rather than the interpretation of collective representations. Much of what S. B. remembered of his father emerged when I was ghostwriting his biography in 2001–2. As for Tina Komé's last years, and the story of his firstborn son, who inherited the name Kulifa from his paternal grandfather, I would only glean these details when the hitherto taciturn Abdul opened his heart to me during my visit to Firawa in 2008.

It was the middle of the afternoon. The village was still. People had gone indoors or sought some shade in which to wait for the cool of the evening.

But Abdul was deep into his account of Barawa's troubled history, and I was hanging on his every word.

He had begun with the years immediately after his father's retirement in 1942, when Teneba Sewa was still chief. After almost two decades in the Court Messenger Force, Tina Komé was ready to return to Firawa, and insisted that his firstborn son accompany him, even though Kulifa was at that time a student at Bo Secondary School for Boys. Kulifa refused, arguing that he wanted to finish his secondary schooling and did not want to live in the bush where there were no schools, no hospitals, no decent houses, and no amenities.

Abdul threw his hand back over his shoulder to describe the ritual gesture of disowning one's child.

"It was like a curse," Abdul said. "Our father turned his back on his eldest son. He did not care about him now. He told him he would suffer in life."

"Because he could no longer expect the blessings of his patrilineal ancestors? Because he was now outside their protection?" I asked.

"Exactly."

I had encountered this oedipal parting of the ways many times before. Indeed, the vexed relationship between a father and his firstborn son was an inevitable outcome of the rule of primogeniture. While the father doubts his eldest son's ability—continually testing his mettle, requiring him to oversee the household in his absence and allowing him to punish his younger sons should they misbehave—the son becomes discouraged and oppressed by the demands being placed upon him. At the same time, the oedipal tension between father and firstborn son is displaced onto the relationship between elder and younger brothers, which may explain S. B.'s constant disparagement of Noah, not to mention S. B.'s unforgiving attitude toward Kulifa.

A son's yearning for his father's praise, or the tendency of a younger sibling to look up to older siblings for approval, is frustrated by the elder's refusal to show affection on the grounds that feelings are inimical to the structural relationship between them. "The eldest son is looked upon as the father's rival," Noah once told me. "So, in public, they avoid all contact and familiarity." In his ethnography of the Tallensi, Meyer Fortes is explicit about the oedipal overtones of the ambivalence between father and heir. "Your oldest son is your rival" (*I bikpeem a i dataa*), the men say bluntly, and Tallensi speak of an ongoing struggle between the Yin (personal destiny) of the father and his eldest son, in which the son's Yin seeks to destroy the Yin of the father.[1] Among the Kuranko, the father emotionally resists the inevitability of his son succeeding him, for this would be to admit his own mortality, while the son grows impatient with his father's coldness and carping, for he needs to show the world that he is equal to the tasks that his father declares him to be incapable of. Something of these oedipal tensions finds expression in the prohibition on the son wearing his father's underwear, trousers, gown, or cap, or sleeping on his father's mat, for any of these acts may suggest a usurpation not only of the father's authority but of his sexual relationship with his wife.

There is another compelling rationale for why a father should mask any affection he might feel toward his firstborn son. If a man favors one of his sons, it will cause resentment among the others, in the same way that favoritism toward one wife will cause envy among her cowives. These two relationships are, in fact, entangled.

I suspect that these tensions found expression in Tina Komé's relationship with Kulifa and contributed to Kulifa's dramatic rejection of his father's expectation and his equally dramatic departure for Liberia and thence to America, where he remained for thirty years without any direct communication with his family.

Kulifa only returned to Sierra Leone in his dotage, and the stigma of his reneging on his duties as firstborn was still as keenly felt as when his father had been alive. I retain a vivid image of him standing under the mango trees beyond the perimeter wall of S. B.'s house at Thompson's Bay, dressed in a navy blue suit, white tie, and red suspenders, and wearing polished black shoes. "A clown," S. B.'s wife called him. "S. B. will not let him in the house. Even the mother has said she will kill herself unless he stops bringing shame on the family." Kulifa threatened to blow open the gate with dynamite. And as he shouted slanderous comments, loud enough to be heard by all the neighbors, Rose encouraged her children to shout back. "You useless beef!" they cried. "You teef-teef [thief]." The kids then ran terrified and tittering from the balcony.

The slanging match was soon over, and Kulifa began his slow walk back up the lane, a small boy toting his suitcase, as Rose's kids took their parting shots. "Send sweet for me. Send chocolate for me!"

"He don shame," Rose said.

I later learned that Kulifa had been arrested, manacled, and taken to Kissy hospital for observation. He died a few years later, a half-crazy beggar on the Freetown streets, still shunned by his family.

Perhaps the aftereffects of Kulifa's youthful decision to continue his education rather than do his father's bidding explained Abdul's attitude toward schooling.

"I did not want to go to school if it meant leaving Firawa," Abdul said. "I wanted to stay and take care of my mother. In fact, I am the only one who has remained rooted in Firawa. I have never regretted this. I am proud of it."

"It's like the difference between your father and his brother Tina Kaima," I said, "and in your own generation, the difference between S. B. going into national politics while you remained in Firawa, keeping the home fires burning."

"*A ko sebe*, that is true."

"Do you mind me asking," I said, "why Barawa refused to vote for your father in 1946?"

"The eight heads of the main clans voted against him. As the only literate Kuranko man in Koinadugu, people identified him with the British. One time, he brought picks, shovels, hoes, and handcuffs to Firawa to make farmwork and gravedigging easier, but rumors spread that if he was elected chief, people would have to work for the British, making roads in addition to their farm work. So they voted for Pore Bolo. My father was bitterly disappointed. He left Firawa and rebuilt Kurekoro. Pore Bolo went to him there and begged him to return to Firawa, saying there were no hard feelings, that he had nothing personally against Tina Komé. But my father refused."

Recalling this moment, Abdul was fighting back tears. The shock of his father's political defeat, and the misinformation and misunderstanding that led to it, were too hard to bear.

"*I maiye*, you see," Abdul went on, quickly recovering his equilibrium, "it was the same then as it is today. What I am going through now is nothing new to me," he added, alluding to his fight for the Barawa chieftaincy against an outsider.

Wanting to bring our conversation back to the subject of Tine Komé, I asked Abdul how old he was at the time Pore Bolo won the chieftaincy.

"I was born in 1935. The election was 1946."

"So you were eleven."

"I was initiated in Firawa during the dry season that followed Barawa's amalgamation into Nieni. I was the head of the *bilakorenu*, the young boys. And I was a great wrestler—"

"Kin gbilime [Heavy-Foot]," I said, using Abdul's nickname and moved by how easily his imperturbability had been undermined by the memory of his father's defeat so many years ago.

"The past is heavy," Abdul said. "It cannot be moved easily. You cannot easily put it behind you."

I made a note of this metaphor of wrestling with the past and underlined it as Abdul began recalling the year of his initiation.

"That dry season, I led a group of the other bilakorenu on a tour of the newly amalgamated chiefdom, paying our respects at the chiefs' compounds, visiting kin and notifying them of our forthcoming initiations. Everywhere we went, we were given hospitality and small gifts.

"My father had given me a gun. And the keminetigi [leader of the young men] who accompanied us had two small drums. Whenever we approached a village or town where we wanted to pay our respects, I would fire a shot to announce that we were coming, and the drummer would beat his drum. You had to show off a bit. Dancing. Singing. Showing people how happy you were that you would soon be a man. We went from Firawa to Momoria, to Bandakarafaia, Kondembaia, Yifin. At Yifin I spent a night and a day, lodged with the chief. Then we went on to Alikalia to see my father's sister. As we neared the compound I fired a shot, careful to point the gun away so that its back blast did not hit the house. People asked, 'Who is that?' Someone said, 'Sergeant-major's son from Barawa. The one that betrayed us.'"

"Why did they say that Tina Komé had betrayed them?"

"Just as I told you. They thought he had the interests of the British at heart. They did not see that he was trying to improve the well-being of his own people. Before Barawa was brought into the amalgamated chiefdom of Nieni, my father argued against this, saying that we would lose our traditional right to rule, and that Nieni would dominate us, as it had in the past. And you know how rumors spread like a grass fire. Once they have started, you cannot stop them.[2]

"I was taken with the other five boys to chief Da Bonso, who poked at our heads and verbally abused us. I was frightened. But I knew I would have to master my fear and speak out. So, I asked if I could speak.

"I told the chief that my father had sent me to pay my respects. I had not expected Alikalia to arrest me.

"There was a big crowd now. Word had got around that the gunshot was some kind of sacrifice, and this was why I had been arrested. I was told that pretending to fire a gun was all right, but it was a crime to actually fire one in the village.

"I pleaded that my father was a man who knew the law. Therefore, I knew it was no crime to fire a gun. What is more, I had fired the gun and we had beaten our drums in many villages since leaving Firawa.

"I was detained. The chief allowed people to abuse us verbally but not physically. So, there we were, for a day and a night, unable to leave. But the chief's daughter was a friend of mine, and though the chief had refused to allow us food, she managed to smuggle some to us.

"Early the next morning, an old man with a walking stick came to the compound and ordered the chief to release us. We were not to blame for the quarrels caused by the amalgamation acts and the struggle of each chiefdom to maintain its own traditional right to rule. 'We're all in the same struggle together,' he said. 'When there is a problem you don't molest the messenger. These kids were paying their respects before their initiation. The gunshot was part of their way of celebrating, that's all. We have problems, certainly, but let us not take them out on these boys.'"

According to Abdul, the palaver went on for some time, with the old man's view vying with old suspicions and rumors. Finally, the boys were released. They finished their tour but did not dare fire their gun or beat their drum again. When they reached Kulanko and told their story, word went ahead of them to Firawa.

"Barawa was much feared in those days," Abdul said. "We still had a reputation as warriors. If anything had happened to us, the initiations would not have taken place. Who knows what else might have happened. . . ."

Abdul paused and looked me in the eye. "You know, Michael, I cannot believe that with all this history, people have not learned the lessons of the past. They listen but they don't understand. That is why I shed tears before. This trouble between people. These misunderstandings. The way politics affects ordinary people, who become enemies and betray their leaders. But you know, we have that saying, 'A palm wine tapster may have a dog with him, but that doesn't mean that the dog drinks palm wine.'"

I must have looked mystified.

"Those who follow a chief cannot become chiefs," Abdul said.

Later, pondering my conversation with Abdul, I thought long and hard about the tragic ironies and echoes with which the story of Barawa was replete: Tina Komé's rejection of his firstborn son, for example, and the repercussions of that irreversible gesture, not only in his son S. B.'s act of turning his back on Barawa, but in S. B.'s coldness toward his own sons because, like Kulifa, they had chosen to follow their own destinies in England rather than respect their father's wishes.

That these fault lines between father and firstborn and between siblings are universal suggests perennial and possibly unresolvable differences between the rule-governed, established order we associate with the old, and the emotional but unregulated energy we associate with the young. How this energy may be controlled and stabilized on the one hand, but released and celebrated on the other, is a central problem of social existence.

In Meyer Fortes's essay on the firstborn, he speaks of the widespread assumption "among tribal and oriental peoples" that "there is underlying and essential to parenthood a fund, but only a strictly limited fund, of male vitality and female fecundity, which is partly physical but largely metaphysical . . . which must be transmitted to the filial generation to ensure the proper continuity of the family and thus of society but which can only be transmitted at the cost of the parental generation. There is no alternative for parents but to sacrifice themselves for their children."[3]

This implies an ethical tension between the life of any particular person or creature and life itself, for life in this broadest sense of the word—the life of one's lineage, community, or nation, or life everlasting—is often seen as the greater good to which lesser goods must be sacrificed. It goes without saying, however, that the gift of life is for the individual to surrender; it is not something that a heroic cause, or another person, can simply take.

Doctrines of reincarnation spring readily from this notion that particular lives flow into and out of the stream of life itself.[4] By this reckoning, death is never final but simply a stage on the way to becoming another form of life— albeit a form of life predetermined by tradition.[5]

If Tina Komé judged his firstborn harshly, it was because Kulifa was acting for himself, and by implication had made his own particular life the greater good. And yet Tina Komé had passed, in his own lifetime, from honoring his own lineage and his own chiefdom as the greater good, to embracing the higher ideals of Islam and espousing the value of a Western education.

This was poignantly brought home to me when Abdul recounted the story of his father's final days.

"He never became chief of Barawa or Nieni. But the British regarded him as an able man and backed his appointment as court president at Yifin [the main town of Nieni]. But even then, Barawa whispered that the government favored him. That he was their puppet. It was the stress of fighting these rumors that brought upon him the illness that killed him. I was in Firawa at the time, and he had gone to a council meeting at Yifin. When my father fell ill, Paramount Chief Kali Koroma decided that he should be carried back to Firawa. The journey took two days, and news of his illness went ahead of him. My mother and my twin sisters left Firawa and met him at Yankakoro. They were there when he died. His last words were these. He opened his eyes and said, 'Manse' [chief]. My mother asked him, 'Which chief?' She thought he might be referring to Chief Kali Koroma. He said, 'No, I am calling God the chief [Dale Mansa, lit. creator chief].'"

At this moment of one man's death, a historical transition was presaged from foregrounding relationships with ancestors, country, and kin to relationships with God.

Limitrophes

Even when divine and secular powers are not metaphorically coalesced, as in the Kuranko notion of God as Dale Mansa (creator chief), or the Christian image of Christ as King, or the institution of divine kingship, it seems that the right to rule in this world always requires the backing of some extraworldly authority. This may be because the flaws and foibles of mortals contradict the images of moral superiority associated with men in positions of power, and some transcendent reference point is needed to redeem human shortcomings and shore up collective ideals. Thus, the adoption of the Islamic high God (Altala or Allah) provided heterogeneous Kuranko polities with a unifying symbol, even as rulers remained stubbornly agnostic.

In any case, even military might, protective fetishes, and a command over lightning and thunder were not enough to guarantee the dominance of the Barawa Marah. Hence they turned to other means of consolidating their power: the invocation of first settlement, alliances with powerful djinn, or affiliation with Islam. Such powers were drawn from worlds beyond the village, and because they could not be fully controlled or comprehended by mortal men, they were wild. Accordingly, to venture beyond the village was always hazardous, for one might either lose one's life in the wilderness or receive blessings and bounties beyond one's wildest dreams.

If fieldwork was my gamble, throwing in his lot with me was Noah's, and these uncertainties were equally evident in Kuranko attitudes toward djinn.

On a moonless night toward the end of the dry season of 1970, I stepped outside our house at One-Mile and was bitten by a night adder lying in wait for frogs from the nearby swamp. Pauline immediately drove me to the local clinic, where I was given shots of antivenin, but for several days afterward my leg was paralyzed, either from the snakebite or from the serum. Rather than take a break from fieldwork, I decided that Noah and I should undertake our planned trip to the Loma Mountains, where I hoped to research the history of the Marah clan in Woli chiefdom.

After driving twenty-five miles to the Seli River, we parked the Land Rover, crossed a hammock bridge, and began our trek to Firawa. In the grasslands, the wan light of the oncoming day showed us the path. Noah walked ahead, his sandals padding on the dusty ground, but I was dragging my right leg and struggling to keep up.

Noah was all for turning back, but I would not hear of it. I was still convinced I could will my paralyzed leg back to life and was determined to press on, at least as far as Firawa. Only years later did it occur to me that my lameness might have been a physical symptom of a growing ambivalence about anthropology—pushing myself to attain an intellectual goal but in the process neglecting the human relationships that were the true source of my well-being, including my relationship with Noah.[1]

As the sun rose, we rested and shared the peppery venison and cassava that Noah's wives had prepared against our journey. But a couple of hours later, exhausted from limping, I accepted Noah's argument that we needed to rest and should spend a day and a night in Firawa.

That evening I took a stroll outside the village to test my leg and passed a group of women on the path that led to their section of the local stream. Momentarily captivated by the grace with which they carried pails of water on their heads, the coy smiles they threw me, or their sudden gusts of laughter, I was also shamefully aware of their mocking comments, for once again the *tubabune* had invaded their space.

We pressed on next morning before first light. Entering the forest was like entering a cage filled with cackling and hooting animals. Had our journey been dreamed, it would have been interpreted as a sign that a plot had been hatched against us. Neither of us spoke. Perhaps it was because we had been walking for so long in the hypnotic circlets of lantern light. Perhaps it was because we unconsciously deferred to the forest djinn, who, according to Noah, could capture our names and use them to do us harm. The path led through swamps. The mist clung to us. The stench of decaying vegetation was overpowering. In the distance, the rapids of the Bagbe sounded like a rising wind.

Around noon we entered a small farming hamlet—several thatched huts surrounding a compound of tamped earth and dead hearths. Noah introduced me to the town chief and explained to him where we were going, though not why. Then we plunged once more into the rainforest, stumbling over exposed roots and outcrops of stones, getting closer to the Bagbe River.

Overhanging trees and lianas threw shadows across the turbid water. Noah said that crocodiles lurked in the deep pools, but all I saw animate the sullen surfaces was dappling sunlight and falling leaves. He also pointed out the trail that diamond smugglers used. "They make a dog swallow the stones," Noah said, "or they put them in a banana and eat it themselves. Sometimes the women put them in those cloths, the ones they use when they are bleeding."

We crossed the river on a hammock bridge and entered forest even more dense and overpowering than before. The narrow path was aswarm with ants. Myriads of butterflies illuminated the occasional shafts of sunlight. Green tree snakes slowly uncoiled along the trail, and the spoor of monkeys was everywhere.

About half a mile before reaching the village of Bandakarafaia, we stopped to rest by a massive granite boulder. Men and women passed us on their way to their farms. Most greeted us warmly, asking where we were headed and where we had come from. Some recognized Noah and asked after his family. Some referred to me as Noah's white man (tubabune); others called me his djinn.

I was well aware that such pacts were fraught with ambiguity and danger. Though a djinn might give a barren woman a child, empower a dancer, inspire a musician, or enable an ambitious politician to succeed, it might take as repayment the life of someone near and dear—as though the improvement of an individual's fortune logically entails a social loss. When, in 1972, I suggested to Noah that he come to New Zealand to further his education, his mother dissuaded him from leaving Sierra Leone. In Aisetta's opinion, whatever Noah stood to gain from going abroad, it would mean the attenuation of his ties to home. In this advice, was Aisetta echoing the misgivings of her late husband, who had also thrown his life away to become a child of the white man, not to mention the fate of her firstborn, Kulifa?

Beneath the stone, raw and cooked rice, kola, bananas, and strips of white cloth had been strewn and, as I rested in the shade, several women returning to Bandakarafaia from farms deep in the bush scattered some of the palm nuts they had gathered that morning. When I asked Noah why they did so, he cited the Kuranko adage, "Nyendan bin to kile, an wa ta, an segi," alluding to a particular species of soft grass, used in thatching, that bends before you as you pass through it, then bends back the other way when you return. Though this logic of reciprocity holds true even of one's relationships with the extrahuman world, I would learn that it also contained the seeds of both life and death since, in Kuranko parlance, the path along which blessings flow may become blocked or darkened.

It is seldom humanly possible to ascertain when a gift has been returned, respect shown, honor satisfied, words heeded, justice done, or a fair apportionment of scarce resources secured. Accordingly, everyday life involves endless uncertainty as one seeks to make the most of what one has while keeping an eye open for new possibilities. As I watched the women making their small sacrifices to the stone, I wondered what I would risk on a Faustian bargain with a djinn for academic or literary acclaim.

We reached Bandakarafaia in the heat of the day and paid our respects to Chief Damba Lai Marah, whose house stood in the shadow of an immense granite escarpment. The chief explained that he was accustomed to having white men lodge in his village. They would make it their base before scaling Loma Mansa (also known as Bintumani). But I was the first white man to have passed that way in many years, which undoubtedly explained why the small children of the village, some stark naked, some in rags, fled in fear from my presence only to be dragged back by their older siblings and shoved before me, eyes wide with alarm.

In the course of our conversation, I asked the chief about the stone we had passed on our way to the village.

It was called Mantene Fara (Mantene's Stone), Damba Lai said, adding that he was its custodian (*tigi*, lit. owner or master). As for Mantene, she was a djinn who had come to the chiefdom in Damba Lai's grandfather's time.

To seal a political alliance, Damba Lai's grandfather had been given a woman in marriage by the chief of Kombili, the capital of Morfindugu chiefdom to the northeast. Because this woman knew how to address and praise Mantene, the djinn followed her to Woli and made its home there.

In other chiefdoms, I would discover that most ruling lineages were once associated with a djinn and made sacrifices (*dugu ma sarake*) to them to secure the well-being of their chiefdoms. The Mansaré clan led the sacrifices for the upper Kuranko chiefdoms at Yalamba (west of the Loma Mountains, in Guinea), while the Koroma clan led the sacrifices for the lower Kuranko chiefdoms at Bonkoroma. When I asked the Woli chief why these sacrifices had been discontinued, he said it was because adulterous affairs had spoiled relations between the clans involved, and no sacrifice could be made, either to ancestors, God, or the djinn if such undeclared intrigues, either political or sexual, existed between the parties involved. Could it be, however, that the decline in sacrifices to the land reflected the declining power of chiefs during the colonial period, and later, the dwindling influence of genii loci? In chiefdoms where rulers had embraced Islam, no major sacrifices were offered to the djinn, and as Islam extended its influence among the Kuranko, imams outlawed sacrifices to djinn and even banned the telling of folktales in which djinn appeared. Where people once turned to djinn as a source of insight into their fluctuating fortunes or as an extrahuman power on which they might pin their hopes, they now turned to Allah or, in the cities to the south, to political big men and benefactors, to Pentecostal ministries, schools, colleges, and NGOs, or set their sights on migration to Europe as their best chance of a better life.

The intimidating wall of rain-blackened rock was like a materialization of the falling darkness, and as Noah hastened away in search of his kith and kin, I attempted to make myself at home in the derelict house that had been allocated to me.

After lighting a fire in the yard and boiling some water in the small country pot I found there, I sat on the front porch—or what remained of it— with a cup of tea clutched between my hands, hoping that Noah would soon return with something to eat.

Nearby, two mangy goats were nibbling at the grass. I picked up a stone and lobbed it toward them. One had a deformed hind hoof, and limped away to safety, bleating pitifully in protest, reminding me of my own partly paralyzed leg. The other goat joined its mate, hovering and trembling in the shadows of another ruined house.

It was dusk by the time Noah reappeared, bearing a calabash of parboiled rice and a peanut and chili sauce. Having discharged his obligation, he left.

I could not sleep. Despite scraping a hollow in the hard earth for my hip and pummeling my rucksack into the shape of a pillow, I could not get comfortable. At first, I was unnerved by the silence. Then, from the far end of the village came the sound of wooden clappers, followed by a dull, hoarse muttering, as though someone were stuffing words into the mouth of a horn.

My fretfulness gave way to real fear as the sound came closer, but then silence fell again, and I heard only the unsteady thumping of my heart and the intermittent shrieking of a night bird in the bush.

As the night dragged on, I was plagued by a skin rash. Desperate for sleep, I scratched and clawed at my midriff, wondering what the hell I had touched or eaten that might have caused this reaction. I lost track of time. And when at last I dozed off, it was only to wake in a cold sweat from a dream of a clear blue sky suddenly darkened by smoke or cloud.

As dawn broke, I got up and paced about, shivering with cold and still tearing at my skin.

I passed the day in a stupor. The rash bothered me less, but still I could not sleep, and I was now besieged by fragments of long-forgotten poems, passages from novels I had read in my teenage years, and hallucinatory flash-backs to Cambridge.

As darkness fell and my second night in Bandakarafaia began, I prayed for sleep. Noah appeared in the half-light for a moment, took one look at me, and left. Perhaps he was afraid of me or bewildered by his inability to know what to do. Perhaps he had not been there at all, and I had imagined him.

I lay in a delirium, a sodden log drifting on the stream, experiencing slight vertigo as the current rolled me this way and that. I thought, I am not lying on the earth; the earth is suffering my lying upon it. I am disembodied now watching myself lying on the ground, but I am not lying here. I have been placed here, to suffer the darkness, claustrophobic, hot, and the shrilling of a single cicada, but I am not feeling anything or hearing anything. These things are happening to me. I am having them happen to me.

Then I was looking down at my own supine body, my awareness drift-ing away from it like smoke, upward through the shattered roof, toward the stars, and I found myself looking back with a kind of calm pity at my aban-doned body, thinking, I am dying. Is this dying? Because I knew I could choose to go back into that prone form if only I made the effort.

In the lantern's dull penumbra, dark forms stir into life. I am aware of myself walking, of Noah's presence in the half-light ahead, but I am not so much moving as being moved, as in a dream. Out of the depths of the forest, howls and shouts give voice to scampering shadows.

Not a word passes between us. I walk in a daze, limping like the goat at Bandakarafaia. I think only of what I will do when I get back to Kabala.

At the farm hamlet, we rest for a few hours. I catch some sleep in the town chief's house, stretched out on a raffia prayer mat. My first sound sleep for two nights. I wake to an enamel plate of pineapple slices and bananas. Even Noah seems to feel relief now, nearing home. This strange white man, with his woes and silences, no longer a burden. And the rainforest already giving way to patches of open grassland, the mist lifting.

We stop again at the Bagbe, and I clamber down the riverbank, strip, and wade into the unmoving water. It is cold. It momentarily shakes the fever out of me and brings me to my senses. On a boomerang-shaped beach, swallow-tail butterflies quiver and flap in the early morning sunlight, before settling back on the dung. In the nearby shade lies the sloughed skin of a snake.

Noah's Story

Our daughter was born in Freetown with the rains. We were woken in darkness by violent gusts of wind, the curtains flung back from the open windows, billowing and flailing. The sky was being ripped apart at the seams. Thunder crackled. Lightning laddered the clouds. Mere hours later, Heidi Aisetta came into the world, and our lives were changed. On returning to Kabala, I limited myself to one-day excursions to villages within easy reach, and when Noah came to our house at One-Mile, he would often bring his children, Kaimah and N'na, and we would spend more time talking about the challenges of parenthood than about my research.

If I felt uncertain about my future, whether as a writer or academic, Noah appeared no less ambivalent about what he would do when I returned to the UK: resume teaching, further his education, or go into business—all options he entertained, albeit without much passion.

Inevitably, our concern for our own children made us remember our own childhoods, and so, one afternoon, as rain drummed on the tin roof, making conversation all but impossible, Noah quietly tape-recorded his story as Pauline and I sat opposite, taking turns holding Heidi, and occasionally interrupting Noah to ask him to repeat something we had failed to catch or fully understand.

I was not surprised that Noah's story echoed many of the motifs of the traditional tales I had collected, including the tension between brothers and the plight of orphans.

Born in Firawa in 1942, Noah was his mother's last-born child. His father, Tina Komé, was employed as a court messenger and often transferred to various parts of Sierra Leone. "I was my father's favorite," Noah said. "I started school late because my father wanted me to be with him. I was all the time with my father, sleeping with my father, moving with my father, until his death in 1954. Only then did I really get to know the woman who bore me."

In 1953, under circumstances Noah would never fully understand, his elder brother S. B. took him out of school and pledged him to a Mandingo trader to whom he probably owed money. Noah found himself embarked on a seemingly endless journey driving a herd of reluctant cows down boulder-strewn roads. His taciturn companion, whose name was Kemo, gave him corn and curdled milk. He watched women in the fields, hoeing up mounds of lumpy black earth. He saw children his own age splashing and laughing in river pools below the girder bridges they crossed. The air was fragrant with the perfume of flowers after rain, but in the towns the streets were quagmires that stank of cow piss and dung.

In a southern town called Bambatuk, Kemo took leave of Noah, telling him that he was to remain there and work for Mammy Kasan.

Noah saw money change hands before an enormous woman, whose brow was creased with an expression of intense disapproval, gathered her flowing blue robe about her and led him to the shed where he would sleep.

In the eyes of the small boy, the main house was a mansion. The walls of its central room were covered with framed photographs of men in army uniforms and women in voluminous white gowns and towering head kerchiefs. Padlocked doors led to rooms Noah was forbidden to enter. All the windows in the house were barred against thieves, and it was Noah's job to see that the shutters were securely bolted every night. Along the front porch of the house ran an ornate concrete balustrade, painted bright yellow. At one end of the porch was Mammy Kasan's shop. Its ceiling was hung with lengths of coarse cotton cloth, hanks of rope, metal buckets, and kerosene lanterns. Its shelves were filled with packets of Tate and Lyle sugar and Bryant and May matches, bars of soap, bottles of pills, and enamelware. On the worn counter were piles of onions and arrays of okra and red peppers.

Mammy Kasan sat behind the counter frowning at the street. Hardly an hour passed without her summoning Noah, whose name had become Kekura (New Boy), to do some chore for her.

"Ke-kura, Ke-kura, Ke-kura," she called monotonously. Then stridently, "Kekura!"

Noah came running from the back of the house, his hands dripping with soapsuds.

"Kekura, do the ironing," she commanded.

He left the laundry and heated the heavy smoothing iron by filling it with coals from the fire. Then he struggled with one of Mammy Kasan's crumpled gowns on a rickety table that creaked ominously as the huge iron was pushed along a fold of the cloth. No sooner had he made some headway than Mammy Kasan summoned him again, her voice somnolent then peremptory, "Ke-kura, Ke-kura, Ke-kura," and as he sprinted around the side of the house, dodging the puddles under the eaves, he heard the voice raised into an angry demand: "Kekura, come now, Kekura!" Arriving breathless at the bottom of the steps, he was told that he still smelled of Kemo Sisé's cows.

Noah quickly learned that Mammy Kasan made such remarks to give herself time to remember what it was she wanted him to do. When the chore came back to mind, she indolently lifted and extended her right arm and with her left hand hitched the billowing sleeve of her gown up onto her shoulder. "Kekura, fetch firewood," she snapped, or simply, "Bring water!" Noah lowered the bucket into the well, and as it hit the water he saw his silhouette jolt and shatter, and a blue half-circle of sky turn to mud.

He found solace in the company of Mammy Kasan's husband, Yandi, who had been blinded by a spitting cobra not long after enlisting in the army in 1939. Gossip circulated that Yandi's mind was a bit touched as well.

The blind man, feeling his way along the scarred plaster wall of the house to the back steps, liked to come into the yard where Noah was working and, for no apparent reason, throw himself into a display of parade-ground drill as Noah hastily pushed basins aside and kicked firewood out of the way lest the blind veteran trip over them.

Yandi marched up and down, shouting orders to himself: "Lep rite, lep rite, lep rite, lep. Riiiii wheel. Lep rite, lep rite, lep. Squaaad halt," before springing to attention facing the mango tree, his hand quivering at his forehead in salute.

"I am over here," Noah said, obliging Yandi to wheel toward the voice and repeat his salute.

The boy flinched as his blind companion stumbled over outcrops of pitted rock or waded into a puddle, scattering the ducks. But Yandi was tireless. "Give me the pestle," he ordered, and taking it from Noah he shouldered and presented arms while the boy dodged the flailing pole.

At first Noah was unsettled by Yandi's ghostly eyes. They reminded him of the spectral gaze of the people in the parlor photo gallery and of the locked rooms he suspected were occupied by the spirits of the framed figures. But familiarity soon allayed his fears, and lying awake at night on his mat in the outhouse, he was lulled by the sound of Yandi's flute warbling and trilling above the rain, until Mammy Kasan's voice broke the spell, calling, "Ke-kura, Ke-kura, Kekura! Come now."

From time to time Mammy Kasan went on an errand to another town. Yandi said she went to collect debts. Noah went as Yandi's guide. Each held an end of a long pole, the boy steering his blind companion down the narrow bush paths while Mammy Kasan bustled ahead, her gown catching the breeze and filling like a sail.

One morning at Sirabo, Mammy Kasan sent Noah off to buy some bananas.

Sauntering along a row of stalls in the market, he was startled to hear snatches of Kuranko. Looking around, he spotted three men, one of whom wore an indigo gown like his father's. He sidled up to the men and cautiously greeted them.

"Eh, m'bonnu!" one of the men exclaimed to the others. "The boy speaks Kuranko."

"I toge kama?—What is your name?" asked another.

"N toge le Kekura."

"Kekura!" said the first man, surprised. "And where do you hail from, New Boy?"

"From Kabala."

"Kabala! Eh m'bo, you are a long way from home."

"We are also from Kabala," the second man explained.

Noah fumbled in his pocket for the penknife his father had given him.

"My father gave me this when he sent me away to school," Noah said.

The first man took the knife and turned it over in his hand. "He sent you to school here? In Sirabo?"

"No, in Kabala."

"It's a fine knife," said the second man.

The first man made to go. "Awa," he said, "mi nala—we will see you later."

Noah felt a lump in his throat as he watched the Kuranko men disappear into the crowded market. He hung around until late afternoon in the hope that they would return, but dreading Mammy Kasan's ire, he finally gave up his vigil.

At this time, Noah's eldest sister Ai was married to Alhadji Momodu Salloh, who lived at Bonthe. On a trip to Bantai chiefdom to buy rice, she chanced to meet the Kuranko men with whom Noah had talked at Sirabo.

Noah's father, Tina Komé, had written to Ai about Noah's disappearance, and when the travelers mentioned the small Kuranko boy with an army knife, Ai was certain it must be her little brother. Though puzzled by the child's nondescript name, she immediately took a truck to Sirabo, where the market people told her about Mammy Kasan and her houseboy. Ai came on foot to Bambatuk the next day.

The town was on an island in a tidal river lined with mangroves and shell banks. The only way across to the island was by a wooden ferry, given buoyancy by empty oil drums, which the ferryman winched across the river by means of a cable attached to trees on either bank.

After asking directions from the ferryman, Ai proceeded to Mammy Kasan's house.

Mammy Kasan was ensconced behind the counter of her shop. Ai greeted her and asked casually if she was the trader who had a small Kuranko boy called Kekura working for her.

Mammy Kasan's frown deepened. "He is there," she said, tugging at the sleeve of her gown.

"I am sure that Kekura is my brother," Ai said. "The last we heard of him, he was in the care of a certain Kemo Sisé, a cattle trader."

Mammy Kasan said nothing.

"May I see the boy?" Ai asked.

"He is there."

Ai walked into the house, calling, "Noah, Noah, are you there?"

Yandi, sitting in a gloomy corner of the parlor, muttered as if to himself, "There is nobody here called Noah."

Ai asked if he knew of a boy called Kekura.

Yandi at once sprang to his feet. "Att-en-shun," he barked. Then, tilting his head as if expecting some ethereal reply, he called, "Kekura, Kekura, come here."

At first Noah hardly recognized his sister in the dim light, but Ai led him to the back door to get out of Yandi's hearing. Noah, seeing her face clearly, could not suppress his joy.

"Keep calm," Ai whispered. "You must pretend you do not know me. Just wait. I'll come back this evening."

Ai returned to Mammy Kasan and asked if Noah could go back to Bonthe with her. "Perhaps only for a little while," she added, noticing Mammy Kasan's deepening frown.

The trader's blunt refusal convinced Ai that further pleading would be a waste of breath.

"Even if you were the boy's mother, which you are not," Mammy Kasan pontificated, "I would not let him go with you. He is pledged to me, and Kemo Sisé has gone to Liberia."

"Then may I spend the night here?" Ai asked. "I'll go on my way in the morning."

Mammy Kasan gave her gruff assent. "Kekura!" she shouted. "Bring food!"

That night Ai stole down to the shed and explained to Noah that he was to run away in the morning. She carefully outlined her plan, making him repeat what he was to do and impressing on him the need for calm until they had made their escape. It was well after midnight when she returned to her own room.

The day dawned, bringing high cirrus clouds like rubbed tobacco and a sea breeze. Ai thanked Mammy Kasan for her hospitality, said a curt good-bye to Noah, and walked away quickly along the path to the ferry landing.

Noah waited for Mammy Kasan to go into her shop before approaching her with his heart thudding.

"I am going to cut firewood," he said.

He was wearing two pairs of trousers and two shirts and was fearful that Mammy Kasan would notice. But she was preoccupied, counting out pills from a brown bottle into the palm of her hand.

Noah raced through a coconut grove and on through the scrub and grass, taking a roundabout route to the ferry landing. Ai had tipped the ferryman a pound note and told him to wait for Noah. He grinned as he watched the boy squelch clumsily across the mudflats, then stumble breathlessly down the landing stage.

"My sister . . ." Noah began.

"Come, Kekura," the ferryman laughed, "let's go."

As the ferry slid slowly out into the stream, Noah looked back anxiously at the path to Bambatuk. He half expected Mammy Kasan to appear, with her gown billowing about her, and order them back.

"You were lucky," the ferryman said, straining at the rusty winch. "If your sister had chosen to cross in the evening, the tide would have been out and you would have been stranded."

Noah watched the distorted shadow of the raft in the olive water. Mangrove pods drifted with the current, and butterflies caught by the river wind flapped and flurried near the surface.

As the ferry bumped against the landing, Ai seized Noah by the arm and hurried him away from the river.

They skirted the first village they came to, using a grove of mango trees to keep themselves out of sight. But they were close enough to hear the murmur of voices and the thud of pestles and feared that some kind of alarm would be shouted at any moment.

Once clear of the village, they regained the path and walked on through the heat of the day. The air was heavy with humidity, and Noah's ears throbbed. He complained that his legs were numb and his throat dry, but Ai insisted they press on. All night they walked, picking their way down the moonless path through a wilderness of mangrove forest. Occasionally they disturbed a nightjar resting in the warm dust of the path, and it would fly up clumsily and break the heavy silence with its churring cry.

At noon the following day they reached a town where Ai had friends.

That night Noah woke from a dream in which Yandi was fumbling in the darkness for his flute. It was the first time he had thought of the blind man since the morning he had left Bambatuk. "I must whittle him another flute if he cannot find that one," he thought. Then weariness overwhelmed him and he fell back to sleep.

Two days later they reached Bonthe, where everyone fussed over Noah and urged him to recount his adventures. Ai had scarcely seen her brother in the eight years since Tina Komé had left Moyamba, and as Noah spoke of his vicissitudes, she responded with reproachful sighs and exclamations of incredulity.

"Han!" she cried, as Noah listed the chores he had had to perform for Mammy Kasan. "That woman made you work so?"

Though Ai knew that Noah was pining to rejoin his father, she was unsure how to arrange for him to get home. Days passed, until one day a friend of the family who worked in the colonial administration, Mr. Banya, dropped by to announce that he had been transferred to Port Loko. On hearing of Ai's predicament, Mr. Banya said he would be only too pleased to take Noah north as far as he was going.

With great trepidation, Noah passed into the charge of another stranger. Yet by the time Mr. Banya put him on a truck at Makeni bound for Kabala, the boy's anxieties had vanished.

It was past midnight when the truck pulled up outside the Kabala post office and Noah clambered down and hurried into the shadows, bent on avoiding his relatives in Kabala and getting home.

He arrived in Firawa two days later, footsore and alone. His father clasped him in his arms and fought back tears. His mother Aisetta's joyful crying brought neighbors running. Yeli Foré, the praise singer, put all his heart into his xylophone, and the thrilling, melodic phrases took such a hold of Tina Komé that he shouted to the whole town to come and celebrate his son's return.

That afternoon, when the excitement had died down, Tina Komé sacrificed a cow in gratitude to Allah and vowed that his son would never again leave his side.

Noah would make these events an allegory of his life. He would recall the idyllic period before his separation from his father (who died within a year of Noah's reunion with him) and compare it to life before colonial rule. And he would complain of hardship and betrayal in the same breath with which he expressed his perennial hope of rescue. In years to come, all these themes would be echoed in the stories of his son Kaimah and his grandson Michael.

"Since my father's death," Noah explained, "I have had to paddle my own canoe," and he recounted what his life had been like in the years after Tina Komé's death when he went to live with his married sisters in Kabala and attend school.[1]

"It was not an easy time I had then. I remember one time my sister Mantene remarking that my father had petted me; now that my father was dead I would have to fend for myself. So I was there, struggling—going to find food, laundering, doing everything in the morning before going to school. I had to take care of myself."

Noah described this period as one of domestic servitude and virtual slavery. But though he felt hard done by, there was always rescue at hand.

"I remember one Lebanese, Mr. Hassan Mansour, who took pity on me at one time and told me I could always go to him when I needed help. As a small boy I often went to Hassan Mansour."

His relationship with his elder brother S. B. was very different. "When the 1957 elections came round," Noah said, "my younger [half-]brother Kaima and I went all over ferensola [the Kuranko area] campaigning for S. B. I was like his propaganda secretary. When I returned to school, the principal warned me that further absenteeism would not be tolerated, but in 1962, S. B. again enlisted my support. I was at Magburaka Secondary School at the time, and Parliament had been dissolved, with the elections about three months away. S. B. sent a telegram, asking me to come and campaign for him. I asked the principal, who said no, so I sent S. B. a telegram saying I could not join him. S. B. then sent a second telegram, ordering me to come. The same thing happened in 1964, when S. B. decided to campaign for the Paramount chieftaincy in the amalgamated chiefdom of Sa Nieni. I had to leave school to help him, but this time the principal did not permit me to return.

"At the time of the general election in 1967," Noah went on, "S. B. was already in Parliament. But many of the younger people urged me to run as a candidate for the opposition APC [All People's Congress]. When Sir Albert Margai [the leader of the SLPP, Sierra Leone People's Party, and prime minister] heard that I was with the opposition, he ordered me to Freetown. The DO provided a Fiat lorry to bring me. I can remember leaving Kabala at exactly 4:30 to attend the call of the prime minister. We reached Freetown late at night, and I slept in the lorry. Next morning I was taken to the prime minister's office on the eighth floor of the Administration Building. Mr. Kande told the prime minister I had arrived. I thought this could only mean that I had been the subject of some discussion. The prime minister told me that he'd heard many reports about my activities. But his displeasure was not the real reason I dropped out of the race because, by then, S. B. had set our mother against me. She began to pester me, crying to me all the time that she would be blamed, and people would mock us, if I ran against my brother. She said, 'People will laugh at us and say, Oh, these two brothers fighting each other!' You see. So, mindful of all this, I dropped out."

Though Noah saw himself as unfairly hindered in his ambition to make something of himself, he often received help from unlikely quarters — though none of these benign interventions appeared to have worked out. One day in Kabala, for instance, he was sent to buy kerosene at Lansana Kamara's shop and ran into Wing Commander Macdonald, the district officer. "We talked for a while," Noah said. "And he asked me whether I would like to work. I told him I would, but there were no jobs. He asked me to find him in his office the next morning. I went to the office and found him. He offered me work as a native administration court clerk. But I had nothing of my own. He had to give me 20 leones to buy some soap and clothes.

"After I had been there for some time, he posted me to Musaia in the Fula Saba Dembelia chiefdom. I was there doing clerical work. Then I decided to leave the native administration work because I felt I was deteriorating educationally. I then decided to pick up teaching. I was given an appointment in the District Council School, the same school I had earlier attended as a pupil. So, I was there, fighting hard. At this time, while my contemporaries were still at school, I was struggling hard to earn my living.

"As it happened, the SLPP lost the 1967 elections, and the APC came to power. From this moment on, my life became very difficult. I was harrassed. At one time I was detained. I had met a man called Babande in the village of

Koba, who asked if I could help him find a cure for his sickness. My cousin Dr. Osayon Kamara was then at the Kabala hospital. So I told Babande to come to Kabala, and I promised to take him to my cousin. What I did not know was that Babande was a juju man. The APC people in Kabala knew this, and when they found out that I had sponsored Babande's trip from Koba to Kabala, they had him arrested, and accused me of hiring him to kill the prime minister, who was then Siaka Stevens, as well as Dr. Forna [minister of finance] and S. I. Koroma [the deputy PM]. The police came to my house that same night and arrested me. I was charged with sorcery. But the case against me failed, and I was discharged. But District Officer Gorvie, and the then Paramount Chief Baruwa Mansaray, decided I should be tried in the Native Court. This time I was fined 50 leones. I immediately came to Freetown to hire a lawyer and file an appeal against my conviction. Cyrus Rogers-Wright was willing to help me, but when I told S. B. what I planned to do he ordered me to drop the case.

"At times, really, I feel very bitter when S. B. tells me I am not serious. People who really know him blame him for what I am. In fact, some people feel I would have been in a better position and been a better person had he not tampered with my destiny. But you know, I hold no grudge against him, except when he makes these remarks about my not being serious. I used to agree with him. I used to say, 'You could say I am not serious: if I were serious, I wouldn't have gone all out to make you what you are today.'"

S. B. had, as one might expect, a different take on the events that Noah chronicled, pointing out, among other things, that he had urged Noah to complete his secondary schooling, but Noah himself had decided against it, and he had often secured jobs for Noah, including the position of trade inspector in Kono.

Although Noah's and S. B.'s views are irreconcilable, they reflect differences in power as well as personality, and I hesitate to reduce the latter to the former. Yet it would be impossible not to conclude that their vexed relationship encapsulates a recurring motif in societies that make birth the measure of a person's worth. The privileging of the firstborn and the marginalization of the young create similar resentments. And similar fantasies of redress arise whenever hierarchies based on age, gender, and inheritance are given primacy over equalities based on common humanity.

That I never felt obliged to choose between loyalty to one brother or the other was partly because neither ever sought to enlist me in their cause, and partly because I loved them both. But often, watching Noah playing checkers with a friend, I was tempted to interpret his moves symbolically and sympathetically as strategies for getting his pieces to the back line where they would be crowned and, as kings, become free to move in any direction and decimate his opponent's remaining pieces.

The complementary relationship between political and occult power fascinated me. That both forms of power are ever-present potentialities for us is evident in accounts of Kuranko chiefs who periodically drew on supernatural powers to bolster their secular authority and accounts of cult leaders who exploited their alliances with djinn or Islam to undermine or influence secular rulers. At any given moment, one form of power may be brought to the fore and the other eclipsed. Transposed to the field of individual consciousness, this oscillation is one between focal and peripheral frames of awareness. "Lived experience," observes Sartre, "is always simultaneously present to itself and absent from itself."[2] Although at any moment we may have a fair idea as to who we are and what we might become, we tend to be blind to who we are for others and to the many unknown forces that bear upon our fate. In Noah's case, he fantasized becoming a man of substance like his brother S. B. His consciousness latched onto a specific objective and determined a specific course—the assumption of political office. He recognized no other possible form of being for himself. But when thwarted in his desire to realize himself politically, his ambition fastened on an image that had, until that moment, lain dormant in his mind—the image of occult power.

Such transformations seldom occur painlessly; they are the outcomes of crisis. This alternative form of power suddenly presents itself to Noah, accused of sorcery, as another way of seeing himself—an analogue, as Sartre calls it, because this new identity is initially mere potentiality, an object that is still absent and irreal. In an act of what Sartre refers to as "provocative impotence," Noah now imagines himself, not as someone who will simply follow in his brother's footsteps, but as someone potentially capable of accessing higher powers and possessing great influence.[3] Moreover, he now becomes free. For in beginning to imagine he might actively become the person that he has been accused of being, he turns a stigmatizing identification to his own advantage, liberates himself from the humiliating position of existing in his brother's shadow, and acquires powers that, while marginal, nonetheless have a recognized place in the Kuranko social order.

Taking Stock

After a year in the field, Pauline and I returned to England by sea. Impatient to get my PhD out of the way so that I would be free to embark on writing in a less academic vein, I quickly completed my dissertation and, thanks to the timely intervention of Meyer Fortes, found funds for a further stint of fieldwork in early 1972. Although my academic future was uncertain, when my former master's degree supervisor in New Zealand, Hugh Kawharu, wrote asking if I would be interested in a position at Massey University (where he had been recently appointed chair of the newly formed Department of Anthropology and Māori Studies), neither Pauline nor I hesitated. The prospect of raising our daughter in familiar landscapes, close to family and old friends, left us in no doubt as to where we wanted to be.

Though two of my new colleagues, Hugh Kawharu and Te Pakaka Tawhai, lived in Palmetston North, Apirana Tuahae Kaukapakapa Mahuika commuted by car from his home in Wellington. On Api's weekly one-and-a-half-hour journey to the Manawatu, he would recite whakapapa (genealogies), committing to memory details gleaned from Ngāti Porou elders and rehearsing his considerable knowledge (*mātauranga*) of the vital connections not only between his generation and past generations but between "animate and inanimate, known and unknown phenomena in the terrestrial and spiritual worlds," since whakapapa "binds all things," mapping "relationships so that mythology, legend, history, knowledge, tikanga (custom), philosophies and spiritualities are organised, preserved and transmitted from one generation to the next."[1]

Is genealogy a core ontological metaphor for all relationships? "That every individual life between birth and death can eventually be told as a story with beginning and end" is, for Hannah Arendt, "the prepolitical and prehistorical condition of history, the great story without beginning and end."[2] Similarly, relationships with divinities are everywhere conceptualized in terms of kinship and descent, and the devolution of religious authority in Judaic, Hindu, Islamic, and Buddhist traditions is also understood in genealogical terms. Examples also abound of genealogy as a metaphor for both social and cosmological relations. Writing of the relationship between *ambwerk* and *tuman* (elder and younger siblings of the same sex), Kenelm Burridge notes that the terms are "categories of more general understanding as well as categories of specific relationship," while among the Iatmul, "every thing and person has a sibling, and the polysyllabic names are so arranged in pairs that each pair is the elder sibling of the other."[3]

Though not wanting to reduce all models of relatedness to kinship, or sentimentalize societies in which genealogy was the prevailing metaphor for comprehending the connectiveness of all life forms, I envied the depth and breadth of Api's genealogical knowledge and the association of this knowledge with key locations, notable *rangatira*, and epochal events. By contrast, my own family history felt shallow, bereft of any stories that might give moral rather than merely legal legitimacy to my nationality. Moreover, Api could trace his descent to Porourangi and beyond, to Māui-tikitiki-a-Taranga, who fished up the North Island (Te Ika a Maui) from the sea. As an ordained minister of the Anglican church, Api's genealogical perspective also encompassed God, leaving me, an atheist, with a further reason to bemoan the absence of a wider frame of reference for my identity. When called upon to speak on a *marae*, I spoke as a stranger (*manuhiri*), and while I could cobble together some putative connections with the ground on which I stood and the *tangata whenua* (people of the placenta) whose *tūrangawaewae* (standing place) this was—alluding to the mountain in whose rain shadow I was raised and to Māori friends who hailed from the region—it was always with an embarrassed awareness of my lack of fluency in *te reo* Māori, and my longing for a place I could unequivocally call my own.

The politics of land tenure also implicated whakapapa. From the beginning of large-scale colonization in 1840, disaffected Māori sent thousands of letters to the New Zealand Land Commission, reclaiming land that had been confiscated, wrongfully sold, or traded under false pretenses. Almost

150 years later, the Treaty of Waitangi became the basis for redressing long-standing grievances and settling land claims. As with the 1976 Aboriginal Land Rights Act in Australia, genealogical connections between indigenous people and their traditional lands were vital to securing restorative justice. But there were other equally important functions of genealogical knowledge, as I had discovered during my Kuranko fieldwork, notably its critical use in establishing claims to positions of authority, often according to the principle of primogeniture, and determining lines of succession and inheritance. By contrast with the Kuranko, Ngāti Porou recognized the role of women in tribal life, and Api's whakapapa provided numerous examples of women achieving positions of rank and authority, while knowledge of the matriline was equal in importance to knowledge of the patriline.[4]

This gendered construction of social reality interested me less, however, than the complementarity of what Meyer Fortes called politico-jural and domestic domains—a distinction that roughly corresponds to the Greek distinction between polis and domus. For Fortes, the "web of kinship" and the "dynamics of clanship" were both structurally and metaphorically connected and echoed the Greek view that microcosm and macrocosm mirrored each other, as well as the fractal model of the self-similarity of small-scale and larger-scale phenomena. Nevertheless, what mattered most to me was not the epistemological question of which preferred frame of reference was intrinsically truer, better, or more fundamental than any other, but the existential question of when and why people invoked ethnic, sexual, religious, geographical, genetic, historical, or political images of belonging.

Although structural-functional anthropology showed how genealogy provided a framework for social order, it tended to pay less attention to its role in creating a sense of collective belonging in which personal identity was subsumed by a field of relationships that went back many generations in time and even encompassed other life forms, such as totemic animals, divinities, and the ancestral dead. Nor did this extension of kinship and affinity beyond the confines of one's immediate family simply provide a moral basis for claiming support in times of crisis; it sometimes gave persecuted peoples a consoling sense of presence and power: the Israelites in Egypt, the Mormons driven into the wilderness of the southwestern United States, the Muslim notion of the *umma*, Aboriginal people's invocation of the Dreaming. That is to say, genealogy often functions as a theology, or form of communitas, offering individuals a sense of being-at-home-in-the-world in which the distinction between I and We is annulled.

Clearly, genealogy is but one of many possibilities for imagining that one's own life participates in, and draws its ultimate meaning from, the wider field of life itself. But whether we think of this existential matrix in genealogical, geographical, ecological, theological, or political terms, human interconnectedness is universally conceptualized in remarkably similar ways.

For Ernest Gellner, "the way in which time and its horizons are conceived is generally connected with the way . . . society understands and justifies itself."[5] Thus, it may be argued that the Kuranko adoption of the Islamic notion of a supreme being enabled a community made up of different estates and diverse lineages to imagine itself united in terms of a common "creator chief" (dale mansa) as well as able to overcome the gap between the remembered and the unremembered past.

But genealogy has more immediate and intimate relevance, and touches on the significance of regeneration and natality in human life.

Consider, for instance, the analogy Kuranko draw between custom and birth (namui, lit. mother childbearing), both of which are facts of life that are given rather than chosen. Birth suggests firstness (in English, natality, nativity, and nationality all share the same root); hence, Kuranko invoke the ancestral past with such phrases as "That is how things happened," or "That is how our ancestors let it happen" (ma bimban' ya to nya na), or "That is what we met" (maiya min ta ra), or "That is what the first people did" (fol morgonu ko dane). During my first fieldwork I was given to understand that to not pay heed to ancestral words (bimba kumenu) would spell misfortune. Hence the proverbs "Long life is in listening" (sie tole lto) and "Your ear is only as wise as your ancestor's words" (i toli kina i bimba ko).

Even though time (wati) was thought of in terms of phases of the moon, seasons of the year, times of the day or night, or stages in the life cycle, it was always described as repeated oscillations rather than a succession or lineal progression of unique events. Even death was assimilated to this way of thinking, since a person's name is recycled in alternate generations. Genealogical time was similarly understood as a perennial recurrence of five generations—one's grandfather's time (the word bimba connotes both grandfather and ancestor), one's father's time, one's own time, one's children's time, and one's grandchildren's time. Since the old became ancestors when they passed away, they effectively live again, sustaining the life of the lineage through the blessings they bestow rather than the children they father.

Relationships are, however, never simply a matter of birthright. They have to be fostered and sustained by conscientious work (*wale*), which, for Kuranko, implies a continuous exchange of goods, services, and words. Universally, these elementary forms of sociality include greeting, hospitality, intermarriage, pressing noses and inhaling each other's breath (the Māori hongi), breastfeeding an infant or feeding a family, and friends exchanging kola, beer, wine, betel, or blood. Melanesian boys ingest the semen of older men in order to grow;[6] West African villagers share specific cuts of meat from a sacrificed animal. Even when a relationship is not mediated through such acts, it will be imagined in similar ways—through metaphors of blood (consanguinity),[7] money,[8] material property,[9] layers of earth,[10] sonic echoes,[11] prenatal destiny,[12] inherited valuables, matrilineal or patrilineal essences,[13] divine grace,[14] transmigrating souls, mirroring,[15] myths,[16] a tree with roots, trunk, stem and branches, lines,[17] dendrites, a house with many rooms, a braided rope or chain of several links, a body with left and right sides, flesh and bones, limbs and joints.[18]

The ontological metaphors for human relationships are clearly as diverse as the conceptual frameworks used to theorize them, whether genealogical, theological, historical, mythological, or metaphysical. More difficult to pin down, however, are the diverse ways in which these abstractions are idiosyncratically experienced and expressed. In his phenomenologically nuanced study of the Sora of southern Orissa, Piers Vitebsky describes "what may be the most elaborate form of communication between the living and the dead documented anywhere on earth. Almost every day in every village, living people engaged in conversations with the dead, who would speak, one after another, through the mouth of a shaman (kuran) in trance. Together, living and dead would chat, weep, or argue for hours at a time."[19] Although the Sora cultivated the experience of communicating with the dead to an extraordinary degree, and often depended on ritual experts to put them in touch with their forebears, this experience should not be strange to us, for don't we also inhabit a social universe in which ancestors are remembered with the help of photographs, archives, and family anecdotes, albeit without the dead being assigned active roles in the lives of the living or this experience becoming systematized as a worldview? In the course of my fieldwork among the Kuranko, it had become clear to me how important one's ancestors were for one's well-being, and how imperative it was to recognize and nourish one's relationship with them through sacrificial offerings and gestures of respect. But not everyone dreamed of their forebears or entered into the kinds of intimate and everyday relationships with them that Vitebsky describes for the Sora. Nonetheless, when one dreamed of an ancestor, this was not construed as Westerners would, as a memory of someone who no longer exists, but was said to be a glimpse of someone who continues to exist, though in altered form, in a parallel universe. The phenomenological similarity here between personal relationships with forebears and with God would become central to my fieldwork over the next two decades.[20]

Ferensola

Seven years passed before I revisited Firawa, accompanied by Pauline and our daughter, Heidi Aisetta, and joined for several weeks by Noah and three of his children (Kaimah, N'na, and Jeneba). Though the village appeared physically unchanged, I was soon struck by the new idioms of collective belonging that were in circulation. Genealogy was still significant, to be sure, but it was often submerged by new forms of solidarity based on regional, political, and religious affiliation.

We reached Firawa late in the day to find a large crowd assembled in Tala Sewa's compound. People from villages throughout Barawa were there, as well as delegations from neighboring chiefdoms. It soon became clear, however, that the reception was not for us. The message I had sent four days before, announcing our arrival, had been garbled, leading people to expect S. B., now minister of energy and power, as well as the assistant district officer and a bridge engineer. But Tala Sewa received us without a hint of disappointment, acknowledging my intervention with Prime Minister Siaka Stevens to secure S. B.'s release from detention in 1975, and my 1977 monograph *The Kuranko*. Addressing the crowd without the mediation of his speaker, Tala Sewa declared, "We want this man to make Firawa his home, and to live here in peace with his wife and daughter, not just as our friend but as our brother."

Talking later that day with Tala Sewa and several elders, I heard the shadow side of the story of Barawa's struggle for political representation and economic development.

"The rains that germinate the rice also breed mosquitoes," Tala Sewa began, before regaling me with a litany of grievances about the government tax collectors who came to the village after harvest like scavenging birds, and magisterial clerks who removed court cases from his jurisdiction and took them to Kabala. "In our father's time," Tala Sewa said, "tithes would be repaid with benefit, but now we receive nothing in return for what we give."

Echoing Tala Sewa's dismal observations on the lack of reciprocity between Freetown and Koinadugu, one elder commented that in the old days, "Our heads were in the hands of our chief. Now who is it that holds our lives in fee?"

Tala Sewa also reminded me of the chaos in Freetown. The coups and countercoups, the bungled conspiracies and brutal retaliations. When the smoke cleared, it always became evident that nothing was going to change the government's indifference toward the north.

Only once in the years since my last visit had there been any hope that the Seli would be bridged. Tala Sewa recruited all the young men of Barawa to cut a vehicle track from Firawa to the riverside. But the bridge did not materialize, and within two years the earthworks washed away, log bridges collapsed, and scrub reclaimed the track, reducing it once more to a single laterite path, winding around outcrops of stone, blindly honoring the original contours of the land.

To salvage his own dignity as much as to fulfill his promise to his people, Tala Sewa took matters into his own hands and began the construction of the bridge. "You cannot cross a river on a bridge that is in your head," he said, urging his people to contribute money, cows, rice, cement, and labor to get the work under way.

I told Tala Sewa I had seen the four box pillars of reinforced concrete on the bedrock of the Seli but had not realized the work had been done by local people. I now understood why so many had gathered to meet S. B. and begin the final stages of the work.

One of my happiest reunions was with Saran Salia Sanoh, an elderly medicine master with whom I had formed a friendship during my first fieldwork after successfully treating his septicemia with antibiotics. He now insisted on putting his house at our disposal, and that afternoon I helped him move his few belongings, including herbal decoctions and fragments of horn, shell, and mica, into one room, leaving us free to occupy the other rooms.

Within days we had resurfaced the interior walls and floors, found some sticks of furniture, constructed a latrine in the yard, and repaired the back porch. Though Noah stayed with Abdul at the other end of the village, Heidi hung out with his children most days, and we ate together as a single family.

As I went about the village, I was intrigued by the number of faded, yellowing fliers everywhere. In the past, hardly a house did not have a white flag and small bell hanging outside as a safeguard against the nefarious forces of the night, so I wondered whether the political notices served a similar magical purpose.

Whatever their occult value, they conveyed a rough record of the tumultuous run-up to the 1977 general elections.

Some of the fliers advertised the All People's Congress Party—a rising sun surmounted by the words "A. P. C. Live For Ever." Others announced regional political candidates from both the APC and SLPP. Most, however, were for S. B. Marah, the SLPP candidate for ferensola.

What, I asked Noah, was the meaning of *ferensola*? And what had persuaded S. B. to return to politics after his traumatic fourteen months in solitary confinement as a political detainee?

Noah reminded me that S. B. had been an MP in Milton Margai's post-independence government, but when SLPP was defeated at the polls in 1967, S. B. vowed to quit politics. That's when he went to work for Tony Yazbeck, running the Alitalia Agency in Freetown. In 1973, he turned down the nomination for Koinadugu South, but in the following years, Noah said, the whole of ferensola mobilized to return S. B. to power and elect a Kuranko to Parliament. S. B. was no longer his own man, Noah said. He now belonged to ferensola. Everyone wore the ferensola cap and ferensola gown. Praise singers composed songs to stir people's hearts. Even my 1977 book became known as the ferensola book, a sign that the Kuranko were now known throughout the world.

Before I could press Noah to be more specific about the meaning of the word *ferensola*, we were interrupted by an elderly man called Fore Kandé, once a renowned wrestler but now suffering from conjunctivitis. Earlier in the day, I had promised to give him some chloromycetin drops, and he was wondering if I had them with me.

"We are all in this ferensola business," Fore said. "We all stand united behind S. B. Marah."

That evening, Yeli Maliki Kuyaté came to my house with his four-stringed harp (*konné*) against whose droning accompaniment he sang the praises of the lords of Barawa, naming them all in successsion. "In the end," he said, "chieftancy will be with the Marah as it was when dawn first broke on the world. Manti Kamara Kulifa, Tina Kaima, Tina Komé, S. B., they were all born into a ruling house. This is not the first time that the Marah have been the protectors of ferensola. In this our Barawa, Tina Komé went away to the army in order to open up the country and make it prosper. He alone did that. Ferensola depended on him. It was his ancestor who first ruled here, and it is through him that ferensola is now being returned to its rightul owners. If you hear of ferensola, you should know that Barawa is the seed of ferensola."

When Yeli Maliki paused, I asked what the word *ferensola* meant.

"It means twin town."

I knew the etymology, but it was the symbolic connotations of the word that escaped me.

"There were four founding rulers," Yeli Maliki explained. "Mansa Morfin, Mansa Yira, Mansa Borsingbi, and Mansa Yamisa. Yamisa ruled in Barawa. Because Barawa was the most powerful and impregnable of the four countries, the first three rulers placed themselves under Yamisa's protection. When Yamisa accepted the overlordship, he declared that the whole country should be known as ferensola so that he would not appear to hold the prestige of chieftaincy alone. Thus the countries of Morfin, Yira, and Borsingbu became one moiety in the twinned lands. Whenever we say *ferensola* we mean oneness, despite our differences. And the four corners of the ferensola mark the boundaries of Kuranko itself."

There was a dance that night in celebration of ferensola, and as I picked my way along the darkened lanes of the village I pondered the echoes of Yamisa's story in the story of Bol' Tamba: the same alliance and the same crisis attributed to different actors at different times, as if history was bound to repeat itself and myths inevitably draw upon the same handful of plots and leitmotifs. But mainly, I was struck by the dialectic of identity and difference that found expression in the ferensola image—the perpetual oscillation in life between individual and collective forms of identity, and the tension between cultural or ethnic distinctions on the one hand, and images of our shared humanity on the other.

By the light of kerosene lanterns, xylophonists were striking up, and the crowd had begun to form a circle in preparation for dancing.

Entering the close-pressed, shuffling circle, I half closed my eyes as Senewa Kamara's exhilarating anthem filled my ears. Be ara kanye—we are all one.... Ma lkoinya—our common cause.

We danced until we lost track of time in an ecstatic commingling of xylophones, flutes, and singing. We danced until the beat of the gourd rattles and bells was no longer necessary to cajole us into moving as a single body.

S. B.'s Story

In the years since my first fieldwork in 1969–70, anthropology's focus had steadily shifted from local to global realities as if in response to the supposed disappearance of the relatively remote, small-scale, kinship-based lifeworlds that anthropology had once regarded as its definitive stamping ground. In fact, these village lifeworlds had never been cut off from the wider world, the nation-state, or history.[1] Nor did globalization spell their demise, for even today greater numbers of West Africans live in rural villages than in towns and cities. Moreover, while my Cambridge mentors took great pains to locate a person within a kinship universe that itself nestled within a social order consisting of lineages, clans, and tribes, and the new anthropology emphasized political economies and world systems, my own interests lay in the indeterminate relationship between idiosyncratic experiences and overarching systems of ritual and belief. I called these relationships existential because they were irreducible to personality, ethnicity, nationality, or evolutionary biology yet implicated all these elements in ever-changing constellations. By focusing on life stories and lived situations, I hoped to disclose the complex intrapsychic and intersubjective aspects of human life without privileging any single interpretive model or discursive form.

In October 1979, I returned to Sierra Leone without my family for further fieldwork. Rather than head straight back to Firawa, I spent several weeks in Freetown, staying with S. B. and Rose.

Not a day passed without visitors coming to the house to pay their respects to S. B. and ask him for help and advice. Many of these visitors were Kuranko chiefs who, on learning that I was the author of "the ferensola book," were keen to offer genealogical information that I might add to future editions. Only reluctantly did I fall back into the role of ethnographer, dutifully recording what they wished to confide, though without a context these lists of names held little meaning for me. As for my relationship with Noah, now working as a teacher in a Freetown school, his help in mediating my conversations with local people was no longer necessary, and I would accompany him on trips downtown where he was documenting the effects of rising food prices and rampant inflation on the lives of the poor.

It was during these weeks that S. B. shared what would become the first chapter of the biography I would ghostwrite twenty years later.

Unlike the chiefs' genealogies, S. B.'s story was at once more personal and more dramatic, and I was riveted by it.

In 1925, Tina Komé was elevated to the rank of sergeant major in the Court Messenger Force and sent to build the barracks at Panguma (Kenema District). From there he was transferred, first to Sefadu (Kono District), then Moyamba, where he was again promoted—to staff sergeant major. S. B. was born on August 19, 1934, the third child of Tina Komé's fifth wife, Sanfan Aisetta Mansaray. His earliest memories, he told me, were of Moyamba. "I remember the day war broke out. We saw, or heard, the sound of a plane passing overhead. And as a small boy, I remember the governor's special train coming to Moyamba, and the governor awarding my father a medal. In prison," S. B. continued, alluding to his period as a political detainee, "I also found myself thinking about my boyhood friends in Bonthe, where we went to live in 1939.

"In Moyamba my father was on friendly terms with the district commissioner, and my elder brother Kulifa and I used to go to the DC's house and retrieve tennis balls. At the end of the day's play, the DC would give us a penny, which was a lot of money for us. My father was also a close friend of Siaka Stevens's father. [Siaka Stevens was president of Sierra Leone from 1971 to 1985.] He was a short man. He had a shop and some Limba chaps working for him. He used to supply the prisons, I think. Anyway, my father and Siaka Stevens's father, and Sergeant Braima Koroma used to eat together every day, taking it in turns to go to one another's house. They were at my father's house one day when something happened that I will never forget. I had often watched my mother breaking eggs into a bowl, and wanted to try it myself. So I picked up an egg and broke it. When she saw what I had done, my mother took me to my father. I hadn't meant to steal the egg, but it looked as if this was indeed what I had tried to do. Siaka Stevens's father said to my father [whom he called Kau]: 'Kau, this boy must not become a thief. We will have to take him to prison.' And believe me, they took me to prison that night. I know my father didn't want to, because the matter had been so trivial, but his friend said, 'The boy must not continue this way. You must put him behind bars.' So I spent that night in prison.[2] When Siaka Stevens detained me in 1974, I said to myself, His father has already sent me to prison! Three years later I told this to his face. I told him that I bore him no grudge for having detained me, and that the law had to take its course. Then I thanked him for my release. When the 1977 elections came round, and the Kurankos wanted me in government, Siaka Stevens said he would send a helicopter to bring me from Kabala and Freetown. When I told him I didn't want to fly, he sent his car from State House. He wanted to make me a minister in his government. This was when I told him the story of how his father had sent me to jail. Today I see it as no bad thing. For it made me afraid of stealing. All my life, I have never taken anything that did not belong to me. In all the years I have been in politics—and I would say this proudly on the floor of Parliament—I have done nothing corrupt. So I told Siaka Stevens, 'Your father put me in jail the first time, and you put me in jail the second time.' And I explained why I called him Pa, even though he was, strictly speaking, my brother. 'Now that our fathers are dead,' I said, 'I will call you father.'

"After Moyamba we moved to Bonthe. In those days, court messengers had considerable power. They were second only to the district commissioners, who were our colonial masters. So people regarded the sergeant major as the most powerful man in the district. My father always told us, 'You are Kurankos.' He did not want us to speak any other language. He used to say, 'If you don't speak Kuranko my kith and kin will laugh at me.' And he was right. But this did not stop me learning Temne, Susu, and Mende. I learned them all, all the languages of our country. And this has stood me in good stead, because wherever I go I can speak the local language fluently.

"Tina Komé retired in 1942 after the death of his beloved brother, Tina Kaima, whom he had always called Daddy. For many years, Kaima had worked as speaker under the Barawa chiefs, Belikoro, Teneba Sewa, and Pore Bolo, so Tina Komé now decided that the time had come for him to return to his native soil and take charge."

S. B. traveled up from Freetown the following year and joined his father at Kurekoro. But he did not stay long, because his elder brother Kulifa wanted him to continue his schooling in Freetown.

"These were the war years," S. B. explained, "and it was not easy to get to Freetown. You needed a permit from the District Office. But I got my permit, showing that my purpose in going to Freetown was to join my elder brother Kulifa and attend school. I remember arriving by train at Waterloo, where you had to show your permit. I did not know where I had put it. I was scared. I kept searching for it, until I finally found it and gave it to the officer. In Freetown there was no one to meet me. But I told a Mende woman—I cannot remember her name—that my brother lived in Waterloo Street. She said she lived at Upper Waterloo Street, and that I could spend the night at her place. She would help me find my brother in the morning. This she did. I had a bag of rice that I had brought with me—the only thing I could really bring from home. So I lived with Kulifa and attended the Government Model School, though I had to repeat Standard Six.

"When Kulifa went to Liberia for a while, I lived with my aunt at Smart Farm. My uncle was a charcoal burner, and I had often gone there in the weekends to help with the burning and sorting and bagging of the charcoal. Life was not easy. We lived on dried cassava when there was no rice. But I paddled along until I went to St. Edward's Secondary School. I remember many of my friends from that time.

"When I left school, I immediately returned home to see my father. The district commissioner of the Northern Province at that time was Victor Ffennell-Smith. My mother's uncle worked for him as a cook. Because Mama and Papa were in Firawa, I stayed with this uncle in Kabala and got to know him very well. Then one day my father sent word that I should go to Tekaw, near Makeni, and see my uncle Sori Marah. My uncle Sori introduced me to Mr. Dave McBurnay, who was a New Zealander, like yourself. He was planning to establish an animal husbandry project in Musaia and said that he would send me to New Zealand to study. But not long afterward, he was killed in a road accident and I ended up in Musaia with another white man—a West Indian by the name of E. S. Capstick. While I was there, District Commissioner Ffennell-Smith said he wanted to build schools in Koinadugu District, and needed some boys to study at Njala Teachers College. After teacher training, we would return home to teach our kith and kin. He suggested that I go to Njala.

"Among the others who went with me were A. B. M. Kamara, who became minister of transport and communications, Sieh Mansaray, who became paramount chief in Kabala, Almami Kalla Kamara of Makeni, who was my best friend, and Thomas Bobo Mansaray, who died not long after we graduated. At Njala I studied hard, and the principal, Mr. Ted Evans, a Welshman, remarked that I was the best student of my year. I was also very popular among my classmates, partly because of the dances I organized. I told the principal that we didn't really want to go off campus in the weekends, especially those of us from the north. We didn't want to get involved with other men's wives. So could we organize Saturday night dances? He agreed, and so we borrowed drums from the Mendes and created our own entertainment. We even had a flautist, called Besema. And this provided the music we wanted for our comfort.

"When I had completed my teacher training, I went to see my dad in Firawa, to tell him I had passed my exams. As usual, my father said he had high hopes for me. He knew I would do well in life. My mother's eldest sister's son, whom we called our eldest brother, used to say that a man can always tell his child's destiny. And so, because my father said I would do well, I am not surprised that I have. And I shall continue to do so, because I always think of my father, who is very dear to me.

"My first posting as a teacher was Kitchon. The headmaster was I. S. Kahn. I worked with him through 1951. The students liked me. I organized football matches and concerts. Taught well. Many of my students went on to do well in life. Dr. Abass Bundu, who became a successful businessman, was one of my students. And Momodu Wusu Munu, who became a lawyer and permanent secretary, then clerk of Parliament and secretary-general of ECOWAS, still insists in calling me teacher. In fact I was so liked that when I was transferred to Kabala, many of my students, including the school band, accompanied me on the boat to Rokupr, singing my praises and imploring me not to go.

"I did not stay in Kabala long. I was transferred to Falaba as headmaster, then to Fadugu, before taking leave in 1954 to attend an intensive teachers' training course at Fourah Bay College. It was while I was there that my father died. Though I returned to Fadugu for a year, I was beginning to think of becoming a lawyer. It was all a question of funds. I first thought of going to see my elder brother Kulifa, who was diamond mining at Tongo, but I went instead to my uncle Pa Sheka Mansaray, who was speaker to our grand-uncle, the late Paramount Chief Kande Baba. I appealed to him, but he could not help me. So I went to appeal to my cousin-in-law, the Reverend J. S. Mens, who was very sympathetic to my request. The Reverend Mens told me that my uncle had not been able to help me because he had given his money— 700 or 800 pounds—to Paramount Chief Almami Dura for safekeeping. I went to Binkolo to see Chief Dura and ask for the money, but the chief said I should come back and see him the following day. I hardly slept that night.

I was very happy, very excited. I thought I had struck a deal and would soon be on my way to England to study law. Next morning I went back to see the chief and thanked him for receiving me the previous day. Again he asked me to wait another day. This went on for a week, so I made up my mind to go and see my elder brother in Tongo field in the hope that he would help me. I ran into him at the lorry [truck] park, and he told me he was on his way to Freetown. I was happy, because I had not seen him for some time. We traveled to Kenema together and stayed the night there. Next morning we came on to Freetown. He stayed with our cousin, S. B. Daramy, who was then financial secretary, while I stayed with another cousin, the late Alhadji Mamadi Kabba, who was living at Magazine Court. For the next week my brother went around buying musical instruments and ignoring my request. It was futile.

"I had promised a friend of mine, Fam Bulleh, who was on my staff at Fadugu, that I would spend some of the holidays with him. So I went down to Zimmi and stayed a week with him. I then traveled north, via Kenema, Blama, and Bo, to Makeni where I stayed with my friend, the late Almami Kalla Kamara. Kalla told me he was going into politics, and that Chief Dura and others were supporting him. This inspired me. I said, 'Well, I had better change my mind. Since I do not have the money to study law, I'll go into politics and represent my people.' The following day I went on to Kabala and discussed my plans with my brother-in-law, the town chief Almami Amadu Koroma, whom we also called Kassi. No sooner had I announced my intentions than he wanted to begin canvassing [for] support."

As with the chiefs who had prevailed upon me to record their histories, I sometimes felt that genealogical time was measured in names rather than years. Yet, as S. B.'s narrative suggests, names locate one not only in time but in networks of relationship that collectively and adventitiously shape one's destiny. In contingent events and unhistorical acts, one's life is drawn in one direction rather than another, and I liked to imagine that the small part I came to play in S. B.'s life completed what the New Zealander had been about to do for S. B. before he met his death in a road accident so many years ago.

One of the most compelling things about S. B., as I came to know him, was the tension between his strong sense of determining his own destiny through hard work and his equally strong sense of being a part of a social field that encompassed his Barawa forebears, his filial and affinal connec-

3 S. B. Marah (in white gown) presiding over a political meeting, Kabala, 2002.

tions, and the people he represented in Parliament. This tension is perhaps most keenly felt by those in power, struggling to reconcile self-interest with the interests of the people they serve. Hence S. B.'s recurring declarations that he was incorruptible, even when enjoying the privileges of high office.

The other thing I remarked as S. B. recounted the events of his early life was the care he took to identify the constellation of people and events that had shaped his journey. Though all were tributary to the course of his life, the only person to whom he attributed a defining role was his beloved father. In this respect he confirmed a view I heard often in the course of conversations with Kuranko villagers, that you are nobody if you do not know your origins or have forgotten those on whom you first opened your eyes. By extolling his father, S. B. was not, however, denying the equally influential role of his mother; he simply followed the Kuranko protocol of publicly acknowledging the social primacy of patriliny over matriliny and measuring the value of one's life in terms of the family or peer group to which one is beholden.

I was fascinated by these oscillations between what a person foregrounded in one situation and backgrounded in another, this oppportunistic code-switching and shape-shifting. Thus, in S. B.'s narrative he proudly evokes his Kuranko ancestry, his fluency in several Sierra Leone languages, his regional background ("a son of Koinadugu"), and his political allegiances, depending on whom he wishes to impress or what he hopes to gain. There was a lesson here for anthropology, for it is seldom the case that new political, religious, national, or regional affiliations eclipse genealogical and tribal identifications; rather that the potential of these frames of reference will be realized differently in different contexts.

After the War

In one of his theses on the philosophy of history, Walter Benjamin claims that to articulate the past historically does not mean recognizing "the way it really was"—it means to seize hold of a memory as it flashes up at a moment of danger. I remembered this line in January 2002, as Sierra Leone prepared to announce the end of a brutal decade-long civil war, and I returned to the country I had first visited thirty-three years before.

I had been back to Firawa only once since 1979 when, following Pauline's death at age thirty-nine, I made a lonely pilgrimage to the village under the illusion that I might find her there. I encountered only a country descending into economic ruin and political chaos, and even Noah's and S. B.'s fortunes were at a low ebb. On my return to Australia, where Heidi and I had moved to make a fresh start, I discovered that my applications for a university position had come to nothing, and so resigned myself to living on the dole, at least until Heidi finished her high school years and I could search for employment further afield. These years in the wilderness were not, however, bereft of joy. I fell in love again and dedicated myself to new writing. But when I finally did secure a university position (in Bloomington, Indiana), war had engulfed Sierra Leone, and Francine and I decided to embark on fieldwork together in Aboriginal Australia. It was only after a series of further moves, first to Australia, then to New Zealand, and finally to Denmark, that I at last returned to Sierra Leone.

Miraculously, Noah and S. B. were still alive, though still at loggerheads, so when S. B. asked me to join his entourage on his first trip to Koinadugu for many years, Noah was not invited to accompany us.

Before the outbreak of war, Noah had been employed as a trade inspector, first in Koidu, then in Port Loko, Makeni, and Lunsar. By the time of his final transfer, he was suffering from glaucoma, and within a day of his undergoing surgery, Lunsar was overrun by rebels. Before Noah's two expatriate doctors fled for their lives, they bandaged his eyes and gave him medication, but when the rebels broke into his house and took him captive, he had to leave everything behind.

"The rebels taunted me," Noah said. "'Pappy, here, drink,' they said, and thrust a bottle of beer into my face.

"I don't drink."

His tormenters pushed a cannabis cigarette into his mouth.

"I don't smoke either," Noah said. "Would I eat if I were not hungry?"

From Lunsar he was force marched to Masimera, where the rebel brigade stopped for two days. Noah asked if he could talk to their commanding officer.

"What! A civilian like you wanting to see our co!" One of them lifted his weapon to show what would happen if Noah continued to push his luck.

Four days later, Noah said, the rebels abandoned him in a Temne village. His eyes were no longer bandaged, but he was in a lot of pain. In the months that followed, he lost the sight in one eye, and now had only limited vision in the other.[1] Unable to return to schoolteaching and with little hope of finding any other work, he survived in Freetown on his wits, scrounging money to buy rice and food for his family and pay school fees for his kids.

One of the first things I did on returning to Freetown was to visit Noah's mother, who was living with her daughter in the East End. Sanfan Aisetta was in her ninetieth year, and little more than skin and bone. She was lying on a palliasse on the floor of a back bedroom. I had never expected to see her again, and as I touched her shoulder and greeted her, I felt as though I was reaching across an unbridgeable gulf. Then her eyes flickered open. "How is Heidi?" she whispered, without stirring. "Is she there?"

"Yes," I said. "She is in Australia. She promises to be with me next time I come, and she sends her love." When Aisetta closed her eyes, it was as though she were closing them on a world of unutterable sorrow and disappointment.

By the time Noah and I returned to the city, the narrow, potholed streets were clogged with traffic and the air thick with exhaust fumes. Along Kissy

Road I saw the destruction left by the rebels during their invasion of the city in 1999—the fire-blackened laterite walls of public buildings and churches, concrete facades pockmarked from gunfire.

An unbroken stream of people flowed and eddied around the stalled lines of poda-podas, overladen lorries, broken-down taxis, *omolankeys*, and white Land Cruisers. UNHCR. Save the Children Fund. Child Rescue Mission. Planned Parenthood. Save the Youth. Sight Savers International. I could not but wonder how many people were actually helped by this influx of NGOs and foreign aid, and, thinking of Noah's impaired vision, I asked if he had ever sought help from any of these agencies. His attitude was both stoic and skeptical. Despite all the rhetoric of reconstruction, rehabilitation, and re-settlement, he knew the odds against anyone receiving immediate benefit. "The leg that steps forward is soon enough the leg that steps back," he said, citing the Kuranko adage. "What can one do but accept things as they are, and live one day at a time without great expectations or undue hope? Things change," he added, "but seldom because of anything we say or do."

"Nonetheless," I said, "we must see what we can do for you."

In a small yard, some young men in shorts were playing soccer with a half-inflated football. Whenever we came to a standstill, kids clamored at the window of the car with packets of bubble gum and biscuits, bottle openers, disposable razors, key rings, and pocket calculators. Along every street, women sat at small tables, selling onions, tomato paste, bunches of cassava leaf, cubes of bouillon, bottles of palm oil, bundles of split firewood, groundnuts, charcoal, kola nuts, loaves of bread, and peeled oranges. In small booths made of lashed poles and corrugated iron, men and women plied their trades—making furniture, dying cloth, cutting hair, selling enam-elware, shoes and sandals, stationery, and lottery tickets.

So many people waiting, I thought. Waiting for a transaction or lucky break that would make the difference between having food and going hun-gry. I found myself reading the slogans emblazoned on the poda-podas and lorries around us—Allah Is in Control. God Is Great. Better Days Are Com-ing. Be Yourself. Respect Education. Never Give Up. Still with My Paddle Nevertheless. Labour and Expect. No Condition Is Permanent. Then, mind-ful of Noah's long wait for a change in his fortunes, I asked him if he was still *sunike*.

"I have never embraced any moral system," Noah said, "and I hope I never will."

Yet we all find meaning in something beyond ourselves, and although Noah appeared to have long abandoned any political ambition, and kept his distance from orthodox religion, I was surprised when he confided a belief in occult power.

Sitting together in the downstairs parlor at S. B.'s house, the daylight fading, Noah spoke of his paranormal gifts.

"There was a certain Dr. Kawa," Noah said, "a senior consultant surgeon at Connaught hospital. Kawa's sister had borne a grudge against her brother from early childhood, jealous of his successes in life and his prestigious social position. She therefore bewitched him. He began to suffer dizzy spells and blackouts, sometimes during surgery. Following the deaths of several patients, Kawa was suspended. He became known as Killer Kawa."

Noah, who had acquired the powers of an alpha or mori-man, "cleansed" the doctor. The sister died not long afterward, punished, according to Noah, for her evildoing. Kawa was reinstated, and Noah submitted to an appendectomy and hernia operations under him, confident in the surgeon's skill now that he was free from his sister's baleful influence.

Within These Four Walls

As for S. B., he was leader of the House and President Tejan Kabba's right-hand man, and though I had long been accustomed to the distance between Noah and his elder brother, that distance not only had widened with time but reflected the widening gap in Sierra Leone between the powerful and the powerless.

Although I had agreed to write S. B.'s biography, I had cautioned him against expecting a hagiography. My interest lay in how his political fortunes and misfortunes echoed the life and times of his father and how their personal stories implicated the history of Barawa.

Sitting beside S. B. on the veranda of his house day after day, recording installments of his biography, I was aware of how painful many of his recollections were. At times his voice was barely audible, and he leaned forward against the rail of the balcony as if to protect his face from being seen.

The focus of his story was not the war. At least not at first. It was the period of his detention. And he had already decided that the title of his biography should be *Within These Four Walls*.

He first described the layout of the detainees' wing. The two rows of thirty cells. Each row two-tiered. His own cell on the lower level, with two small barred windows, each seven feet above the floor—one on the back wall and one above the steel door. Night and day, the cell was lit by a single bulb that made the walls appear yellowish. By standing at the back wall, S. B. was able to see through the transom window above the door and so observe the movement of people on the catwalk that ran between the lower and upper tiers. Food consisted of one pound of cooked rice per day, with some thin soup. No pepper or salt. No fish or meat. The toilet bucket was removed once a day by an ordinary prisoner. "But there never was much in it," S. B. said, "because we ate and drank so little."

"As a political detainee, I was never allowed out of my cell. And I was not allowed to wash. In the first few months we were given half a gallon of water each day, but one day, when several of the detainees were taken to the high court to be charged, it was discovered that Dr. Forna had used some of his drinking water to wash his jacket during the weekend so that he would look presentable in the courtroom. As punishment, they took away our water supplies and gave us a communal bucket which was placed outside the cells. If you wanted a drink you had to bang on the door, and a prison officer would come and dip your cup into this bucket. It was a plastic cup. You could do this no more than twice a day. The day he was taken to court, Dr. Forna was handcuffed. I had known him years before as a brilliant scholar at Bo School. I had known him when he was a medical officer at Wilberforce Hospital. And I had known him when he was minister of finance and acting prime minister, being driven in a motorcade with motorbikes going ahead of him. Now I saw him going to court in handcuffs, as later I would see him going to the gallows."

When S. B. paused, I asked him how he passed the long hours alone in his cell, how he kept his sanity.

"I would close my eyes," he said, "and clench my fists, and pretend I was running from my office, along Siaka Stevens Street, passing Barclays Bank [as he spoke, he mimed his routine of running on the spot, imagining himself jogging through the city]. The law courts now, passing the cotton tree, Pademba Road, the petrol station, the bridge, Hill Cut Road, Hill Station Junction, Bottom Mango, home. I would remember every detail of the route; at every place I passed, I would say aloud where I was. I am approaching my house now, I am getting close to home, I am coming to the compound, I am saying to Rose, 'How are you? How are the children?' That was my exercise. Running in my mind's eye. Daydreaming. Another thing I used to do was sing quietly to myself. Kuranko songs. Making up the words. Go tell them all around the Loma Mountains that I am here and that I am well. Tell my mother to pray for me. Tell them that I remember what my father used to say to us—a man must endure hardship. Today I am passing through such hard times, but I am sure I will conquer. Tell the people around the Loma Mountains that I will not give up, I will not relent. I will not disappoint them.

When I am released from this place I will fight for them, to see that they are recognized."

"What was the worst thing you had to endure?" I asked.

"Not being with my family, not seeing my children. At Christmas, at midnight, I called out to them, 'Merry Christmas, Rose. Merry Christmas, Fatmata. Merry Christmas, Abu. Merry Christmas, Aisetta, Merry Christmas, Aisha.' . . .

"One day," S. B. said, "I asked for the doctor. I told him it was not healthy that we should all be drinking from the same bucket. One of us might have TB. We could contract the disease and contaminate our families when we went home. But my pleas fell on deaf ears. In fact, none of our questions was ever answered. None of our requests was allowed. We lived like slaves. We were not even permitted to speak, except to say good morning to the prisoners in the cells next to our own. One morning I greeted a fellow prisoner whose name was Alhaji Salam. He was a very soft-spoken man, and I was not sure he had heard me. So I raised my voice: 'Alhaji Salam, Alhaji Salam.' An officer came to my cell, opened the door, and took away my blankets. He said I was making too much noise. I said, 'Sir, I was only saying good morning to my neighbor. I wasn't sure he could hear me. That's why I kept repeating his name. I am sorry.' The officer ignored me. He took away my blankets for two weeks, and I had to sleep on the bare floor. He said I had broken a rule, and that was my punishment.

"I was a very poor sleeper in prison. I pleaded with the medical officer to give me Valium or something to help me sleep. I found it difficult to get my family out of my mind, even for a moment, especially at night. My mind would wander, thinking of them, how they were in the house. But the medical officer told me that if I took Valium it would get into my system and when I left prison I would not be able to sleep without it. I told him that if I could only sleep in prison I would gladly face sleeplessness when I returned home. 'While I am here,' I said, 'I want to forget about my family.' It was terrible at night, thinking about them all the time, and not being to sleep.

"I had been in prison for a year when one night my ulcer burst. I pleaded with the prison warder to open the door so I could breathe fresh air. I was finding it hard to breathe. He said he did not have the keys with him and that I would have to wait until morning, when he could see the director. That night I thought I was going to die. But in the morning the doctor came and directed that I be taken to the infirmary. I had not seen sunlight for twelve months, and when I was taken out through the main gate of the prison the sun blinded me, which is why I now have to use reading glasses. In the infirmary there were two condemned prisoners. They were in chains. They wore black, with 'Condemned' written on them. One day a prisoner, whose father was actually a prison officer, told me that I should be extremely careful of these men. If they happened to kill again, the government would set them free. You can imagine how I felt. I could not sleep properly after this, fearing that these men might strangle me to win their freedom. Even though I knew that this was surely impossible, I also knew that anything could happen to a person in prison. So I slept during the day.

"There were many deaths during the time I spent in Pademba Road. Many people died during an epidemic. Their stools were bloody, and they died within days. I remember a young Fula chap, very handsome . . . and then there were the Mammy Yoko murderers. They were only boys, about eighteen or twenty. Two of them I knew very well. One was the son of Mr. Sheku Jabi and my cousin Fanta. I remember when he was born. The other, Sila, was another cousin's daughter's son. They were tried and condemned to death. They were in the cell above mine. When I learned that they were to be executed next day, I could not sleep. Imagine someone you know well, who you have known as a baby, going to the gallows. I cried that night. The third boy, who I did not know personally, managed to communicate a message to Bedor Bangura, one of the detainees in our group. When you are released, this boy said to Bedor, please tell my parents to forgive me for all the pain I have caused them. Let them pray for me. And tell them that I did not murder Kabiya.

"Bedor never left Pademba Road prison alive. So the message was never delivered. And since I did not know the parents of this boy, who was hanged that night, I could not deliver the message either. Had I known them, I would have done so.

"I remember another man too, a soldier from Murraytown Barracks. He had gone mad, and was kept in chains. At night you could hear him singing Poro songs in his cell. The prison officers would order prisoners to flog him. They said that flogging was the best medicine. Then he was tried and condemned to death. I saw the medical officer arrive the night of the execution. I had known him in Kabala, though I forget his name. . . .

"Then one morning, while I was still in the infirmary, a friend of mine whom I had known outside prison (he used to come to my Alitalia office and do the football pools with me), came to me with news that all the detainees that had been tried and found guilty were to be executed that night. My friend's name was Renner. He sometimes brought me iced water to drink. When he told me this news, I implored him not to tell anyone else. I did not want the others to know. But they were in my thoughts all day. Dr. Forna. Ibrahim Taqi. All of them. I was thinking of them all.

"I will never forget that night. The main electrical supply was disconnected, and a generator turned on. I tried to sleep by persuading the nurse to give me a double dose of Valium. I was scared. You can't imagine how I felt. It was terrible. I did not want to be conscious of what was going on. But the pills did not work, and every hour, from one in the morning, I watched from my bed as the medical officer went to the execution cell and then returned. I saw corpses. Eight were executed that night, at hourly intervals. The last was my friend N'Silk, paramount chief of Makarigbanti. I had known him for years. He was a school teacher like myself. At one time he was captain of the protectorate football team. He went to Parliament as APC, but later went over to SLPP. I'm sure Siaka Stevens never forgave him. When he was found guilty of treason, he was not spared. He was a friend of mine. His children called me uncle. I hate to remember that night. The deaths of Paramount Chief N'Silk, of Dr. Mohamed Forna, of Ibrahim Taqi. It is something terrible, an execution. I would hate to sign the death warrant of any man. This part of politics I find abhorrent.

"After that I did not know what would happen. Though I played no part in the coup attempt, anything could have happened. I was very worried. The chap in the cell next to mine at that time was Alhaji Lamine Sidique. We used to joke around. 'Cousin,' he would say, 'I've got over three hundred bedbugs here in my cell.' 'Well, you're a Fula man,' I'd say. 'These are your cows!' It was fun, but it wasn't fun. Life wasn't easy. One day, about a month after the executions, Lamine told me that he was going to ask the prison director for pen and paper so that he could write to Siaka Stevens. 'I have been here for a year,' he said. 'I have done nothing wrong. I am going to ask him why I should be detained.' At that very moment, his cell door was opened and he was taken away. A prison officer then told the rest of us that further charges of treason were to be laid. This was to frighten us. We became very uneasy. But next morning we learned that Lamine had been released. I was very happy for him. I thought, Perhaps now he is free he can use his influence to get the rest of us released.

"The following day, an old man called J. J. Davis, an ex-serviceman, told me that he had overheard some prison officers saying that some of the detainees would be released. And he started planning a celebration at Brookfields Hotel. 'Even if we are released,' I said, 'I do not want to go anywhere except home, to be with my family, to see my wife and kids. Anyway,' I said, 'if we all went to Brookfields, wouldn't the CID arrest us again, and accuse us of plotting against the government? We would have to meet in the open.'

"Ten minutes later we learned that Pa Davis was dead. It was incredible. My temper rose up and I banged the iron door with my fist. How could he have died in that short space of time? I was distraught. I did not sleep that night.

"But the next morning, Frederick Carew and I were freed.

"It was a Thursday. I had not had a bath for thirteen months. After collecting my shoes, my ring, my watch, and my coat, I took a taxi to Tony Yazbeck's. He was not home, and his children did not recognize me. I said, 'I am Marah, S. B. Marah.' So they gave me a lift to Wilberforce, where I lived. I had a beard. I was shabby. I went straight to Rose. She hugged me. I think she knew I was going to be released. Then the children came. I had dark glasses on. Rose said, 'Look, Aisetta, it's Papa.' Aisetta thought I might be Father Christmas! She did not remember me. When I left her, she had been four years, four months old. She said to me, 'Take off your glasses.' She was still afraid. Abu was very small. He did not know who I was either. Rose prepared my bath, a warm bath. She gave me a good scrub, brought me a towel, got me a new shirt and trousers. I was now united with my family again.

"After I left prison, several friends suggested that I should go and pay my respects to Siaka Stevens. However, the president had been involved in a road accident the day before my release, so it was not possible to see him at that time. A few weeks later, Tony Yazbeck gave me and my family air[plane] tickets to Abidjan, Beirut, and London. Rose wanted to visit her elder sister in Ivory Coast. And I needed a medical checkup in England. We stayed in London for a month, where I managed to see S. I. Koroma, who was then vice president. I first knew him when he was at Bo school, though we were never close. I never followed anyone. I was always my own man. S. I. Koroma told me, 'I do not have anything against you. I don't know whether or not the Old Man has something against you, but in my opinion we should not molest people like you.' I told him that I had been arrested and detained. Nothing more. I did not know why. But this was the price one has to pay in politics."

Though moved by S. B.'s equanimity as he recounted his story, I also felt bitter and angry. For his remarks had brought home to me the paradox of power—which, for all its promises of a brave new world, invariably generates envy and resentment. For this reason, whoever attains high office must perforce divide his energies between nurturing this illusion of a better future and defending his hold on power. What Max Gluckman so perceptively calls the frailty in authority is born of this gap between the expectations we have of rulers, both secular and divine, and the flaws and failings we all too readily see in them.[1] This is why dissent and rebellion are endemic to political life. When a country is impoverished, like Sierra Leone, a leader may, through no fault of his own, fail in reconciling high expectations with everyday reality, and end up bearing the brunt of people's disappointment. Perhaps this is why politicians sometimes give up on the idea of the general good, and focus on feathering their own nests—throwing occasional sops to their faithful followers, consolidating their power base, silencing dissent. In the 1967 general elections, Albert Margai's SLPP was narrowly defeated by the APC. As his successor Siaka Stevens was being sworn in at the State House on March 21, a young army officer and aide-de-camp to the governor general, Lieutenant Hinga Norman, stopped the ceremony on orders from his force commander, Brigadier General David Lansana, whose justification was that the results of the chiefs' elections had not been taken into account. Martial law was declared, and two days later Siaka Stevens and several of his ministers were driven in a military Land Rover to Pademba Road prison. By the time a countercoup reinstated Siaka Stevens in April 1968, the new incumbent had doubtless had ample time to decide what he must do to remain in power, and how he should deal with his opponents. Understandably distrustful of the army, he created a paramilitary unit consisting of many recruits from Guinea, called the Internal Security Unit (ISU), though it would subsequently be known as the State Security Department (SSD), or Siaka Stevens's Dogs. These, then, were some of the background events and experiences against which Siaka Stevens's shadow state began to emerge— with its insidious control of the nation's diamond wealth by a ruling elite, the deployment of spies and thugs to intimidate enemies, and finally the stage-managed dynamiting of C. A. Kamara-Taylor's house, followed by the trumped-up charges, the litany of lies, the confessions under duress, and the abuse of high court protocols that in the early hours of July 19, 1974, culminated in the judicial murder of S. B.'s colleagues and friends.

A few months after hearing S. B.'s account of his detention, I read Aminatta Forna's *The Devil That Danced on the Water*, in which she speaks of her search for the truth about her father's life and death. In his final hours, Aminatta writes, Dr. Mohamed Forna used the paper and pen supplied to him for his mercy plea to compose an account of his life from boyhood to his death, and she goes on to describe, on the basis of an eyewitness report, his walk to the gallows, and how, on the morning after the executions, her father's body, and those of the seven other men who had been hanged, were displayed in open coffins before the crowds outside Pademba Road prison. That night, she concludes, the bodies were loaded into military trucks and driven to Rukupa cemetery on the road to Hastings where they were doused with acid and dumped in a mass grave.

Passages

Back in Copenhagen, my work on S. B.'s biography was interrupted by a phone call from S. B. in Freetown. S. B.'s and Noah's brother Ali was dead. S. B. said he wanted me to be the first to know and to convey to Heidi the sad news. We talked for twenty minutes or so—of Ali's descent into insanity, of the tragic death of his son, and the devastation of the war. I remembered Ali with heartbreaking vividness, his immediate smile, his unfailing generosity, and the day Pauline and I left Freetown on our way back to England in 1970, when Ali ran up the gangway minutes before we sailed, with oranges for Heidi.

> *He is still standing on the Freetown wharf*
> *in police uniform as our ship prepares to sail,*
> *his hands empty of the oranges*
> *he brought on board for us . . .*
>
> *But this was thirty years ago*
> *before madness claimed him*
> *before war engulfed his country*
> *before his son was killed*
> *before my daughter became a woman*
> *before his brother phoned me this morning in Copenhagen*
> *with the news that he was dead.*

"Send me that photo you took of Ali on the wharf,"
S. B. said. "And come back soon.
We are rebuilding the house.
The road is now open to Firawa.
Everyone remembers you."

My fingernails feel for the hard, thin rind
of African oranges.
I squeeze the bittersweet juice
into my mouth,
and sit in my office after S. B.'s call
in absolute silence.

Within weeks, I received a second call from S. B. Sanfan Aisetta had passed away, coincidentally on the birthday of my daughter, Heidi Aisetta.

Six months would pass before I returned to Sierra Leone and heard the full story from S. B. Sitting on the veranda at P.K. Lodge, overlooking the city and the sea, with the distant thrum of traffic in our ears, S. B. began by describing the general and presidential elections in May 2002 that returned the SLPP to power. "I had been involved in deciding ministerial positions in Tejan Kabbah's new cabinet," S. B. explained. "As I dressed that morning, I was looking forward to the interviews. But then the telephone rang. It was the Honorable Alhaj Ali Sheriff on the line. He said, 'Korto, anything can happpen in this world. One must take courage. It is with a heavy heart and sympathy that I have to tell you that your mother passed away this morning.'

"I was shocked and stunned, because I had not seen her for some time. In fact, it was painful for me to visit her. I would always leave her in tears, not knowing if I would see her again. Now I thought of the years she had nursed and cared for me, right up to the time I became a man. But I was in a dilemma. That morning I had these interviews beginning at eleven o'clock. My mother had passed away in Kissy, and I was at P.K. Lodge [on the other side of Freetown]. I thought to myself, I have my national duty to perform. The nation is waiting, the world is waiting for the new government to be set up. And the nominees and their families are anxious to know who will be selected. I then reached the conclusion that just as my mother had performed her duty very well, bringing me into this world, caring for me, I should now follow her example. So I said, 'Honorable Sheriff, I would like you to take her to the funeral home while I go to Parliament and do my duty.' At the Parliament I informed my colleagues of the sad accident that had taken place. Well, as always happens, people think of the moment, and so it was in this case. Everybody was with me, and they appreciated the fact that I had the courage to leave my mother in the mortuary while I went to do my job. I then did the interviews, and we buried her that Friday. My children and neices from abroad, and a few relatives, wanted me to take the corpse to Kabala, but I told them that I wanted my mother to go home to her people where she belonged. I had decided to send her to her nephew Kande Sayo in Kalangba, beause he had requested her to be with him so that one of his wives could keep vigil over her. I had agreed to his request. My mother had served her husband and his people well. It was now time for her to return home, to her origin, to her people, like a hunter returning home from the bush. But as fate would have it this was not possible, because the president said that if I took her to Kalangba or Kabala he would go with me. I knew what that meant. If he traveled with me, most of my parliamentary colleagues, many civil servants, and most government ministers would come too. So I decided to bury her in Freetown.

"It rained heavily that day. But many people were there to pay their last respects. The president himself, most of my parliamentary colleagues, permanent secretaries, people from all walks of life including Lebanese businessmen and several ambassadors."

S. B. went on to describe how he clung to his mother, crying bitterly, when the time came to take her body to the cemetery. "From P.K. Lodge, the cortege moved through the city with a police siren clearing the way, and people along the roadside were telling one another, 'That's S. B. Marah's mother. That's S. B. Marah's mother.'"

His face hidden behind his hand, his voice a hoarse whisper, S. B. recalled his last glimpse of his mother as she was lowered into her grave. "May God bless her for all she did for us after the death of our father fifty years ago. May her soul rest in peace."

Relationship and Relativity

In the same way that the course of history comprises a succession of turbulent events interrupted by periods of comparative calm, the course of our lives is punctuated by the deaths of those we love. It is in these breaks that we take stock of our situation, come to terms with what has occurred, and begin anew. These are also the moments when we foreshadow—in the ways we speak, think, and act—the shape of things to come, which is why ethics is a matter of how we respond creatively to our situations in life rather than an abstract moral imperative or normative prescriptions we obediently endeavor to adhere to.

Storytelling is one of humanity's oldest and most vital ways of turning the tables on events over which we have no control, a kind of *esprit d'escalier* whereby we retrospectively take the sting out of events that deprived us of meaning and compromised our humanity. This is the message of Akira Kurosawa's great film *Rashomon*. The truth of an event is relative to our vantage point and interests, but the outcome of any event hinges on how successfully we claim final truth for our own view of it, and how successfully we convince others of that truth.

Three days before I flew to Sierra Leone on January 9, 2003, I read the following report on the Sierra Leone website:

Election violence in the northern town of Kabala Saturday caused polling officials to flee the town and forced a premature end to Sengbe Chiefdom's efforts to crown a new Paramount Chief. After the first round of voting, polling officials said, no candidate had received the requisite 55 percent of the vote necessary to avoid a runoff. But, according to several reports, the supporters of Ali Marah claimed their candidate had won a first round victory and demanded that the staff [of chieftaincy] be handed over immediately. Supporters of Ali Marah stoned the home of parliamentary leader S.B. Marah, whom they accused of supporting Alhaji Balansama Marah, Ali Marah's principal opponent. Glass was broken from the windows, but S.B. Marah was not injured. The mob also attempted to attack Mohammed Fasilie Marah, a brother of S.B. Marah, forcing him to flee for his life. S.B. Marah, reached at his home in Freetown, acknowledged his backing for Alhaji Balansama Marah, but he insisted it was a private matter on behalf of a man who had supported him throughout his more than forty years of political life. "I am supporting my brother who was supporting me all my political career," he told the Sierra Leone web. "Everybody knows that. I have been supporting somebody who has been good to me. I want to repay him in his own coin. Is that a crime?" S.B. Marah decried the political violence directed against him because of his support for another candidate. "That doesn't mean that they will go and stone my house . . . Is that democracy?" ("Election Violence," January 6, 2003)

Because I would be staying with S. B. and Rose in Freetown, this report both troubled me and aroused my anthropological interest, not only in the background to the divided loyalties but in the entanglement of the politics of the state and the politics of chieftaincy.

My flight from Brussels reached Freetown via Abidjan shortly after nightfall, and I took the first available helicopter from the airport to the city. For some reason, however, my bag was put on a later flight, so though S. B. was at the heliport to meet me, we faced a possibly long wait for the next helicopter. S. B. was with a political colleague who was clearly impatient to get back to the house where he, S. B., and others had been discussing "that Kabala business." I urged them to leave and send a car back for me. It was therefore after dark by the time I finally got to S. B.'s house, greeted Rose, had dinner, and went to bed.

In the morning, I found S. B. sitting in the parlor, preoccupied with visitors and phone calls, so it was Rose who first recounted to me details of what had happened in Kabala. In her opinion, S. B. had been largely responsible for what had befallen him. "The president had given strict instructions to all parliamentarians not to interfere in chieftaincy elections," she said, "but S. B. blundered in."

Rose went on to say that Ali Marah, a son of the late paramount chief, had spent the war years in the U.S. and had stayed with her and S. B. when he returned to Sierra Leone in 2002. He had shown no signs of ill will toward S. B., nor indicated that he had any political ambitions. As for Ali's main rival in the election, Alhaji Fatmata Balansama Marah (a younger brother of the late chief), Rose was frankly critical, accusing him of having squandered the money given at his elder brother's funeral, and reneging on his obligation (under the levirate) to take care of his brother's two widows. In Kabala, Rose said, many people regarded Alhaji Balansama as selfish and corrupt, so there was widespread anger when S. B. supported him. Rose then spoke of S. B.'s second error of judgment. Apparently Ali had claimed that Vice President Solomon Berewa backed his candidacy. On hearing this, S. B. criticized the vice president to his face, without first ascertaining whether Ali's claim was true. "Yesterday morning," Rose said, "the vice president came here and ex-onerated himself." But the damage was done, and she was afraid her two sons would not be able to go to Kabala and claim their inheritance: Abu, the house that the mob had destroyed; and Chelmanseh, the second house near the swamp. Rose was also critical of S. B.'s expectation that the president would sort things out simply because they were close friends and brothers-in-law (President Ahmad Tejan Kabbah's late wife, Patricia, was Rose's elder sister). "Even yesterday," Rose continued, "the president reminded S. B. of the need to be careful what he said, and to whom he said it"—an allusion to a court case eighteen months before in which S. B. had been accused of slap-ping a police officer on point duty. Although acquitted, S. B. had, it seemed, subsequently bragged about treating the officer as he deserved.

In Lawrence Durrell's novel *Balthazar*, a young English writer, having rendered an account of his love affair with a beautiful Alexandrian woman called Justine, is shocked by the realization that his understanding of the events in which he and Justine were embroiled is only one of many possi-ble interpretations. "We live lives based on selected fictions," the character Pursewarden writes. "Our view of reality is conditioned by our position in space and time—not by our personalities as we like to think. Thus, every interpretation of reality is based upon a unique position. Two paces east or west and the whole picture is changed."[1] When Rose mentioned S. B.'s confrontation with the police officer, I was immediately reminded of other episodes when S. B. had behaved as if he was above the law, or a law unto himself, and I was not surprised when S. B. later told me not to set much store by what Rose had confided to me, and proceeded to share his version of what had happened.

First, he showed me a report he had written to the inspector general of police the day after his house had been attacked, beginning with details of his arrival in Kabala on December 28 to spend the New Year period with several parliamentary allies. "Although some of these friends soon returned to Freetown," S. B. wrote, "I had to stay behind because I had taken some tools for roadworks, which I had to distribute to my people in the district."

On the morning of 5 January, between nine and ten, I received information that Ali Marah, a candidate for Sengbe Chiefdom PC election and others were coming to attack my person and burn down my house; this was said in public, so I sent Umaru and Balacun Conteh [two of S. B.'s servants] to inform the police and tell them that I needed their protection. After fifteen minutes they came to report that the police said they were coming. It took an hour for the police to arrive. From my verandah, I saw a police Land Rover drive toward Ali Marah's place, where a big crowd had gathered singing in Kuranko that Ali had won the election. As soon as the police Land Rover moved away, Minister Ibrahim Sesay, Munda and myself then observed the crowd moving towards my house. Just at that moment one or two policemen arrived. One was in plain clothes with a walkie-talkie. The crowd was then busy making road blocks and raining abuses on us. We tried to send a second message to the police, but the whole place was blocked. It was Allie Sheriff who went to UNAMSIL [UN Mission in Sierra Leone] to ask for help since we were not satisfied with the way the police were handling the situation. The crowd came as close as ten yards from my house, then started stoning it. They had machetes and clubs which they used to start breaking down the doors and windows of my house, and they were singing and at the same time raining insults on my parents in the forecourt of my house. We were barricaded [in] and the police stood there doing nothing to stop them.

There was a crowd of about three hundred. Our lives were left to fate as they smashed all the windows of my house. Then the Bangladeshi arrived. They met me at the corner of my house, and told me that they were peace makers, but that they would do their best to protect and evacuate me, so I must remain cool, but it took some time to make the security arrangements.

After they left and went to get more security men, and after my house had been completely damaged, that was the time that the police started throwing tear gas. We were barricaded for four good hours, in the end the place was dark, and the Bangladeshis started making arrangements for our evacuation.

S. B. concluded his report by listing his material losses—Indian mango trees and cassava plants uprooted, all the windows of the house broken, a satellite dish "broken to pieces," a large wallet (containing 2,150,000 leones, equal to U.S. $1,000) stolen, together with two wristwatches (one gold), and S. B.'s sunglasses. The mob also beat to death two cows tethered in his compound (one a gift to the resident minister, another that S. B. had purchased for himself). Furthermore, two goats were taken to Ali Marah's house, together with a motorcycle (valued at Le 10.7 million, equal to U.S. $5,000), 20 bundles of corrugated iron sheets, 25 bags of rice, 1,200 palm oil seedlings, 500 machetes, wheelbarrows, and shovels for road work, and some cooking pots—all "under the very eyes of the police." Finally, S. B. observed, "I told Christopher Johns (Regional Commissioner of Police, North) and Chief Police Officer Mustapha that they had seen everything that had been done to me in their presence."

Because numerous visitors from Kabala were coming and going at this time, I had plenty of opportunities for expanding my picture of what had happened on January 5. Balacun Conteh's comments were particularly interesting, if only because he, like Rose, had an axe to grind with S. B. This had became evident the morning after my arrival in Freetown, when S. B. humiliated Balacun in front of the visitors sitting in the parlor. Balacun had just reentered the room after carrying two buckets of hot water into S. B.'s bathroom. Convinced that Balacun had spent more time than was necessary in his room, S. B. said, "I hope you didn't steal anything from my room while you were there." Balacun did not respond but, hurt and indignant, he later told Rose that he would quit working for S. B. if he was spoken to in this manner again. (Indeed, he did walk out the following day, after a similar upbraiding.) When S. B. left for his parliamentary office that morning— after Balacun had laid out his clothes and helped him dress, put on his shoes, collect his diaries, papers, mobile phone, and car keys, and carried his bags to his car—Balacun fetched a deep sigh of relief.

"Thank God," he said to me, with a wry smile. "Thank God."

Seizing the moment, I asked Balacun to give me his version of what had happened in Kabala.

That the police had done nothing to prevent the attack on S. B.'s house, even after Balacun, S. B., and others had phoned them for help, was, in Balacun's opinion, a result of S. B. having smeared the chief police officer in the days before the election, and because he had not been forgiven for the time he verbally abused and physically assaulted a police officer on traffic duty in Freetown.

"But why should Ali turn against S. B.?" I asked.

Balacun thought it was a matter of political expediency. Since Ali's main rival was associated with the SLPP—the party in power—Ali decided to throw in his lot with the traditional opposition, the APC. Many ex-combatants had done the same, smarting from their defeat in the civil war by the SLPP government of Tejan Kabbah. The mob was made up of many dissident soldiers and Revolutionary United Front (RUF) combatants, Balacun said, who were aggrieved at losing the war, or looking for a quick way to enrich or empower themselves. "We were very frightened," Balacun added. "They wanted to kill us. Now they are going around Sengbe, looting and threatening section chiefs."

That afternoon, Noah shared his view of Ali's conduct.

By contrast with Balacun, who interpreted it politically, Noah referred to Ali's upbringing.

"Ali's father, the late Balansama Marah, was never a strong chief or father," Noah said. "Nor did Chief Balansama demand that people respect the protocols governing relations with a chief. He was too lenient. He let his children do what they liked. He was kind to a fault. And Ali's eleven years in the U.S. may have set him on the wrong path."

As to what this "wrong path" might have been, S. B.'s nephew Sewa Koroma, who had also been caught up in the Kabala affray, said that Ali probably used drugs, like his cohorts, many of whom were ex-rebels and sobels (renegade soldiers who had fought with the RUF). "He's also a tool of the APC," Sewa added, and described how he had been spotted by Ali's boys while buying gasoline at a Kabala garage. "Look at the wutètè [many] boys coming, those S. B. Marah boys," Ali's followers shouted as Sewa jumped into his Suzuki four-wheel drive and drove straight to the police station. The four policemen there said they could not protect him, and advised him to go to UNAMSIL headquarters. It was there that Sewa listened in on the radio-telephone conversation between the Bangladeshi field commander and his men at the beseiged house, and heard the police complaining that they were tired and wanted to go home, as well as reports on the mob's attempt to burn a Bangladeshi armored personnel carrier, and details of the final rescue.

The next fragment of the mosaic that was slowly emerging from the various conversations and accounts of the Kabala incident was a report, written by Christopher E. F. Johns, regional commissioner north (Makeni), and addressed to the inspector general of police in Freetown. If S. B. had a contentious relationship with the police, Johns's report made it abundantly clear that the police had their own bones to pick with S. B.

Acting on intelligence reports from Kabala, Johns dispatched police reinforcements to the town on January 3. His report then described the election on January 4. Of the nine candidates for the paramount chieftaincy, Ali Marah received 105 votes, and Alhaji Balansama Marah 91. Under normal circumstances, a second ballot would have been held an hour after the first to decide between the two leading contenders. At 5:30 p.m., Ali Marah, some counselors, the electoral commissioner, the provincial secretary north, police officers, and representatives of UNAMSIL and the United States and International Civilian Policing were all at the courthouse waiting for the runoff to begin. Alhaji Balansama arrived at 7:10 p.m. with some of his counselors and supporters, but when the supporters were told they could not enter the courthouse (*gbare*), they "started insulting their opponents and throwing stones at the police, thereby rudely dispersing the crowd." At 7:15 p.m., according to Johns's report, the two assessor chiefs summoned the electoral commissioner and the provincial secretary to a nearby house for urgent discussions. Twenty minutes later they returned to the courthouse and advised Johns that the runoff be postponed for security reasons. One chief even said that he feared for his life. Johns said that he had reinforced the police, so there was no reason for any delay; indeed, he wanted to avoid "agitating the impatient crowd." However, the electoral commissioner and parliamentary secretary, fearful of the anger of the crowd, fled, taking the ballot papers with them, so at 8:00 p.m. Johns was obliged to announce a postponement of the runoff.

Convinced that "the police and UNAMSIL were on top of the situation," Johns then left for his headquarters in Makeni, seventy-five miles to the south.

The next day, Sunday, January 5, Johns phoned Kabala for a report. Though informed that everything was calm, he consulted his superior, Mr. M. Kamara. On the strength of what he heard, he decided to return to Kabala, where he arrived at 3:07 p.m. Hearing of the attack on S. B. Marah's house, he went immediately to the scene. "I saw over three hundred people armed with sticks, stones and branches shouting at the top of their voices, demanding the 'head' of Hon. S. B. Marah and the chieftaincy 'staff.' The group was a blend of men, women, youths (male and female), and children. I noticed a lot of damage had been done to the house. I was able to talk to the crowd and the situation was partially brought under control."

Johns observed that people were converging on the house from all sides. Because it had no perimeter walls or fences, protecting it was not easy. However, Johns noted, the Bangladeshi troops under the command of Colonel M. H. Saladhudin, and troops under the command of Bambett Seven, "were on standby."

On learning that S. B. and his family were "held up in the house," and after conferring with Colonel Saladhudin, Johns said that he then entered the house to talk to S. B. "We convinced him to move out to safety, but he was not ready to go, instead insisting in having his belongings with him. After much talking he agreed to leave. At about 20.30 hours we were finally able to get the crowd off the road. At about 21.00 hours Hon. S.B. Marah and family were smuggled out of his house in a convoy to the headquarters of Bambett Seven, where final arrangements were made for his movement to Makeni. SLP 294 was provided for him with a police driver OSD 4700 and one guard. I led the way to Makeni."

Johns's report concluded with an account of the journey back to Makeni—how S. B. ordered a halt at Fadugu, where he "said a lot of bad things about the police" and then later, at police headquarters in Makeni, where S. B. and the resident minister north "hurled invectives at the police," threatening the police driver who had driven them down from Kabala with "a lesson he will never forget." In his final "comments," Johns noted, "I have observed that the Hon. S. B. Marah and the Minister are in the habit of provoking the police and subjecting us to a lot of ridicule and embarrassment in the eyes of the public. Even where we went all out to rescue him and his family from possible death, instead of saying thanks, it was molestation."

In the course of a telephone conversation with the inspector general of police, Keith Biddle, on January 11, S. B. sought to rebut several of the assertions Christopher Johns had made in his report. "I am the target of misinformation," S. B. began. "I've seen the report by Christopher Johns. Quite honestly, I was not alone in Kabala. There were other important people there. Moreover, whenever I am in Kabala I never step out of my house. I stay there. But one thing I do—I've got a musical instrument [an amplifier and sound system] that the kids love. I try to arrive in Kabala in time to play music, so the kids can dance. And before I go to Kabala I always inform the police. It was alleged I didn't notify them, but in fact I did—for security— even though I've never feared for my safety in Kabala. But I wanted security in case the kids quarreled at the dance.

"On the day of the election I was never in the court gbare. I was in my house. I heard the results of the election there. Ali and his followers declared no need for a second ballot because they had won a majority in the first. Ali accused me of being responsible for the stone-throwing at the court gbare. But nobody can accuse me of interfering in the election. I favored Alhaji Balansama because this man was in Fadugu when I was a teacher there many years ago. He used to bring me bread. He supported me all out in the 1956 election. He later went to Kono to mine for diamonds. He would often assist me with money. During the war he provided food for the CDF [Civil Defence Force]. He was SLPP chairman. He is progressive. He has houses in Freetown that he built with his own money from diamond mining, yet he returned to farming. I gave Alhaji Balansama money because I owed him as a human being. Is it a crime to support someone? If I've broken the law, let God be the judge of that.

"Someone came and told me that Ali had announced his intention of attacking me, killing me, and burning my house. I sent for the police. They said they would come. They took an hour—and only after going to Ali's house first, which was two hundred yards away from mine. I could see the crowd.

"Ali's people blocked the road a hundred yards from my house. The man I sent to the police told me that the police were unwilling to interfere. I got a message to the Bangladeshis. They came and explained they were only peacekeepers. The police came two hours later."

After giving details of how the cows were beaten and killed, and his property looted, S. B. described the worsening situation in his house.

"Stones were thrown. They even tried to burn a Bangladeshi armed vehicle. We had to move from one end of the house to the other as windows were broken and doors were smashed. I had some extra doors, and we used these to barricade the broken windows. In the evening the army came. 'We could not come until the police requested it,' they said. We were told to gather our luggage in the parlor. The Bangladeshis took videos of the damage. Then we were taken to the Bangladeshi barracks. The first and only time I saw Christopher Johns was at the end of the day, as we were about to leave Kabala. I talked to him in the Bangadeshi compound for the first time.

"Believe me, Keith, if you had been there you would not have thought I would come out of it alive. It was a sad spectacle for me to be molested like that. I can be difficult at times. I am difficult to people who try to get things without working. That's what I am down on. Even the public sometimes. That's the trouble with this country—people trying to get things without working for them.

"Even this morning there have been reports from Kabala of Ali's people beating people up, terrorizing them. Everyone is scared now.

"As for the police, they say that I removed their CPO from office, but even this CPO, when he left school, he came to me; I sent him to college, helped him, advised him not to drink or quarrel. And Christopher Johns, I helped him get back into the police force after he was jailed by the NPRC [the military junta—the National Provisional Ruling Council—that seized power in 1997] in Makeni. I don't know why the police are holding grudges against me. I am not antipolice. I'm against people who don't work hard. And I want justice done. Because Alhaji Balansama's supporters are really scared now. Ali's people are beating people up, saying they must be for Ali Marah.

"I am grateful to you for listening to me, because I have been made the culprit in this business. People have given you the wrong picture, Keith."

In the days that followed, S. B. urged whoever had been witness to the events in Kabala to make statements to the police. He even sent a somewhat reluctant Alhaji Balansama downtown to do this, phoning Freetown police headquarters to say he was on his way. It was S. B.'s hope that these depositions would lead to charges being laid against Ali Marah, and that the runoff would be delayed until a police investigation had been completed. He therefore urged Alhaji Balansama not to be intimidated by his political opponents, but to cultivate support, make friends, and confirm old alliances in preparation for the second ballot.

Such hopes were soon dashed. The president ordered a thorough and immediate investigation, the outcome of which was that S. B. was cleared of any wrongdoing, and the runoff went ahead as scheduled on January 24. S. B. confessed that he was mystified as to why the president should make this decision. In any event, a few days before the runoff, Alhaji Balansama decided that he had no support, in part because of the widespread intimidation of local chiefs, and he withdrew his candidacy. His box was nonetheless included, and he received five votes. Ali got 148 and was declared the winner. For S. B. it was "all wrong." Alhaji had been chairman of the SLPP for many years, had spent millions of his own money during the war, buying food for the army and CDF, and he was owed this position.

"Will you make your peace with Ali now?" I asked.

"I'll never work with him," S. B. said, despite the president's decree that he and Ali make up. S. B. considered this idea "childish and insulting" and was annoyed that the president should ask this of him. "I couldn't do this," he said. "I would betray all Kuranko. Ali insulted my mother and my family. He destroyed my house, my property. How could I accept an apology?"

When the moment came for S. B. to hand over the staff of chieftaincy to Ali Marah, he abruptly told the new chief, "Get out of my sight."

Events quickly and imperceptibly become stories.[2] In S. B.'s telephone lobbying, and in the numerous discussions that went on every morning and throughout the weekend in S. B.'s parlor, during which the Kabala affray was recalled, recounted, and analyzed, and declarations made as to what ought to be done to resolve the issues arising from it, I witnessed this transmutation of what had happened into what people now thought should happen. Clearly, this process of retelling and remembering an event draws on formal reports as well as anecdotal accounts, and involves the transformation of a lived reality, which is open to many interpretations, into a discursive reality that is both conclusive and consensual. After ten days, the event was no longer recounted as it had been lived, but as it had been reworked in order to validate and give legitimacy to the interests of those whose fortunes had been most deeply affected by it. In the same way, secondary elaboration occludes our memory of our dreams; photographs impair our ability to recollect the events or persons whose images they have apparently captured; and anthropological texts erase the immediacy of a lived moment, rendering it in a form that already anticipates purposes that belong to another place and another time. Accordingly, the causes of an event are almost impossible to disentangle from the rationalizations and interpretations that are born of it, and why we so readily, though fallaciously, claim that our *post festum* conclusions may be treated as primary causes.

During the period when the events in Kabala dominated almost every discussion among visitors to S. B.'s house in Freetown, I often had a sense of déjà vu. What occurred in Kabala had not only been anticipated by S. B.'s assault of a police officer in Freetown and his alleged smearing of the chief police officer in Kabala; it echoed historical events. For instance, one of the agitators in the crowd at Kabala was a son of A. B. Magba Koroma, whom the twenty-three-year-old S. B. had defeated for the seat of Koinadugu South in 1957, following his first political campaign. Informants told me that the humiliation of this defeat had never been forgotten or forgiven by the older man—an ex-serviceman and close associate of Albert Margai. There were also memories of APC thugs during the years of Siaka Stevens's autocratic rule—the same intimidation of voters as the police stood by, doing nothing—not to mention the violence of dissident soldiers and rebellious youth in the recent civil war. "It's like the APC period all over again," Balacun remarked, only a few days after a report appeared in a local paper on the problem of restructuring and reforming the Sierra Leone army. "Many soldiers after their training [go] 'AWOL,'" *Concord Times* reporter Regina Thomas observed, "and go in search of money as they had been used to at-tacking civilians during the war." It seems, she concluded, that "as the adage goes, 'money nor go lef hin black han biyen' ('money would not leave its black hand behind')."[3]

I was also struck by the tension between different modes of conceptu-alizing power. Though S. B.'s authority derived from both his political and hereditary positions—as leader of the House of Parliament and scion of the ruling house of Barawa—he was still subject to the law of the land. It was this law, in the police view, that S. B. continually flouted. But, invoking cus-tomary Kuranko notions of work and duty (the Kuranko word *wale* covers both), S. B.'s argument was that the police had a duty to work for and obey senior parliamentarians. Understandably, the police saw this as putting one-self above the law, and they complained of the "ridicule and embarrassment" they had suffered from S. B.'s behavior. This conflict of wills—between con-stitutional and civil law on the one hand, and the politics of patrimonialism on the other—discloses a state that is not so much failed as conflicted. Net-works and alliances based on friendship, kinship, provenance, party mem-bership, and commercial interest all vie to determine the nature of truth and the course of events.

Any event discloses biographies as well as histories. This was borne home to me in Noah's comments on Ali's upbringing, in S. B.'s reasons for support-ing Alhaji Balansama (both S. B. and the SLPP were indebted to Balansama for what he had given them over many years of loyal service), and in S. B.'s remarks about Christopher Johns (having helped him in the past, he was owed loyalty now) and the chief police officer (who owed S. B. for similar reasons). It was also evident in Balacun's personal reasons for criticizing S. B. (though well educated and deserving of respect, he was obliged to do menial work for a Big Man who treated him like a slave), as well as in Rose's resent-fulness. Clearly there are unresolved ambiguities here concerning what is owed or due between men of different rank, or a husband and wife, as well as whether power confers a right to lord it over others rather than care for and protect them. S. B.'s autocratic disposition was so at odds with Noah's self-abnegating demeanor that I was inclined to see them as embodying the extremes of authoritarian and pastoral power that had, as far as I could see, always vied for dominance among Kuranko rulers. Moreover, the compet-ing claims of the candidates and their supporters during the Sengbe elec-tions disclose the deep rift between a traditional gerontocratic order, with all its symbolic privileges, and a generation of young men and women who demand equality, inclusion, and respect based on modernist conceptions of social justice. That so many ex-combatants threw their weight behind Ali suggests that the root causes of the civil war continue to find expression in a simmering desire among many of those on the margins of power to assert their right to break with a history of what they see as corrupt, arrogant, and unjust title holders, at both local and national levels, and assume a vital role in determining the destiny of the nation. Whether this necessarily signaled a growing redundancy of genealogical knowledge, I was yet to discover.

Endings

I was in Uppsala, Sweden, when word reached me that Noah had died. I had seen him in Sierra Leone only a few days before, and he seemed to be on the threshold of a new beginning. Our last conversation was a fervent exchange on human rights, occasioned by Noah's participation in a training course to become a justice of the peace. It was like old times—his casuistry and independence of mind, his confident dismissal of my dissenting views, his wry humor.

For several days after hearing of Noah's death, I could not settle to work. Walking the snowbound streets of Uppsala, my mind was filled with random recollections of experiences we had shared over a period of thirty-three years. I remembered how villagers once saw me as a djinn who would favor Noah with wealth and power. I recalled Noah's habit of emphasizing blessings over hard work, insisting that his mother had been such a dutiful wife that his father's ancestral blessings were sure to smooth his path through life. Now he was gone, I found it hard to accept that I was the one who had been blessed by our association, and that he, by contrast, had died before his time.

When S. B. died a few months later, I felt that with their passing, my long asociation with the Marah had come to an end. But on visits to London during the next few years, I met S. B.'s sons and spent time with one of S. B.'s daughters, Isata, who was working for a prestigious private bank. It was around this time that Noah's firstborn son, Kaimah, who was only a year older than Heidi, begged me to help him with his education, which had been disrupted by the war and by years of penury and displacement. Now living in Freetown, dejected and unsure of his future, Kaimah dreamed of one day studying abroad and pursuing his interests in political science, civic administration, and literature. Despite the anarchy and violence he had lived through, he had managed to complete his A-levels and qualify for university study, but without money he could not enroll.

Noah had had high hopes for Kaimah. He once told me that he wanted his son to reap the reward of his suffering, as if, in Nietzsche's words, the value of a thing sometimes lies not in what one attains with it, but in what one pays for it—what it costs us. So when I met Kaimah almost a year after his father's death and promised to pay his fees, it was partly in recognition of the credit Noah and Kaimah had accumulated through so many years of hardship and indigence.

Kaimah smiled for the first time since we began talking. He stood straighter. But I felt oppressed by the peculiar mix of abject loss and unreasonable hope that I encountered every day in Sierra Leone, and I found it poignant that just as S. B.'s elder brother Kulifa had once spurned his younger brother's plea for help, so S. B. had—at least in the eyes of his younger brother Noah—failed him. Now, with neither an older brother nor a father to support him, Kaimah was, in effect, an orphan, asking me to adopt him. At that moment, I realized that I was also an adoptee, and that the family that had once embraced me as a visiting anthropologist had become an extension of my own family, and that my obligations to Noah's son would prove to be more financially and emotionally demanding than I could have imagined.

Ten years passed. I moved, with my family, from Denmark to the United States, and though I returned to Sierra Leone a couple of times, I mostly kept in touch with Kaimah via email.

One summer evening, the phone rang. Its insistent summons brought me in from the garden, where I had been about to water the dogwood saplings I had just planted.

The voice on the other end of the line was far away, submerged with other voices and interrupted by electromagnetic interference. I pressed the receiver to my ear but could not identify the caller. In exasperation, I shouted into the phone, "Who is it?" but the caller's voice was so badly degraded that I replaced the receiver and walked toward the door. Seconds later, the phone rang again. This time I recognized the voice. It was my friend Sewa Magba Koroma, and he was on the road between Kabala and Makeni in

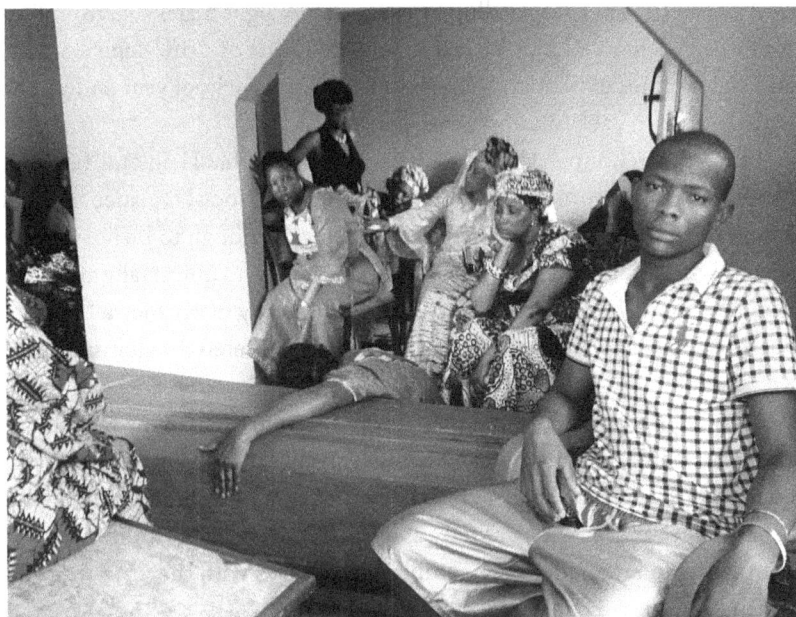

4 Michael Marah with the casket of his father, Kaimah.

northern Sierra Leone. Despite his voice breaking up, I got the gist of his message. "Daddy" Kaimah had died, and Sewa was on his way to Freetown for the funeral.

The interference made it impossible for us to exchange more than a few broken sentences, and I urged Sewa to email me as soon as he reached Freetown. I did not return to the garden. I sat at the dining room table, staring out the window into the trees, and late that night, after another email from Sewa, now in Freetown, I sent my condolences to Kaimah's only son, Michael, whose forlorn face in the photo Sewa sent from his cell phone reminded me of what Emmanuel Levinas once wrote about the face, "as the most basic mode of responsibility. . . . The face is not in front of me (en face de moi) but above me; it is the other before death, looking through and exposing death. . . . The face is the other who asks me not to let him die alone, as if to do so were to become an accomplice in his death."[1]

Not long after Sewa's call, I received an email from Kaimah's cousin Isata, who had been one of Kaimah's most trusted friends. "It is terribly sad," she wrote. "He was very promising and wanted to achieve his dreams. Let us hope that his dreams will be fulfilled through his son." Isata added her thanks to me, "for all your generous support throughout the years."

A few hours after responding to Isata's email, I got a message from Kaimah's sister Jeneba. "I pray he rest in the safe hands of GOD," Jeneba wrote, and she mentioned that, as soon as Kaimah's son's school year ended, she would take him back to Lunsar with her.

I had known Kaimah from the year he was born. That I had outlived both Noah and his firstborn son exacerbated the sense of social injustice that had haunted me for years, for while I had been lucky enough to be born into a society where education and medicine were freely and universally available, and grew up during a period of relative peace, many of my Sierra Leonean peers had failed to realize their dreams and had suffered the devastation of a civil war.

Only days after Kaimah's funeral, I was in Montreal with my wife to celebrate our son's graduation from McGill University. Sitting in the great marquee and listening to the principal of the university extolling the virtues of "knowledge" and "working as one" as keys to "the civilized world's success," I struggled to reconcile these complacent phrases with the grim world in which Kaimah had had to make his way.

In a file in my office I had kept, for eleven years, Kaimah's letters and emails, copies of his academic transcripts and his BEd thesis, essays, poems, and a one-act play. Leafing through this heartbreaking legacy of unfulfilled promise, one of his poems caught my eye. It echoed Isata's comments and brought back memories of the last time I saw Kaimah in Freetown in 2009.

The theme of Kaimah's poem was rebirth. Kaimah had lifted lines from three of my own poems and built his own around them. Describing the visitors that arrive in the northern town of Kabala every New Year's Eve to climb the great inselberg that overshadows the town and celebrate the possibility of miraculous transformations, Kaimah draws a contrast between the verdure of the Wara Wara Hills and the "abject poverty" of the town. His poem ends:

Food, drinks, in no small quantity
as Kabala boasts the birth of another year,
previous hopes dashed,
new promises made.

Such is life

When Noah died in 2002, I took Kaimah under my wing and covered the costs of his tertiary education. But after Kaimah's graduation from Njala University in June 2006, I found myself unable to pay for his further education in the UK or South Africa, and Kaimah reluctantly reenrolled at Njala for an MSci degree in rural development, hoping a second degree would guarantee him employment. With my own two children now at university, Kaimah's fees proved beyond my means, and, like many other young West Africans who had allowed themselves to believe that education would give them a bright future, Kaimah came to the realization that without local benefactors, inside connections, and the means to pay bribes, he would probably never find employment in Sierra Leone, regardless of how academically qualified he became.

When I visited him in 2009, Kaimah seemed close to despair. In the darkness of his single room, his clothes hanging from the ceiling above his bed, and surrounded by the books I had sent him over the years, he cut a sorry figure, and I felt guilty that I could not lift his spirits with an offer of material help. As he shared the story of his misfortunes in that candlelit and claustrophobic room, he expressed his frustration and humiliation at finding himself, at age thirty-eight, still unable to earn a living or support a wife and family.

"What of your girlfriend who worked in the hospital?" I asked. "Are you still together?"

Aisetta had left him. Kaimah knew from the start of the relationship that it would end this way, because she had a beau before him. This man had gone to London with his family to escape the war. When he returned to Sierra Leone, he was able to offer Aisetta security, income, and prospects—so she went back to him. "You can't expect love when you have nothing to give but love," Kaimah said. "Love without money counts for nothing here. You have to have money. Only with children is this any different."

Kaimah then recounted a story that he had never shared with his father Noah.

In 1992, when Noah was employed as a trade inspector in Koidu, and Kaimah was a student at the local high school, Kaimah had fallen in love with another student called Fatamata Massaquoi. Fatamata, who was known as Lango, lived with her aunt and uncle in the same compound as Kaimah's family. Not long before the Revolutionary United Front invaded Kono and only a few months after Lango gave birth to their "love child," the Massaquoi family left Koidu, possibly because of the shame that Lango had brought on them, possibly because of rumors of an impending rebel attack. For the next ten years, war destroyed the country. Villages were burned to the ground, thousands killed or maimed, and every scrap of movable property plundered. Kaimah's family moved, with thousands like them, from one district to another, seeking refuge from the fighting and the atrocities. Despite periodic disruptions to his education, Kaimah passed his O-levels in 1994 and sought admission to Fourah Bay College. Unable to find anyone to help him pay his fees, he completed his A-levels and tried again, to no avail. It wasn't until January 2002, when I returned to Sierra Leone, that Kaimah found the mentor he had been seeking and resumed his studies.

During the war years, Kaimah had done everything in his power to locate Lango. But it was only after his graduation in June 2006 that a breakthrough came. "I began having dreams, the same dream over and over again," Kaimah told me, "and in these dreams Lango was telling me about our child. In the same dreams, an old man appeared, someone I knew in Koidu town when Lango and I were living there. I was sure these dreams meant that I was soon going to see her again. So, one day I went to Koidu with my younger brother, and we found the old man who had appeared in my dreams. I asked him if he remembered Lango, if he knew where she was, and how I could find her. He told me that Lango was dead. She had died in Bo ten years ago. He said she had been seriously ill for some time. So I traveled to Bo next day and found the family. They were where the old man told me they were. I greeted them, and explained who I was, and how much I wanted to see my child. It was very difficult. No one remembered me. No one could identify me. But thanks to God, Lango's Aunty Sarah, who Lango lived with when she was in Koidu, happened to be visiting Bo from Moyamba, and she identified me and told the rest of the Massaquoi family about my friendship with Lango and about our love child."

Kaimah's son was in St. Mary's Children's Home in Bo, and after visiting the boy several times Kaimah petitioned the coordinator of the home to grant him custody, even though he was not married and had not raised other children, promising that he would dedicate himself to his son's education and showing evidence that he had already secured a place for him at St. Edward's Secondary School in Freetown.[2]

As Kaimah concluded his story, and as if what now happened had been carefully stage managed for dramatic effect, Kaimah's fourteen-year-old son appeared at the door, and I was introduced to Michael Noah Marah—named for me and for Kaimah's late father.

Michael sat on the bed beside Kaimah, who proudly showed me his son's school reports. I had a sudden sense of history unfolding before me, and tears welled up in my eyes as I recalled how Kaimah's grandfather, Tina Komé Marah, taught himself to read and write while serving with the British in the Cameroons during the First World War (the first Kuranko man to become literate in English), of how Kaimah's father, Noah, had struggled to complete his education after his elder brother S. B. took him out of high school to help in his political campaigns, of how Noah's mother argued against Noah pursuing studies in New Zealand, fearful that he, like Tina Komé, would throw his life to the winds and "become a child of the white men," and of how, despite Kaimah's years in the wilderness, he was now on the threshold of realizing a dream whose origins lay in his grandfather's conviction that the future lay in a world very different from the world into which he was born.

I asked Michael about his favorite subjects at school. As shy as his father, he spoke little and in whispers. Turning to Kaimah, I assured him I would visit him again when I returned from Firawa, and discuss the possibility of Kaimah going to the UK, just as his cousin Sewa had done, and perhaps enroll in a course of study there. Kaimah said he was ready to give up his MSci studies at Njala. If I could help pay for his airfare to the UK, he would find a college course and stay with his cousins until he found his feet.

"But I am concerned about Michael," I said. "What will become of him if you go to England to live?"

"I have thought about that already," Kaimah said. "My sister Jeneba lives close to here, close to Michael's school. She will care for Michael if I go abroad."

Kaimah did not go abroad. He embarked on studies for an MSci and we lost touch with each other, though I would get regular news of him through Sewa Magba. It was through Sewa that I learned that Kaimah had been hospitalized after suffering some kind of brain seizure. Later, Michael gave me a fuller account of his father's last days.

"At that time my father was doing his master's. One day he came home from class at nine o'clock and was about to have food. In a minute Dad became paralyzed. He was unable to walk. We took him to the hospital for medical treatment, and he became better and was able to walk. We came back home that night with my father's legs bandaged, but I did not know what to tell my family. I could not explain what was wrong with my dad.

"That was how his sickness began. We took him to one of the government hospitals for over three months, but there was no improvement. A woman in the hospital told us that his problem was not medical and we should seek the help of a traditional healer. With the help of my Uncle Komé and Uncle Junior, I took Dad to Lungi, where there are many traditional healers. We were at Lungi for five to six months, but no improvement was made. At this time, I was not in school. I was with my dad for two years, trying to find a cure for his sickness.

"After spending many months in Lungi, we went to Kurubonla, close to Kabala, at the invitation of my dad's friend, the Kabala chief Foday Jalloh. We went there, only me and my father, with no family help. My dad was really suffering when we arrived at the place and called on the herbalist, who performed a ceremony and said that Dad's sickness was not an ordinary sickness. It was caused by sickness among our family members. He tried to heal Dad for over three months but did not succeed. He said the sickness could not be cured.

"Then the friend of Dad's abandoned us. We were in the village suffering. We asked people in the village to have mercy on us and give us money to go back to Freetown. Luckily, we received a phone call from my dad's younger sister, Zainab [Jeneba], who asked us to come back to Freetown. The people of the village provided us transportation, and we were again in Freetown.

"My aunty Zainab Marah was happy to see us, and she shed tears. My dad was taken to the hospital, where he became better for a day. Next day he called me to the hospital. It was only me and him.

"He said these words to me: 'Michael, my son, I am very sorry for whatever wrong I have done to you. I had a lot of plans for you as my only son, for you to study overseas, to have all the joy that a child must have, and for me to become a prominent person in the future.' He asked me to follow his footsteps, so that even if he died my education would be my family [i.e., educational qualifications would provide the benefits in life that a family would have provided] and fulfill a promise for me and him. He asked me to go back to school, and to hold my caring aunty Zainab as my mother from now until death. Finally, he asked me to be a good boy and be happy with my education as there is no dad or mother or even grandparents. He asked me to go in search of you, Mr. Michael, and be in touch with you as my father and helper in education.

"I went back to school that same month. On Wednesday the twenty-first, 2013, on my way coming from school, I received a call that my father had died."

I was arrested by Michael's comment that he had no parents or grandparents. It was as though all connections with the past had been annulled. Ancestry had little value. Barawa did not exist for him. Genealogical time had come to a standstill.

For phenomenologists, one's own world is inextricably connected with the world of one's contemporaries and consociates, as well as genealogical networks that include predecessors and successors. But what defined Michael's lifeworld? What world could he call his own?

One of the most compelling Kuranko stories I recorded in the 1970s touches on what it means to be alone in the world (*telne*, lit. alone, is also the term for an orphan child), and how, in the absence of a loving family, one may find material and emotional succor through relationships with djinn, divinities, or wealthy benefactors.

The story concerns an orphan girl, maltreated by her dead mother's cowife. Ordered to fetch and carry, having to suffer the taunts of her half-siblings and dress in rags, this Kuranko Cinderella one day drops a stirring spoon in the dirt and is sent by her mother's cowife to wash the spoon in a distant river.

It so happened that when the girl's mother died, she was transformed into a crocodile and was now living in the depths of this selfsame river. Reunited with her daughter, the crocodile-mother takes the child beneath the water, where for several years she receives affection and respect and is dressed in fine raiment.

When she comes of age, she is sent back to her village with lavish gifts for her father, her mother's cowife, and her siblings. Despite this generosity, the child's mother's cowife desires only that her own daughter come into possession of such riches, and she sends her to the distant river. This girl is also taken beneath the water, but instead of boxes of money and fine clothing, she receives boxes of scorpions and poisonous snakes. Unaware of what she has been given, she takes the boxes back to her village and gives them to her mother, who, determined not to share her windfall with anyone, opens the boxes in the privacy of her own room and is killed by the deadly creatures they contain.

Kinship's shadow side became increasingly evident in Kaimah's confidences and concerns—the resentment and suspicion that simmer beneath the surface of family life and periodically find expression in oedipal conflict, sibling rivalry, paranoid fantasies, accusations of witchcraft, the persecution of orphans, and malicious gossip (for which Kuranko have a remarkable number of nuanced terms).

I also heard echoes of the past—when Tina Komé was judged harshly for "throwing his life away" and becoming "a child of the white men" and, a generation later, in 1964, when Tina Komé's son, Sewa Bockarie (S. B.), contested the staff of Nieni. Once again, Barawa withheld its support, and the unforgiving S. B. punished those who had failed his father and failed him in turn, declaring he would thenceforth help his own immediate family in Firawa but not Barawa. "You may see an airplane fly over Barawa," he declared. "But it will never land there."

In an email dated December 8, 2006, Kaimah complained about his uncle S. B.'s reluctance to help him:

Even when I was promoted to second year [at Njala University], uncle S.B. kept asking me, "Why are you going to college?" His attitude has extended to the entire family. There is always competition among family members, nobody cares about other family and nobody cares about your difficulties in life. The success and achievement of another person is always a threat. When a member of the family is fortunate to travel abroad, he or she will only help those from his or her biological parents, and even his contact address is kept secret. This is the type of situation our family is operating. This is why, since the death of uncle S.B., no progress has been made. There is no unity among family members, here or abroad. That is why I am so grateful for the generosity you are extending me.

Two years later, as Kaimah and I strolled together along Lumley Beach, the same complaints surfaced.

I was telling Kaimah about my fieldwork in Firawa and how it had brought me to ponder the question of well-being, and the various things that people imagine will make their lives complete, worthwhile, or at least bearable. I had also been led to wonder, I told Kaimah, to what extent the past—in the form of ancestral tradition, the trauma of a civil war, divisions within a ruling house, or family feuds—so constrained our present actions that they effectively denied us any future.

"The war is not on people's minds these days," Kaimah said. "The problem is poverty."

"But people did not complain of poverty forty years ago," I said. "If there was inequality between men and women, rulers and commoners, elders and juniors, it was seen as being in the nature of things. Now it is thought to be the fault of those in power, who have become wealthy at the expense of others."

"That is true," Kaimah said.

"What interests me," I said, "is that people look to God or the government for a fairer deal. But they do not look for a fairer distribution of wealth; they seem to seek windfalls and benefits solely for themselves. In your father Noah's time, people hoped for the blessings of their ancestors, not the beneficence of God." And I mentioned to Kaimah the numerous religious slogans I had seen in the streets of the city. The beaming, chubby-faced preacher, often depicted with his equally cherubic wife, promising everything from a "deeper life" to "miraculous prosperity." "Jesus the Impossibility Specialist," one flier read, while another announced, "The Year of Supernatural Abundance."

"Most of the ministries are run by Nigerians, or by Sierra Leoneans who have trained in Nigeria," Kaimah said. "When the war ended and the Nigerian soldiers went home, several of them left the army and returned to Sierra Leone. I knew one retired lieutenant. His name is Ibrahim Godfather. He told me that Sierra Leone was virgin land, and he began a vehicle spare parts business, though most of the spare parts are cheap fakes. Many Nigerian traders also came to Sierra Leone, selling medicines that do not work, and passing counterfeit 100,000 leone bills. As for the pastors and reverends you were talking about, they build mighty churches, able to accommodate two or three thousand people. But let me tell you, Mr. Michael, they are all drug dealers, even my friend Ibrahim Godfather. During their crusades at the National Stadium, they smuggle drugs in with the musical instruments they use to entertain the crowds."

I was on the verge of making a quip about religion as the opiate of the people, but simply asked Kaimah what kind of drugs were in circulation.

"Cocaine, brown-brown [hashish], anything at all. They distribute it to their agents here, who sell it on the street. It's a big problem now. Many young boys and girls are in the habit of taking these drugs as a form of social life and high meditations. But they steal in order to buy the drugs, and many have got mental problems now and are in the Kissy Mental Home."

We were strolling along a narrow dirt path beside the beach. The mangy grass was littered with plastic, soda cans, cigarette packets, and old shoes. A sordid image of globalization, I thought, knowing that the cocaine in West Africa came from Colombia, destined to be sold on the European market.

I did not want to argue against Kaimah's benighted view of the Nigerian ministries but was fascinated by his implicit comparison between Pentecostal fervor and drug addiction. And I wanted to understand the source of the vehemence and bitterness behind his words.

"Do you belong to any church?" I asked.

"I am a Muslim. The only Christian churches I trust are the Catholic, Presbyterian, and Methodist churches. The older established ones in Sierra Leone. They help people with clothing, microcredit, and schooling. They try to improve people's lives. But these new Nigerian ministries are out for their own fame and fortune. They tithe people. They are based solely on making money for themselves. And they are devil worshippers. They practice human sacrifice. You have to give human flesh, human blood, to get fame. And the ministers use human body parts to make medicines to give people more power, more life, and better chances. Depending on what you ask for, you have to give to God something of equal value. In many cases this is the life of one of your children. You'll have to sacrifice your child for a chance to go overseas, for prosperity."

My first thought was that Kaimah was feeling uneasy, perhaps even guilty, about leaving his son Michael in Sierra Leone when he went to England to continue his education, though, as it turned out, Kaimah did not pursue this option but remained in Freetown. But whatever he did would entail a sacrifice. To migrate would be to place his son's well-being in jeopardy, according to the ominous and unforgiving logic that in return for a favor bestowed by a djinn, one must give up the life of a loved one. But to stay in Sierra Leone would be to sacrifice his own dreams of self-improvement.

It was perhaps this double bind that inclined Kaimah to see renunciation as an invitation to the demonic, and to speak of the Charismatic and Pentecostal ministries as an "underworld" whose "evil works" were done clandestinely. "They perform cleansing ceremonies at night in the hills, rivers, or sea, and sometimes in the forest," Kaimah said. "They use lime, black soap, red candles, kola nuts, alligator pepper, perfumes, and Surrine [a kind of baby oil] from Nigeria. The black soap, lime, and water are common among the Burning Bush churches and the Allajobie churches. They wear white, with a red robe, and walk barefooted with a bell, preaching the word of God and at the same time predicting events that will befall the land. And they instruct people in the sacrifices they have to make in order to avert problems in the future."

"What kind of problems do people bring to them?"

"Many women who are barren go to them. Women who cannot find husbands. People who are not prospering. People who want to block someone else's chances of progress. People seeking political office or employment. People who want control and command over others."

The all-too-human dilemmas that, in the villages, drew people to diviners, I thought as we neared the end of the beach road.

"How far to the bread shop?" I asked.

"It's not far now. Are you tired? Do you want to wait here while I go on to Lumley and buy the bread?"

"I'm fine, Kaimah. But let's rest a little. I want to take some notes so that I can remember all the details of what you are telling me."

When we walked on, I asked whether these new religious practices were essentially different from the old practices of Muslim alphas and mori-men.

"It's all the same," Kaimah said. "It is all based on sacrifice. Like in the gospel of Luke. 'To whomsoever much is given, of him shall be much required.'"

"'And to whom men have committed much, of him they will ask the more,'" I added.

Kaimah was not amused. "To get a better opportunity in life, you have to offer money. Sometimes you have to offer your child. Sometimes you have to pay up front; sometimes you pay only if the work is successful. We Africans are of the conviction that all of these supernaturals have an element of truth. They are not strange to us. Most alphas or pastors have snakes or devils or evil spirits to whom they pledge their loyalty in order to get fame and fortune. This is why they do their work at night, in the sea, hills, or forest. We Africans find it hard to succeed because so many people here are full of envy, grudges, and jealousy, always trying to block your progress in life. You are trying to achieve something, but other people with evil intentions are fighting to block your progress and ambitions. It is very common in polygamous households where every woman is fighting for her own son or daughter to achieve fame. Some go the extra mile and visit alphas or mori-men, looking for a way of spoiling the chances of their cowives' children."[3]

"Was this an issue in your family?"

"My father's second wife never liked me. Even now she makes things difficult for me. The very day you left Freetown for Kabala, she came to my house and said that Ibrahim [Kaimah's half brother] had phoned her from London. He said that you were going to help me go to London and continue my studies. She asked me if this was true. She sees me as a threat, because I am better educated than Ibrahim. This is why I never confide my plans to anyone. You never know what people might do to spoil your plans. I don't say a word about what I am planning to do, except to my friends. Friends you can trust, but not family."

We had reached the Fula bread shop, and I bought several sticks of bread and a bunch of bananas. But Kaimah was less interested in bread than in recalling an incident from his early childhood that illustrated what he had been telling me about occult power. He had traveled with his parents to his mother Yebu Bangura's natal village in Temneland. On their first night in the village, Kaimah fell ill. He was so weak he could not get out of bed. After much discussion, it was decided that Kaimah was bewitched. A local woman with shape-shifting powers had transformed herself into a night owl. She had perched on the roof of the house where Kaimah was sleeping and consumed his blood. But on the second night, the villagers caught the owl and beat it to death. The witch, now weakened and seriously ill, confessed to her crime and explained how she had assumed the form of an owl in order to attack Kaimah. Perhaps she bore some grudge toward Kaimah's mother, Yebu. Her exact motive was never known, for she died soon after confessing.

Kaimah's second story was hearsay. A certain man was able to appropriate his wife's genitalia and pregnant belly. Leaving his own sleeping body at night, he would move around the village as a pregnant man. One morning, just before first light, he found himself unable to reenter his own body. He was discovered, struggling and writhing, with the genitalia and swollen belly of a pregnant woman. He died soon after. As for his wife, she woke that same morning no longer pregnant.

"These things are strange," Kaimah said.

I did not comment. For me it was not a matter of what had occurred but how it was interpreted. There is no mystery in the oneiric experience of journeying to other places, of flying, of bizarre encounters and metamorphoses. Nor is it mysterious that human beings should nurse resentments or bear malice toward a kinsman or neighbor. But where some anthropologists might be inclined to see misfortune as the fallout of historical events or global inequalities, Kaimah suspected foul play, conspiracy, and greed—in a word, witchcraft. Having explored the phenomenon of witchcraft in the course of my fieldwork, I found it easy to see parallels between Kaimah's persecution narrative and the combination of factors that usually precede witchcraft confession. First are the enervating and demoralizing effects of a prolonged and seemingly incurable illness that leads a person to ask the unanswerable question, "Why me, why now, why no cure or respite?" Second is a history of vexed intrafamilial relationship (in Kaimah's case, the rivalry between sons of the same father but different mothers) whose members find themselves competing for scarce spiritual and material resources. That one imagines oneself bewitched cannot be explained solely in terms of the social situation in which one finds oneself, or the existential distress one is experiencing, or even the worldview one has internalized. These beliefs exist in potential, and not every individual will invoke them in the same way, though they afford some kind of understanding of extreme suffering.

What led Kaima to set such store by beliefs that others took less personally? And whence arose his allusions to siblings trying to impede his progress, spoil his chances, and deprive him of the blessings or bounty he had sought through higher education and hard work? Do these conspiracy theories arise from a sense, not only that one cannot act on the world but is overwhelmingly acted upon, as if the existential power and presence to which one is naturally entitled have been wholly appropriated by others?

If they get an education, acquire wealth, or attract women, is it, one asks, at my expense?

At one point, Kaimah touched on the vexed issue of his uncle S. B.'s legacy. It was rumored in the family that when S. B. passed away, a considerable amount of money was left in trust, but that S. B.'s widow Rose or one of S. B.'s most favored children had contrived to prevent this legacy being equitably distributed. Kaimah was convinced that this was the case. It was, as he put it, another sinister example of how people will "go the extra mile" to secure a scarce resource for themselves and disinherit anyone they dislike or regard as "distant kin."

It later occurred to me that Kaimah's frustrations also reflected the critical role one's mother plays in Kuranko society, mediating relations between her children and their patrilineal ancestors. Should her behavior toward her husband be less than dutiful and obedient, the blessings of her husband's ancestors will be withheld from her children. Should she die, her children are left defenseless, for ancestral blessings will now flow to the children of her cowives. But this cultural explanation for why fortune and misfortune are unequally distributed may be seen as a rationalization of the psychological effects of being motherless. Kaimah was a small boy when his mother, Yebu, died. His sense of abandonment and his loss of ontological security translated readily into a sense of being cursed, for without the blessings that accrue to a child through his or her mother's behavior, a person is effectively bereft of the spiritual resources that will enable him or her to survive illness and show fortitude in the face of adversity. In other words, one's capacity to act in the world is contingent on the inner confidence that comes from being loved.

Theoretically, one's destiny is a combination of ancestral blessings and hard work, though patience and forbearance are equally important, since one never knows when good fortune will come one's way or diligence pay off. Undoubtedly, Kaimah's traumatic loss of his mother in early childhood made him more than ordinarily susceptible to the hardships that would subsequently dog his life—his father's and father's brother's inability to support him, the impact of the civil war, the death of Lango, his desertion by his girlfriend Aisetta, unemployment. Each new setback seemed to compound Kaimah's difficulties and increase his despair. Even gifts could turn poisonous, so that when I told Kaimah that I could no longer pay him a monthly stipend because my own children's education had to take precedence, he may have experienced this blow as a replay of the discriminations he had suffered as an orphan child. At the same time, the successes of his close cousins and half siblings were seen as personal slights or read as signs that scarce resources were being secretly siphoned off, benefiting them at his expense.

We were now passing the gray concrete shell of a beachfront hotel under construction. Kaimah said it was being built with money earned overseas by the famous Sierra Leone soccer player Mohamed Kallon. Kallon had been signed recently by AEK Athens, but earlier contracts with French and Saudi professional clubs had made him a lot of money. "But he's the younger brother," Kaimah said, "and his older brothers have squandered much of his wealth. Fortunately, this hotel is in the hands of a private contractor. It is a fixed asset, so he can protect it from the vultures."

What truth there was in Kaimah's story I did not know. But like his other stories, it gave me glimpses into what it feels like to be marginalized, to be "cut out"—as his father Noah often said when comparing his own situation to that of his elder brother S. B.

"The grass is not always greener on the other side," I said. "You should talk to your cousin Sewa Koroma. He will tell you that the streets of London are not paved with gold, but with a lot of human misery. You should know what you are getting into, exchanging Sierra Leone for England."

"I know it will be hard," Kaimah said, "but it will be worth it."

"Yes," I said. "It will be worth it." For hadn't I once left my homeland with exactly the same dreams? And had anyone tried to dissuade me from my course with talk of expatriates returning home with empty hands, ending up in a local mental asylum, exhausted by the cumulative impact of family intrigues, loss of face, endless demands and accusations that one had betrayed one's roots, would this have held me back?

Nevertheless, I had misgivings about the destiny I was visiting upon Kaimah by helping him go to London. Although Kaimah had painted a somber picture of African sociality as claustrophobic and dispiriting, it seemed to me that the ebullience, laughter, and energy generated in face-to-face relations with others were precisely what compensated people for the lack of work, the lack of money, even the lack of food on one's table. But who was I to romanticize a lifeworld that so many regarded as an obstacle to their self-realization?

That evening, as I walked alone on Lumley Beach, my thoughts turned to well-being as the possession of existential power. It might be argued that an emphasis on increasing the size of one's family in the face of economic scarcity reflects high rates of mortality and endemic diseases. By bringing many children into the world (and having many wives to bear them), genealogical continuity is given precedence over individual longevity, and preserving the past (which is tried and tested) is preferable to risking everything on an unpredictable future. But existential potency also lies within, cultivated as hope, and evident in the conviction that one has what it takes to endure one's lot, survive a setback, improve one's fortune, or turn one's life around. Existential vitality is equally contingent on one's relationships with others, and on what the world affords one as opportunity or possibility. These entwined motifs of internal and external potentialities are central to Kuranko notions of well-being. Empowerment comes from a combination of innate giftedness, acquired social skills, inherited status, luck, ancestral favor, and powerful connections. Although money, migration, education, and development are now fetishized as avenues to well-being, a viable life depends on commanding as many resources as one can legitimately locate and exploit. It is not that God, the ancestors, and djinn have ceased to be sources of earthly well-being; rather, that blessedness now depends on other factors as well—though the same reasoning governs attitudes to the new as to the old. Just as sheep, goats, cows, rice flour, and kola are ritually given to the ancestors and to God, so now, in the new churches, money is prayed over, blessed, and purified in the hope that it will, once given, pay dividends or protect the giver from predatory strangers.

It would be tempting to conclude that the most vital sources of well-being for Kuranko are no longer ancestral, genealogical, or spiritual, but monetary. Farm labor is no longer done cooperatively but paid for. Bridewealth and brideservice are calculated in terms of money, not kola or cows. And young men complain that women are only attracted to men with money. Have modernity and monetization ushered in a new age, or can we discern in the growing fascination with the prosperity gospel, money doubling, and migration age-old forms of magical thinking?

Only Connect

It is sometimes said that to share a name is to share an identity and perhaps even the same fate. If this assumption explains my affinity with Michael Marah, it is, however, not because Kaimah named his son after me but because of my inextinguishable sense of indebtedness to Kaimah's father, Noah. This feeling of obligation is undoubtedly what moves people to pay their respects to forebears by making offerings to them, tending their graves, displaying their photographs, keeping mementoes, or setting aside a day every year to remember the dead (e.g., the Mexican Día de los Muertos).

For these reasons, when my already tenuous position at Harvard Divinity School was reduced to a half-time annual appointment, and it became impossible for me to defray more than a small portion of Michael's university fees, I felt guilty. Nor was this guilt assuaged when Michael evoked his father's dying words, as if to remind me of the covenant between me and his family: "He asked me to go in search of you, Mr. Michael, and be in touch with you as my father and helper in education."

I sent Michael emails, explaining my predicament, and even shared a draft of this book in the hope that it would be of some interest to him. To my surprise, my account of his great-grandfather, grandfather, and father filled an almost complete gap in his knowledge of his ancestry. He had never set foot in Firawa, did not speak Kuranko, and never offered sacrifices or prayers to his forebears. In fact, he said, the only people who had "watched over" him since his father's death were his aunt Zainab (Jeneba) and, for a brief period, his uncle Mohammed, who, it seems, had one day driven Michael from his house on the ground that "he had a responsibility to someone else" and could not also take care of his nephew as well. Like Kaimah before him, Michael had experienced the limits of kinship amity. Though lip service might be paid to treating all members of one's family with equal concern, economic scarcity—whether during the so-called hungry time when rice supplies run low, or during periods of economic collapse in the country as a whole—made it impossible to honor this ethical ideal. It was little wonder, then, that Michael had turned to divine providence as his best hope of getting an education and having a fulfilling life. That others sought enrichment through money-doubling schemes was, for Michael, "a waste of time" and evidence of a disenchantment and impatience with ancestral or divine sources of well-being.[1] In this respect, he voices Christianity's ancient antipathy to money ("You cannot serve God and mammon," Matthew 6:24). Yet, spiritual, genealogical, and monetary sources of vitality are symbolically similar: they are scarce and difficult to access, and it is this scarcity and inaccessibility that are the origin of their supreme value. Both money and God embody human desires for love, ontological security, and enhanced well-being.[2]

While many Kuranko villagers continue to make sacrifices to their ancestors, begging them to pass on their offerings to God, Michael approaches God directly. Nor is his God the otiose and ill-defined divinity that Kuranko call Altala or Allah, but a vital presence that he worships as a personal savior, protector, father figure, and friend. For him, genealogy has morphed into theology, and the Catholic Church has become his community and his future.

His conversion was presaged by attending Catholic schools and culminated, in June 2019, in his ordination as a lector in the Catholic Church. He believes that God will provide for him, though God's benevolence will be channeled through people like Jeneba, members of his church, and me. His ventures in street trading might, "with the help of God," augment his income, but as an orphan in an overcrowded city where most people struggle to provide for their own kin and have no surplus to give a stranger, his prospects are as grim as his faith is strong. Indeed, I sometimes feel that his expectations run ahead of reality, and I cannot convince him that even middle-class Americans like me sometimes struggle to make ends meet. When he explains that education is his "weapon" and tells me of his ambition to study for a doctorate and become a professor, I am reminded of the Kabala High School students I worked with in 1970, all of whom subscribed to the belief that even a minimal education would magically enable them to become doctors of medicine, engineers, lawyers, or politicians, and build a brave new world.

In setting store by supernatural agencies rather than his own efforts, Michael sometimes reminds me of Noah's unflagging faith in ancestral blessings and S. B.'s frequent riposte that blessings are conditional on hard work. But in a society with so few possibilities of paid employment, it is understandable that fantasies of ancestral favor, educational success, supernatural aid, patrimonial support, instant wealth, or migration will console one that a better life is possible.

This raises the issue of how an anthropologist, hailing from a world of comparative wealth and privilege, can hope to understand a world in which the exigencies of survival leave little room for intellectual reflection or purely personal pursuits. How can one justify explaining the world when what is urgently called for are ways of changing it? Is it realistic to claim that the abstract relationships on which academic thought depends are based on the same intersubjective logic that informs face-to-face relationships in everyday life, or to point out that no models of relatedness, whether genealogical, theological, economic, or ecological, necessarily reflect lived experience?

Notwithstanding the difficulties of reconciling forms of life and modes of thought, it is important to note what anthropologists share, simply by being human, with those they study. I am thinking here not only of the intimate relationships formed in the course of fieldwork, but of the desire for connectedness and belonging that is common to all human beings. Whether this sense of belonging to a field of relationships that extends far beyond oneself in space and time finds expression in genealogical, historical, geographical, biogenetic, or religious idioms, it remains true that without being encompassed in these ways we would become like the orphans of folk literature, vulnerable, alienated, and alone. Yet belonging is always subject to ambivalence, since the bonds that provide us with our deepest sense of ontological security can also be stifling and constraining, and striking a balance between being a member of a collectivity and finding fulfillment in oneself is seldom accomplished. Nevertheless, to be stuck at one extreme or the other—estranged from the matrixial world of family, friends, or homeland, or so completely assimilated into a community that one loses one's liberty to speak and act independently—are equally distressing.

It would be absurd to draw a hard and fast distinction between traditional and modern societies based on whether they are oriented toward the past or the future, or prioritize individual achievement over the common weal since at various times human beings think and act in very different ways, sometimes putting self-interest first, sometimes foregrounding their unity as a family, or as a community, or even as a nation. This social shape-shifting is as true of a Kuranko village as of an American suburb. We are continually moving among many different modes of connecting our own egocentric worlds with the wider spatiotemporal worlds in which we are a part. "Kinship doesn't run in a straight line but moves in ever-widening circles," writes Stan Grant, speaking of his Aboriginal and Irish descent. And elsewhere, "We are not just alive now, but alive for all time."[3] In Sierra Leone and America alike, cell phones enable people to remain connected despite the estranging effects of distance and dislocation, and new forms of association continue to remind us of age-old imperatives of kinship and belonging.

No life is sufficient unto itself. A person is singular only in the sense in which astronomers use the term: a relative point in space and time where invisible forces become fleetingly visible. Our lives belong to others as well as to ourselves. Just as the stars at night are set in imperceptible galaxies, so our lives flicker and fail in the dark streams of history, fate, and genealogy. One might say that we are each given three lives. First is our conscious incarnation, occupying most of the space between our birth and death. Second is our existence in the hearts and minds of others—a life that precedes the moment of our birth and extends beyond our death for as long as we are remembered. Finally, there is our afterlife as a barely recognized name, a persona, a figure in myth. And this existence begins with the death of the last person who knew us in life.

TRANSITION

Spinning, weaving, binding, threading, braiding, and knotting are not only some of humanity's oldest techniques; they are among its oldest metaphors. In societies throughout the world, human relationships—including relationships with gods, spirits, material possessions, and abstract ideas such as history, society, fate, and destiny—are conceived of as bonds, ties, or strings, while wider fields of relationship are compared to networks, webs, strands, and skeins, or the warp and woof of woven cloth. Even anthropologists have had recourse to such images in their analyses of social relations.

One reason for the ubiquity of these images may be that spinning and weaving are closely associated with clothing, which is itself a core metaphor for social being, as in the cognate terms *costume* and *custom*. That these same metaphors are commonly used of luck or fate also suggests an intimate link between a person's destiny and his or her primary relationships with parents and forebears, a link that begins with the umbilical cord through which nutrients flow from the mother to the fetus, and continues as a symbolic attachment after the cord is tied and severed after a birth.[1] Among the Yaka of southwest Congo, the person "is seen as a knot of kinship relations."[2] Becoming a person (*wuka muutu*) involves "tying together or interweaving" the various forms of exchange that transmit life, emotions, energies, and knowledge among agnatic and uterine kin, as well as between human beings and nature spirits, people and nature, the living and the dead.[3] Among the Kuranko, a person's most immediate social field is compared to the network of ropes that is placed over a rice farm when the crop is nearing maturity. One end of the main rope is tethered to the foot of a high platform on which children sit with slingshots to scare birds away from the ripening grain. When this rope is tugged, the tributary strands shake, frightening scavenging birds away. It is said that "one's birth is like the bird-scaring rope" (soron i le ko yagbayile), or "one's birth is like a chain" (soron i la ko yolke), since one's fate is inextricably tied to the fate of significant others. In reference to kinship, it is said that the main rope is the father, its extension is the mother, and the children are the secondary strands. Kuranko also share a well-nigh universal belief that kinship, fate, spells, curses, and duty are binding. Such bonds often derive from one's birth. As such, they are existential givens and cannot be revoked. "One's duty [is] that which you have to do"—the actions and obligations that are alleged to follow naturally from being male or female, chief or commoner, father or mother, firstborn or last-born, and so on. But while Kuranko invoke the notion of innate essences to explain why certain roles are binding and inescapable, classical Indo-European thought takes the notion of human bonds more literally. In Homer, for instance, fortune is "a cord or bond fastened upon a man by the powers above."[4] At birth, the gods or fates spin the strands of weal or woe that a person must endure in the course of his or her life as invisible threads.[5] And human beings are bound to die. Comparable images appear in Norse mythology, where the gods are called "the Binders" and the Norns spin, weave, and bind the fates of men at birth.[6] For the Anglo-Saxons, fate was also woven, while pain, age, and affliction were spoken of as bonds.[7] Yet in all human societies we find a dramatic contrast between necessity, conceived of as that which a person is bound to do or that which is bound to happen, and freedom, construed as the possibility of loosening, unbinding, or escaping the constraints placed on one by virtue of one's birth and circumstances.[8] Intersubjectivity is vexed and unstable—a matter of both bonds and double binds, of fulfillment and frustration—a point that Kaimah had driven home in his conversations with me. Even hospitality comes with strings attached, and promises may be broken. Indeed, to break a promise and disappoint a friend is compared to the way beads fall from a broken string—*baiya*, referring both to the threaded beads that girls wear around their waists and to a compact or promise.

"What is the worst situation you could imagine?" I would sometimes ask my Kuranko interlocutors. To be alone, they would answer. To be cut off from family and friends. To die without issue. To be nursed when you are ill by people you do not know. To be at the mercy of strangers in a strange land. Social death and the radical disruption of social bonds seemed more awful to contemplate than one's own physical annihilation. Reflecting on his fourteen months' solitary confinement as a political detainee in 1974 and 1975, S. B. told me that the worst of it wasn't the physical deprivations he endured—the unpalatable food, the polluted water, the threat of execution. It was "not being with my family, not seeing my children."

Human beings remember and sustain relationships with absent friends, dispersed kin, and deceased forebears, even when they set little store by keeping extensive genealogies, celebrating their lineages, or paying ritual respect to their ancestors. Who has not peered into the face of a newborn child, hoping to discern a grandparent's or parent's idiosyncratic feature, or some trait that runs in the family? Who does not prize an heirloom or display family photographs or wrestle with memories of injustices and losses incurred many years ago? At the same time as we look back with nostalgia, anger, or regret, we look forward, anxiously contemplating our children's future and wondering whether our parenting has been good enough to guarantee them a happy life. The past persists and the future unfolds, even when our minds are wholly absorbed by what is personally present. Though the young focus on their futures, they will, in time, come to fixate on the past, just as the first generation of migrants try to forget the past only for their grandchildren to seek to recover the life their grandparents left behind. And though we sometimes think we live lineally, consigning the past to the dustbin of history, we unconsciously recapitulate old patterns even as we recite the mantra that those who cannot remember the past are condemned to repeat it.[9]

Here we encounter what may be called the accursed past, reminiscent of the Kuranko view that one may be a beneficiary of ancestral blessings or cursed to live without them, depending on the quality of one's mother's relationship with one's father.

Two documentary films explore the lives of the children of leading Nazis. In the first, titled *Le Serment des Hitler* (2014), the reclusive sons of Hitler's nephew, William Patrick Hitler, appear to have sworn not to bring children into the world lest their lives be blighted by the ineradicable stain of being related to Adolf Hitler. Even though there is no genetic probability of inheriting an evil disposition, and even though such children would not be morally accountable for the crimes committed by their forebears, a genealogical shadow would, they believe, inevitably steal over them, making them pariahs, forcing them to guard a dreadful secret, making their lives untenable. A second documentary, *Hitler's Children* (2011), explores this "guilt by blood" in the lives of the children of Hitler's henchmen: Hans Frank, Hitler's personal lawyer and the ruler of occupied Poland, whose son, Niklas, researched every detail of his father's murderous reign, spurning and repudiating him in public statements and private diaries alike. At one time, Niklas combed through all the data he had amassed, hoping to find one episode, one detail, that might redeem his father, that might suggest some remnant of humanity in his relationship with his wife, his children, even his Nazi peers. Niklas found none. His brother Norman refused to start a family because he wanted "to rid the world of the Frank name," and their sister committed suicide at age forty-six, the same age as her father when he was hanged at Nuremberg for crimes against humanity. Bettina Goering had herself sterilized in order "to cut the line," while Niklas Frank and Rainer Hoess devoted their adult lives to reminding the world of the crimes their fathers and grandfathers had committed before they were born.

What I find compelling about these stories from the shadows of history is both the determining power of the past and the variety of individual responses to the same legacy. The indeterminate relationship, as it were, between genealogical inheritance and personal choice—the same relationship that the Tallensi theorize as an unresolveable tension between one's Prenatal Destiny (Nuor-Yin, lit. Spoken Destiny) and one's Good Destiny (Yin), which stems from one's unique set of ancestors, all of whom can be ritually addressed and potentially persuaded to smooth one's path through life.[10]

For some people, their most fervent hope is that the past can be left behind, that they can escape its shadows. Sometimes, as with Michael Marah, the past is irrelevant, and only the future matters. Other people make forays into "lost time" out of a longing for an enlarged and more significant way of thinking about themselves. It can be empowering to discover that a famous (or sometimes notorious) historical figure was one's ancestor. And who can resist the allure of the BBC's *Who Do You Think You Are?* or fail to be stirred by the possibility that knowing one's past will promise a remarkable future, as in the Helix slogan, "Knowing where you come from is one thing, but knowing where you are going—that's power. Feel it!"

Commenting on such internet sites as Ancestry.com, or Y chromosome DNA testing, Shannon Percy observes that "modern genealogy means big business. Growing numbers of professional genealogists, local historians, and lay family researchers participate in professional certification programs, conferences, local society chapters, national associations, and online webinars."[11] Nevertheless, deep ambivalence may accompany the search for connections, whether across time or space. All too often there are skeletons in the closet, repressed memories, and unresolved conflicts. There may also be bad genes.

While the younger generation of Sierra Leoneans may be more concerned with their own lives than the lives of their ancestors, a curious recovery of genealogical time is taking place in the Global North as biography is supplemented by biogenetics, and researching ancestry becomes a serious scientific means of predicting our biogenetic fate. Suddenly, the behavioral failings of our ancestors pale into insignificance as we confront the results of screening for breast cancer, ultrasonography for ascertaining the viability of a fetus, and genetic testing for inherited diseases. Age-old anxieties about evil spells and accursed legacies give way to forebodings about our genetic fate and anxious questions about our freedom to decide our own futures.

Yet no paradigm completely eclipses its predecessor, any more than any individual escapes the impress of his or her history. And so we continue to ask how much knowledge of the past, whether genealogical, spiritual, historical, or biogenetic, we can accommodate without losing our sense of being in some small measure able to heal the psychological scars we inherit or minimize the biogenetic risks identified by a scientific test. In a comprehensive study of the moral quandaries of Vietnamese women faced with the prospect of bringing a genetically imperfect child into the world, Tine Gammeltoft notes that a fetal anomaly not only "blemishes a family biologically" but reflects negatively on the twelve goddesses "who, according to Vietnamese tradition, are held to have shaped the child in the womb."[12] Other studies also emphasize the repercussions of genetic knowledge for both family relationships and personal well-being. Thus, knowing one's biogenetic risk of cancer may entail an unbearable increase of uncertainty, anger, and anxiety, leading a person diagnosed as at risk to blame herself for lifestyle choices earlier in life, or make a parent feel guilty at having brought an imperfect child into the world, or, in the case of the genetic effects of the chemical defoliant Agent Orange in the aftermath of the Vietnam War, direct a nation's anger at those who polluted the earth in which one grows one's rice and the water one drinks.[13]

A fatalistic motif informs the history of social science, religion, and literature.[14] For Anaximander, things "suffer punishment and give satisfaction to one another for injustice according to the order of time," and Herodotus shared this view that "history was essentially the interval, calculated in generations, between an injustice and its punishment or redress." In Exodus 34:7 we are told that the iniquities of the fathers are visited on the children and the children's children to the third and the fourth generation. Sophocles's Oedipus, Shakespeare's Othello, and Chinua Achebe's Okonkwo all suggest that neither virtue nor heroic struggle can avert one's fate. "The moving finger writes; and, having writ, moves on: nor all your piety nor wit shall lure it back to cancel half a line."[15] The appointment in Samara cannot be avoided. For Thomas Wolfe, "Each of us is all the sums he has not counted: subtract us into nakedness and night again, and you shall see begin in Crete four thousand years ago the love that ended yesterday in Texas. The seed of our destruction will blossom in the desert, the alexin of our cure grows by a mountain rock, and our lives are haunted by a Georgia slattern, because a London cutpurse went unhung. Each moment is the fruit of forty thousand years."[16]

We cannot, however, reduce our humanity to what is socially, genetically, or genealogically preordained, for what makes the difference between hope and despair are the small unhistoric acts of everyday life that lift us from feeling as though we were bit players in a universal tragedy to feeling, if only for a moment, that we are actors in the story of our own lives.

In any event, one can never foretell the implications of a critical event or anticipate the repercussions of a fateful decision. It is as difficult to prospectively judge the wisdom of our actions as it is to retrospectively place blame when things go awry. Who is to say that Tine Komé made a good or bad choice when he taught himself to read and write, or that Kaimah exercised sound judgment when he canceled his plans to migrate? We conspire in our fates, even though it is not always obvious to ourselves or to others how this happens. In not finding a cause for every effect, or invoking notions of fatality or free will, perhaps fiction may prove more satisfactory than either social science or morality in describing the complex ways we actually live through genealogical time.

FATHERS
AND
SONS

Black Mountain

In the country of the Eastern Kuku-Yalanji there is a mountain of black granite boulders, known locally as Kalkajaka, place of spears. This storied place, in whose blind and labyrinthine passages countless individuals have become lost and perished, is said to be the haunt of a tyrannical ancestor who, to escape vengeful hunters, transformed himself into a cannibalistic snake and slithered to safety in the darkest recesses of the mountain. There he transformed his grandmother into a keen-eyed hawk who would alert her grandson whenever local women came to the foot of the mountain to tap grass-tree sap. The snake would transform his victims into birds before devouring them. It seems the mountain was also a refuge for people escaping the predatory incursions of white pastoralists and vigilantes. "Long time you don't see bama welcoming whitefellas anymore," one man said, as if these historical events were as fresh in people's minds as the mythological ones.

When my wife and I revisited the Kulu-Yalanji family with whom we had lived twenty years ago, we feared that we might be returning to a place we would not recognize and to a community for whom we were strangers. We knew that our closest friends, Mabel Olbar and McGinty Salt, had passed on, that Mabel's nephew had committed suicide, and that her niece had died of pneumonia, but of other members of the family we knew next to nothing.

Our borrowed Toyota was a metaphor for depreciation and decay, a heavily dented rust bucket that emitted an alarming grating sound and stank of burning rubber and engine oil whenever we ascended a steep hill.

I had assumed that the road to Wujal would now be paved, but beyond Cape Tribulation we found ourselves on the same gravel track we had driven so often in the past, climbing Donovan's Hill in first gear, tires spinning on the gravel, a last glimpse of the sea through palms and rain forest as we turned inland. An hour and a half later, we were crossing the Bloomfield River and skirting the settlement, its streets now sealed, well-maintained houses on mown plots of land, looking more like a Sydney suburb than the dilapidated hamlet of broken fences, boarded-up windows, graffiti, and litter that we knew in the 1990s.

Rather than search in town for someone we knew, we drove straight through, hoping to find one of the Olbars still living on the outstation at Ayton. Frayed bandages of mist hung over the distant range. The air was ominously still.

At the outstation a padlocked aluminum gate barred our way. After clambering through the gate, we walked down the clay track to the house, which appeared abandoned. Francine called, to no avail. The carcasses of three vehicles lay half hidden in the grass. Nearby, a heap of unburned refuse. The big tamarind tree whose breeze-disturbed foliage Sonny used to read for signs of a change in the weather was unmoved by our presence. It was as if Mabel's and McGinty's deaths had deprived the place of its very life, and we returned to the road, climbed into our Toyota, and drove to Weary Bay.

A breeze-block toilet and changing room had been installed at the end of the road. But running parallel to the sea was the familiar sandy track we used to negotiate every day to fish with the family off the beach or at the river mouth. The buff sand, blistered and holed by witch crabs, the tidal detritus of wrack, mango pods, small chunks of coral, and dead leaves, and the desultory sea licking at the beach intensified our sense of having traveled through time.

Near the river mouth, cordylines and calophyllum trees afforded shade to the people camping there. Francine explained who we were and asked after various people we had known in the past. "They're all at Wujal," we were told, and directions were given to Gladys's house in Jajikal Close.

We sat for a while on a rocky ledge at the riverside and ate crackers with slices of tomato. A mullet splashed in the shallows. Two women sat some distance away from each other, fishing lines lightly held. A young man in a red football jersey and State of Origin cap lay propped on his elbow nearby. Two small children poked around in the leaf litter on the high-tide line.

At Wujal, we asked some kids at the bus shelter to point us to Gladys and Sam's house. We found Lizzie there, keeping an eye on a small child. Lizzie had just come back from Cairns and was recovering from surgery. "Louie and Kimmy are both dead," she said, referring to her two children. We expressed our sorrow and asked about Cheyanne, Lizzie's granddaughter. Then Sam and Gladys walked in, and it was like old times. The talk was all about family and where they were living. The dead were scarcely mentioned. Illnesses were brushed aside—Gladys's diabetes, for example, which required three trips a week to Cairns for dialysis. She showed Francine the welt on her forearm where the needle went in. Many of the grandchildren, like little Mabel, bore the names of their grandparents, as if re-embodying their spirits. Francine took photos of us all, and I took photos of her with the same group. Addresses and telephone numbers were exchanged, and after phone calls had been made to other members of the family, Kelvin led us down the road to Josie's house to see Betty and Rodrick. Their daughters had been digging yams in the bush, and were peeling and washing them under a tap at the corner of the porch before boiling them. On the way to Wujal, Francine had confessed to feeling sad. Now, in the wake of these reunions, she said she was happy.

Why did I find fulfillment in fieldwork? Was it because I found validation in these remote settings, an affinity with other outsiders? Did their world offer the kind of intimacy and acceptance that was absent from my professional life? In this world of kith and kin one had a place. One belonged without question. One was continually affirmed by children, grandchildren, relationships, commensality, and the rhythms of coming together again after being apart, by contrast with the routines of a profession, or the WIN TV programs I had watched two nights ago, contestants competing to cook exotic food, enticements to purchase personal accessories, fashionable clothing, and household gadgets, films filled with fire and fury. One day, Francine's sister took us to lunch at a rain forest resort not far from Mossman. Polished hardwood floors, starched linen on stained cedar tables, white covers on the cushioned cane chairs, wineglasses, stainless steel cutlery, and a veranda restaurant with a view of palms and a deep river pool. Honeymoon couples sat at nearby tables, as if they had already exhausted everything they had to say to each other. They had paid $1,000 a night and spent hundreds of dollars on their meals, yet apart from lovemaking, watching videos, sitting in the spa, and making occasional trips to the reef, what else was there to do or say?

In Wujal, nobody extolled the virtues of their children, treating them as special or vaunting their successes. You accepted your offspring as they were, not as the people they might become if they got a decent education or made a fortune. Constancy was a matter of kinship, not ownership.

A couple of nights after we had returned from Wujal, Francine's sister threw a party so we could meet some of her friends. Weather-beaten cane chairs on the deck, an old steamer trunk for a table, a barbecue that had seen better days, and coconut palms illuminated by light spilling from the house. First to arrive was David, a lanky man in his sixties, wearing rumpled jeans and a tartan shirt. He smoked roll-your-owns from a plastic pouch he kept in the breast pocket of his shirt and was short of breath. When I asked what he did for a living, he said he was a gentleman, but almost immediately, as if aware that his smart answer was a conversation stopper, he added that he made stained glass and jewelry. After a brief conversation about lead lighting, the difficulty of assembling the many small panels, and the weight of traditional stained-glass cathedral windows that required metal bars to support them, David explained that his small business in Cairns collapsed when the tourism industry went into recession. The reason was not unconnected with 9/11, when people stopped flying.

We were joined by Wayne, a tongue-tied middle-aged man, originally from New Zealand, who had been a realtor for many years but now worked as a handyman. It soon became evident that David and Wayne shared various conspiracy theories, including one that explained 9/11 as a carefully planned distraction from a massive Wall Street financial scandal that had been about to break. An unspecified agency had placed demolition charges throughout the Twin Towers, which explained why they imploded so precisely. To my questions as to why some American agency should murder three thousand citizens and how planes were needed to crash into the Twin Towers if explosive charges had already been placed inside them, David and Wayne exchanged knowing glances and assured me that every cover-up must itself be covered up.

I was fascinated by the way these men found consolation in these myths and urban legends, using them as oblique explanations for why events in their own lives appeared to have conspired against them, producing disappointment, frustration, and a nagging sense of impotence. I drifted away in search of a drink, vaguely wondering why the guy standing alone in the middle of the deck was wearing a hat at night. The leather Akubra cast a shadow over his face so that only the rims of his spectacles were visible. I introduced myself and asked him if he had always lived at Wonga Beach.

"I came here after my parents died."

"Was that recently?"

"Not that recent, no."

Not knowing what to make of this remark, I was about to move away when Gil hurriedly explained that he had been trying to make a clean break with the past.

"And have you?"

"Have I what?"

"Made a clean break with the past."

"I'm still trying to figure that one out."

I looked away, wondering where Francine had got to. But like a fly fisherman, Gil cast his line again, tempting me to rise to the bait.

"My mother was always deeply depressed, and my father was perpetually angry, though I never knew why. They died within a year of each other, robbing me of any chance of asking them what I'd wanted to ask them for as long as I can remember."

Gil's abrupt and cryptic confession was reminiscent of some classical myth. The baleful influence of forebears. A curse visited on one's lineage. Laius abducting and raping the son of a king who had given him sanctuary. Laius recovering his own kingdom only to be murdered by a man who turns out to be his son. Doubly accursed by killing his father and marrying his mother, Oedipus blinding himself in an effort to expunge the memory of his fell deeds.

"Had they lived, I would have had it out with them," Gil said.

"I don't believe we are in thrall to the past," I said. "I don't believe in curses."

"It's scientifically proven," Gil assured me. "Sperm can pass trauma symptoms across many generations. I can give you the reference if you like."

I could have given him one, too: "The chemical necklace of DNA that wraps around the neck, sometimes like a beautiful ornament—our birthright, our history—and other times like a choke chain."

Throughout our conversation, Gil's face had remained completely in shadow, and I began to feel that I was talking to a ghost. When I asked why he had chosen Wonga Beach to make his clean break with the past, he told me that his paternal grandparents had spent some time in North Queensland in the 1930s, and he had become convinced that the key to his parents' unhappiness lay in what had befallen his grandparents there.

Was this Gil's conspiracy theory? I wondered. Yet he seemed more rational than David and Wayne, and far more sensitive to the signs and symbols that enable us to shed light on the darkness within us. I was curious to know more about his past, and why he was haunted by it. And so, next morning, I asked Francine's sister how well she knew Gil.

"He's a bit of a mystery," she said. "He makes furniture for a living. He's originally from New Zealand. His house is at the southern end of the beach."

House was a misnomer. When I rapped on the door, Gil (still wearing his Akubra) invited me into what was, in effect, a one-room aluminum-sided garage with a concrete floor. I took in the makeshift kitchenette, the wooden dining table with twin bentwood chairs, Gil's narrow bed against one wall, and the remaining space taken up with a band saw, a large work-bench littered with tools, and a beautifully crafted open-fronted cabinet whose shelves were crammed with large-format books and miniature wooden boxes.

Gil gave the impression of having expected me. Or someone else. Cups and saucers were set out on the dining table, together with a raffia basket filled with mangoes, mandarins, and a pineapple. While he tamped coffee grounds into a stove-top espresso maker, I studied a framed photograph on the wall of a group of Aboriginal people standing in a rain forest clearing. I recognized the photo as from an archive in Brisbane and was about to ask Gil what meaning it had for him when he asked me how long my wife and I would be staying at Wonga Beach.

"We're leaving Saturday," I said.

"That's too bad," he said, though he had planned to call on me later that morning, so was glad I had found my way to him.

"We're both from New Zealand," I said.

"I know. I read some of your poetry a few years back. I also went to Auckland University."

"It's a small world."

"For all the good it did me," Gil said, and mentioned several lecturers I might have known. He seemed disappointed when I said that only one of the names was familiar to me.

"I was probably there quite a few years before you," I said.

"Where are you living now?" Gil asked.

"I teach in the States," I said warily. In the antipodes, I had learned not to associate myself with Harvard, lest I be accused of bragging.

"What do you teach?"

"Anthropology."

"You dig things up or study people?"

Surprised that Gil knew the difference between archaeology and social anthropology, I explained that my wife and I had spent a year living with an Aboriginal family in the rain forest north of Wujal. "We've just been up there, visiting some of the people we knew from that time."

Gil turned his attention to the stove, where the espresso maker was sizzling and spitting.

"I understand you make furniture," I said.

Gil did not answer at once, but brought the coffee to the table and invited me to sit down.

"Mostly I fix broken chairs and tables for friends," Gil said. "But my real passion is miniature boxes. A tourist shop in Cairns sells them on commission."

"You make these?" I asked, carefully taking one of the small boxes from the cabinet and running my fingers across the exquisitely detailed bees and ants that adorned it. "This inlay's amazing."

"It's not inlay. It's marquetry."

"Is there a difference?"

"They might not look different to an untrained eye, but they're technically very different. With inlay you cut a recess into a surface and fill it with a contrasting wood. Marquetry involves piecing together very different materials, like a jigsaw puzzle. That box you're holding has metal, bone, brass, and cedar veneer. Careful how you open it. It might be Pandora's box!"

Gil's expression gave no indication of whether he was warning or teasing me. I replaced the box on the shelf and poured myself a coffee.

The espresso was surprisingly good, and I was about to comment on the difficulty of finding good coffee in the far north, when Gil declared that he had always loved wood. Loved the smell of it, the touch of it. Loved working with it. Loved the look of it, its colors in different lights, its grains.

"I made my first box ever for my son."

"You have a son?"

"And a daughter. In New Zealand. They come over to see me from time to time."

"Do you ever go back there?"

"I durst not."

What Gil O'Docherty meant by this arcane phrase I could only guess.

Clearing Out the Garage

When Miriam O'Docherty died of heart failure, her son's grief gave way to rage, and as he drove through the night, crossing Cook Strait on a ferry whose throbbing engines reverberated with the sobbing within him, and slept for an hour on a lay-by before waking to the sound of rain, he was in half a mind to abort his journey home. As it was, he stayed in Moabite for only a few hours after the funeral, having been repeatedly assured by his elder sister that she would take care of their father and "had everything under control." But Megan had always had everything under control—had always been, as she was also fond of saying, "on top of things." Her brother Gil was her foil, written off for as long as he could remember as a self-absorbed romantic who didn't give a shit about anyone but himself. Though the caricature no longer had the power to wound, he now embraced it. It gave him an excuse to quit this scene of unresolved rivalries and turn his back on his father's desolation. For he could not suppress the thought that Michael O'Docherty, whose demands on his long-suffering wife had worn her out, had finally got his comeuppance. Besides, how could a son fake sympathy for a father who had never accepted him, and why risk revealing his grief to his sister when she had arrogated that emotion to herself, as if he was only a minor actor in the soap opera in which she was the star? Yet on his return to Dunedin, he could not rest for feeling he had fled issues left unaddressed for far too long. What those issues were, however, he could not say. Remembering his mother's reportedly last words, "How will I know what to do when I reach

China?" he wondered how he could save himself from drowning in a sea of sorrows that had been fed by countless tributary streams over more years than he could reckon, and that he was at a loss to name.

Over the next five months he phoned his father every weekend. "I'm feeling a bit down," his father would say. "I miss your mother. I keep thinking she's gone to the shops and will be back any minute to make lunch. I've lost my appetite. I don't feel like eating alone. And you know I can't cook."

"What about Megan? Isn't she helping out?"

"Megan fusses over me too much. And she doesn't listen. Besides, she's got her own troubles."

"Janine, you mean?" Janine was Megan's teenage daughter.

When his father did not respond, Gil asked after his health.

"I get dizzy spells. I have to sit down."

"Have you been to the doctor about it?"

"He wouldn't know his ass from his elbow."

"Come on Dad. What kind of attitude is that?"

"The attitude of someone with a broken heart."

"Would it help if I was there?"

"You've got your family in Dunedin. You can't just drop everything and come back here."

Gil knew that this was exactly what was being asked of him. He also knew it was what, for reasons of his own, he had to do. And so, he took leave from the university bookshop where he worked and flew back to Taranaki, ostensibly to help his father "get his life back on track."

After hiring a car at New Plymouth airport, he drove through suburbs devoid of life. Houses huddled on barren lots, with a solitary camellia bush or row of standard roses on their front lawns. A wintry emptiness and silence enveloped him.

He stopped once, and fell instantly asleep. He dreamed that the saturated greenness of the landscape seeped into him, and that his hands disappeared into its shadows. When he woke, he looked at his hands, half expecting not to see them. Then he heard the sea, though it was only cars swishing past on the wet road.

He reached Moabite at dusk, the inland hills stacked against the waning light. Loath to go home, he parked in the main street, intending to walk for a while and get his bearings.

In the sickly glow of sodium-vapor streetlights he looked like a ghost. He was morphing into the person who once inhabited that place, the hushed house where he scribbled poems about unrequited love or his longing to move away, the mill where his father worked, the town library and cinema that were his sanctuaries.

His footfall echoed eerily under the iron verandas. The tall glass-paneled doors of the Moabite cinema threw back a distorted reflection of a passing stranger. He stopped and stared back, attempting to peer through his own reflected image to the interior of the old cinema. But he could not cancel himself out. Passages from a book he had recently read came back to him, in which a traveler is described watching himself from afar as if one part of him had become detached and floated off, leaving the rest of him behind. "In every departure, deep down and tiny, like a black seed, there is the fear of death." And elsewhere, "The border is a line on a map, but also drawn inside himself somewhere."

He slept for eight unbroken hours, only to be awoken by his father hitting him on the shoulder with a rolled newspaper and asking him for help in cleaning out the garage.

"What garage?" He reached for his watch. "Jesus, it's only 7:00! Let me have a shower and some breakfast, then you can tell me what you want."

"I want you to help me with the garage. Sort out what's worth saving and what's not."

At the breakfast table, Gil waited for his father to explain why the garage had to be cleaned out so urgently. But it was like waiting for his father to ask after Maya and the children, or to inquire after him.

"Maya sends her love," Gil lied.

Mick grunted. "If you want coffee, you'll have to buy some," he said.

"Hannah and Liam painted some pictures for you," Gil said. "Shall I show them to you now, or wait until later?" He was provoking his old man, and enjoying it.

"I don't know how you can drink that shit! What's wrong with tea?"

"There's nothing's wrong with tea, Dad. But I prefer coffee."

Gil took a slice of toast, pushed back his chair, and made for the door.

"Where you going?" Mick said.

"Out to the garage. Mustn't waste any more time."

After unbolting the garage doors, Gil's first task was to get his father's Ford Escort out of the way. But Mick had mislaid the keys, and in any case the battery was probably flat.

Shoving aside cannibalized machine parts, crates of preserving jars, and bundles of newspapers, Gil managed to get to the front of the car and shove it out of the garage.

He then surveyed the scene.

"Well, where do we begin?"

"You tell me."

"What about these?" Gil said, kicking at a bundle of moldy *National Geographic* magazines held together with baling twine.

"Those can go," Mick said. "I only kept them because I thought you might be interested in them."

"Why on earth would you want to keep newspapers?" Gil asked, though he knew exactly how his father would respond. With the same mantra he'd been trotting out for as long as Gil remembered, and probably for much longer than that. The rationale of every hoarder, of anyone who has known poverty or want: You never know when it might come in handy.

"Let's take a breather," Mick said.

"But we haven't even started."

Though it was clear to Gil that his father was in two minds about getting rid of anything, he didn't have the heart to rub it in. After all, his father hadn't thrown anything away for fifty years; why should he do so now? Waste not, want not, was Mick O'Docherty's other favorite phrase, repeated whenever Gil and his sister turned up their noses at the food on their plates or discarded a broken toy. According to their father, everything could be salvaged and repaired. Everything had a potential use. Uneaten food from yesterday's dinner could be fried up for breakfast. Potato peelings, tea leaves, rotten fruit, and ash from the hearth could be composted, and from this worm-filled loam fresh vegetables could be grown.

Gil once teased him: "If everything has a use, what about everyone? What about broken people?" Curiously, Mick's salvage operations did not extend to people. In fact, he frequently lectured Gil and Megan about people who had only themselves to blame for their misfortunes. He had made something of himself, and so could they if they put their minds to it. What about now, Gil asked himself, now that he is broken and bewildered in the aftermath of my mother's death? Will his attitude soften toward others who, through no fault of their own, have fallen on hard times? Does he expect to survive bereavement unaided and alone? Gil knew the answer to this question. It was why he was there, back in that one-dimensional town, to keep his father company, cook him meals, listen to his complaints, and sort through the flotsam and jetsam of his washed-up life, much of it so familiar that Gil was surprised to find himself setting certain items aside, as if he had become as attached to them as his father was.

What was it that Gil O'Docherty could not bring himself to throw away?

4 bottles of vintage parsnip wine, each bearing a label with the date it
had been bottled

What, by contrast, did his father allow to be trashed without a second
thought?

25 half-gallon tins of paint, some half full, some half empty, that he had
kept against the day he might need details of the manufacturer and color
code to buy more of the same

5 paintbrushes, their bristles hardened into slabs

1 motor mower, together with cans of two-stroke oil and gasoline

241 assorted jam jars and preserving jars with hinged glass lids and rubber gaskets

3 broken rail chairs with frayed wicker seat

16 garden tools, including pruning saws, rakes, hoes, spades, shovels,
trowels, forks, sieves

2 defunct TV sets

1 antique val radio

1 stuffed sulfur-crested cockatoo

4 broken umbrellas

1 box of seashells and small river stones

2 rolls of mildewed carpet

44 bales of newspapers, magazines, and brown paper bags

5 leather suitcases filled with old clothing, men's as well as women's

1 saw blade sharpener in need of repair

2 worn whetstones

1 box of tarnished cutlery

1 tea chest of chipped crockery

What did Mick set aside in a special pile, unwilling to see the items
destroyed?

1 pinewood picture frame, washed in rich champagne gilt, enclosing an
oil painting of a brigantine under full sail off the Taranaki coast

1 unhinged rocking horse

2 unused tires that he described as "good as new" and his son described as "good for nothing"

How had Mick O'Docherty previously justified the retention of this "general Magazine of all Necessary things"? And might he be compared to Robinson Crusoe, who drew great satisfaction from having everything ready to hand, so that "it was a great pleasure . . . to see all [his] goods in such Order, and especially to find [his] stock of all Necessaries so great?"

Certainly, Mick found solace in his trove, much as his son found pride in his books or a miser might find satisfaction in his money. But Gil was right in thinking that his father's childhood held the secret to his frugality, and as Mick's hoard gradually passed from the gloom of the garage into the pallid light of that early winter day, it occurred to Gil that this collection of unused things served as a kind of memory museum whereby his father kept faith with his past, a past whose secrets had long resisted Gil's efforts to fathom them.

What possible uses had Mick envisaged for the fifty hunks of ill-assorted wood that formed the bottommost layer of his midden?

He had planned to make fruit bowls from the cherry wood and walnut burl on his lathe, make cutting boards from the kauri, wooden platters from the matai, jewelry boxes from the cedar, and pen holders from the pine.

Would his children or grandchildren be the beneficiaries of these objects? Neither, since the objects were never made.

What happened when Gil hesitated to throw away the four bottles of his father's homemade parsnip wine?

His father told him that there would be no more events in his lifetime to celebrate. "It's easy to forget," he said, "when the going's easy, that you're only ever one step away from being the sole survivor of the wreck that will claim the lives of everyone you know. In the game of life, the last man standing counts for nothing."

What did Gilbert O'Docherty, bookworm and marquetry craftsman, have to say in response to his father's poignant and self-deprecating remark?

He told his father that, in his eyes anyway, he did count for something, though he was at a loss to say exactly what that might be.

Were any memories precipitated in either father or son at this moment?

Gil remembered the first party he was invited to. He was nineteen, and had been given to understand that you did not turn up at a party without something to drink. Being underage and knowing no one who might buy him a bottle of beer from a liquor store, he implored his father to allow him to take a bottle of his parsnip wine. Though his father was a teetotaler, he had planned to open the parsnip wine when Gil turned twenty-one. Gil badgered his father until he relented. The wine proved to be undrinkable, though Gil never told his father this. In now preserving the last of the wine, he hoped to persuade his father that the wine was worth saving and that there would be some future occasion for opening one of those grime-encrusted bottles and drinking to someone's health or happiness.

Gil's father said he did not remember any of this.

That afternoon, after they'd left off work for the day, Gil asked his father if he ever visited the mill that still bore the O'Docherty name, though it had changed hands several times since Mick owned it.

"Why would I want to go down there?" Mick said.

"For old times' sake?"

"Bugger the old times."

"You mind if I go, then? I'll do dinner when I get back."

"Do what you like, Gil. Don't let me stop you."

"I'd prefer to go down with you, Dad."

"I'm buggered. You go. I'll rest."

The sawmill was only two blocks away, on the outskirts of town. Stacks of logs obscured the blackberry-infested paddocks of a bankrupt farm, and hillocks of sawdust engulfed the fence line that had once separated pasture from mill. As a boy, Gil would walk to the mill most days after school, entering a maelstrom of dust, exhaust fumes, and shouts to watch his father winching a pine log into position behind the breaking-down saw, or tinkering with a malfunctioning generator.

"What are you doing, Dad?"

"Making a wigwam for a goose's bridle."

Fobbing him off. Not wanting to be found wanting. Ignorance averse. Or else it was the noise of the mill engine that made conversation impossible.

He remembered the saw's pained labor as it bit into a log, the grinding *churr* followed by a triumphant *tching* as it passed through and his father sent an untrimmed pine board rolling down the breakdown carriage to his sidekick, Jim Tuwhare. His father would signal to Gil to go home or hang around, depending how much more he had to do before calling it a day. If Gil had to wait, he'd wander out into the yard, respecting his father's warning not to clamber onto the log heaps lest they roll on him, and to avoid breathing in the toxic fumes of creosote. He did not dream of one day working alongside his father at the mill, let alone inheriting it from him, but it was definitely where, for want of any other vision, he expected to wind up. That was until his high school history teacher saw another future for him and encouraged him to entertain possibilities that his father, with inexplicable outrage, refused to see as having any value, and that Gil, despite his academic successes, would also come to question, plagued by a sense that in taking the road less traveled he was betraying both his father and his tribe.

When he turned for home, the light was dying. The macrocarpa branches had become obsidian scimitars, and he shuddered at the thought of the mill's cavernous spaces, bereft of life. He thought of his wife, a thousand miles away, and wished she was with him, sharing the shed of unfinished boards that his father had built in the backyard when he sold the mill. As a teenager, Gil had lain awake in the so-called Mick House, hearing the distant barking of a dog, the bellowing of a bull, or the forlorn whistle of a freight train hauling itself toward one of the enchanted cities his history teacher described to him as if it held the promise of eternal life. But against the prospect of a floodlit stage, the dark drapery of the past hung over him like a pall.

"Well?" his father said as Gil walked through the back door.

"Nothing much's changed as far as I can see."

"Nothing?"

"I've changed. You've changed. But there's not a lot we can do about that."

"You're fuckin' right there, son."

"I'll get the dinner started, then."

As Gil prepared the meal his father had asked for—sirloin steak, mashed potatoes, frozen peas—Mick repaired to the dining room to play a scratchy old John McCormack LP on his gramophone. It was a song that had haunted Gil's childhood, though he had never felt its forlorn appositeness as sharply as he did now.

I have heard the mavis singing
His love song to the moon
I have seen the dewdrop clinging
To the rose just newly born
But a sweeter song has cheered me
At the evening's gentle close
And I've seen an eye still brighter
Than the dewdrop on the rose
'Twas thy voice, my gentle Mary,
And thine artless, winning smile
That made this world an Eden,
Bonnie Mary of Argyll.

Gil did not know whether to treat his father's wistfulness with disdain or compassion. He was so used to seeing Mick as the bane of his mother's life that he was blind to the possibility that deep devotion might underlie that façade of brusqueness and indifference. Perhaps his parents did not know how to open their hearts to each other, or even what words to summon. A gesture of sympathy or confession of love made them feel so self-conscious and stupid that they had recourse to silence as the safer bet, or they fell into the habit of bickering and prevaricating as a way of keeping in touch. *Perhaps my father's bitterness and coldness toward me masked something closer to love than I have ever given him credit for.* Quietly, Gil moved from the kitchen to the doorway into the dining room. His father was staring into space. On the table in front of him was a shoebox containing photos of himself and Miriam in their salad days. There they were in their wedding photo, as rigid and expressionless as mannequins. Then, Miriam holding a shawled baby in her arms and smiling for the dicky-bird. . . . Miriam in the garden with Gil. . . . Mick in shirtsleeves with an unidentified buddy. Now, in his shabby cardigan and soiled corduroys, he looked like a hobo, and Gil found it was impossible to reconcile this shocking image of frailty and fallenness with the gruff, muscular hero of O'Docherty's Mill, who would gaff a log with his hookeroon and move it about as if it weighed no more than a bag of chicken shit. Perhaps that strength went deeper; it was also a moral strength that had deserted him as his physical strength declined. When Gil went back to his chopping board in the kitchen he recalled the humiliations his father had endured in that class-divided town—the bank managers who rejected his loan applications after making him grovel for months; the grocer who refused to let the family charge anything, even when Gil and Megan were sent by their shamed parents to beg for a pound of butter and half a dozen eggs; the accountants and small businessmen at the local golf club who made Mick O'Docherty the butt of their Irish jokes. Because Gil regularly accompanied his father to the golf course, scavenging for lost balls and selling them for sixpence each, he had observed it all—his father refusing to tell scatological stories, labeled a wowser for drinking lemonade, or laggardly limping around the fairways, forever marked by a youthful accident when, working in the backblocks as a bushman, he'd splinted and set his broken ankle unaided. But how could he heal his hurt in the face of these humiliations? He remembered, too, his father on payday, laying out the purple pound and brown ten-shilling notes on the dining table before assigning portions to pay for overheads at the mill, home electricity and phone bills and rent, until there was next to nothing left for housekeeping. Given his father's wounded pride, was it any wonder that he had grown increasingly bitter, and that his resentment of class snobberies and the injustice of his lot would be vented on those closest to him? He would "lash out," as Megan used to say, against his wife and children, until they too came to feel responsible for the indeterminate forces that oppressed their family.

Through a kind of osmosis, Mick's quarrel with the bourgeoisie became Gil's. When Gil turned fifteen, his father nominated him for membership in his lodge. He was brought into the Masonic Hall blindfolded, hands tied behind his back, and subjected to a battery of arcane questions, before being obliged to take vows not to divulge the secrets and mysteries of the order. Already a rebel, Gil found the allusions to Robin Hood ridiculous. Remembering how poorly his father had fared among the burghers of Moabite, he grew impatient with the talk of righteous causes and the brotherhood of man. Before his initiation ceremony was over, he had seen through the pretensions of benevolence and charity, of a "multitude of men seeking to help one other with their burdens." Released from his bonds and with the blindfold taken from his eyes, he saw not a banquet table that he would feel proud to take a seat at but a scene of self-deception, drunkenness, and archaic folly. Within a week, and without informing his father, he wrote a letter of resignation to the Lodge's Worthy Chief Ranger in which he mentioned the widows, pensioners, and Māoris in Moabite who received no help with their burdens, and his own father, their own brother, struggling to avoid his property being distrained, who had not benefited in the least from being a member of Robin Hood's Merry Band. Days after sending his letter, he received a reply. "Your resignation was accepted at our last meeting. No comments. Except from myself. I have framed your letter. Never have I experienced such a lot of nonsense. The aims of Friendly Societies are without exception a true expression of Christian Principles. I could write quite a lot, but perhaps it is better left unsaid." As for Gil's father, he too resigned, not in shame at what his son had done but in solidarity. It was the first time in his life that Gil had felt that he and his father were, despite being at loggerheads over almost every issue, bound together in some unfathomable woundedness.

When Gil set his father's steak down on the table, and took his own place opposite him, Mick did not speak, but remained hunched over the table, holding his knife in one clenched hand and his fork in the other, as if spoiling for a fight.

Seeing his father's unbearable sorrow, Gil felt a sudden urge to take the old man in his arms and pour his own life into him. But Mick O'Docherty was no wimp, and Gil knew his old man's policy on emotionality. A real man masters his emotions; he does not succumb to them. When, two nights ago, Gil had turned up at his father's front door, his father appeared not to recognize him, and stood behind the locked steel screen door as if in a cage, wary and cowering. By the end of their long first day together, he asked himself, is this the man who used to order me out into the yard for some minor misdemeanor, make me wait, then come out of the house and find a bamboo cane before laying into me until my buttocks or the backs of my exposed legs burned and throbbed from the flailing? Gil was fifteen and already taller than his father when he finally stood up to him. Without forethought, and with great calmness, he refused to bend over when ordered to. Then he tore the bamboo from his father's hands, cast it aside, and told his father that never again would he submit to his unfair judgment and blind fury. He half expected his father to act like some Old Testament avenger and smite him down. Instead, his father shook his hand, and said he respected him. He had stood up for himself like a man. Now, twenty-five years later, the emotions of that moment were all forgotten, though he retained a vivid picture of his father beating the shit out of him. Yet how pathetic his father's abuses of power when compared with some of the sociopaths he had encountered in the course of his reading on the Holocaust and its aftermath. When Daniel Jonah Goldhagen published his account of the German people's blind assent to the Holocaust, arguing that they had not been brainwashed by Hitler but were the inheritors of a centuries-old culture of anti-Semitism, Gil wondered what he had inherited from his past, and what unresolved questions he might have to address, lest he pass them on to his own children.

He woke before first light to the sound of rain pattering on the tarpaper roof of the Mick House and tried to recall details of a dream before remembering the painting of the brigantine, alarmed that he might have left it propped against the car in the driveway. Throwing aside his blankets, he dashed out into the rain-swept darkness in bare feet, squinting against the downpour, and worked his way around the house toward the parked car. Much to his relief, the painting was not there.

As he began retracing his steps back to the Mick House, a light went on in the main house and he heard his father shouting above the rain, "Gil, is that you?"

He headed toward the back door, and padded to the bathroom to towel himself dry. Then, with a towel draped around his shoulders, he went into his father's bedroom.

"I went out," Gil said, "to see if that ship painting was still by the car where I put it yesterday."

"You brought it in."

"Yes, but I wasn't sure I had."

"It's in the dining room. You asked me if I wanted to hang it up."

"Yes, I know."

"The painting's yours, if you want it. I told you that. It's of no value to me."

Mick sat up, swung his legs around, and stiffly climbed out of his bed.

"Hand me my dressing gown, will you?"

Gil took the all too familiar bathrobe from the back of the chair, and handed it to his old man.

"I'll get your breakfast going," he said.

His father said nothing, struggling to wrap himself in the robe and draw the frayed silk cord around his waist.

When Gil returned to the Mick House to dress, glimmerings of light were visible through the falling rain, though the distant hills were still a formless mass under the murky wash of the eastern sky. He was not looking forward to the new day. It would be impossible to finish cleaning out the garage, and though there were closets throughout the house, chock-full of stuff his father also wanted to sort through or throw away, he was already depressed by the endlessness of this task and the sense that he had been lured into it as a way of preparing his father for death.

Two days before Gil left Moabite, the mountain momentarily sloughed off its shawl of rain cloud, and he could make out the Mountain House on the blue shale slopes below the great bluffs, now covered by the first snowfall of the season. As a boy, he had often cycled from Moabite to the Mountain Gates, then walked his bike the rest of the way, through sludge and snow-deluged trees, to the Mountain House. On a clear day you could see Moabite on the plain below, an insignificant scattershot of houses, lost in the indelible greenness that surged around it. On the mountain, inhaling the ice-cold air, he felt free of his parents' fretting over money, his father's tirades, the untold sorrows that weighed his mother down. He could look to the horizon and imagine what lay beyond. Even the return home was exhilarating. He would climb on his bicycle and coast downhill through the bush and out onto the plains, not having to pedal until he crossed the bridge at the edge of town and, as if returned to the gravity field of earth after a day in space, head home. Today, however, he did not know where home was, whether in the southern city where he and his family now lived or this small dairy farming town where he had come of age. As he walked the streets, he felt it would be for the last time. The place had changed, and he too had changed, and his father would waste away in the wake of his wife's death, bitter, taciturn, and baffled by the suddenness with which everything had drawn to a close. He passed the houses of his boyhood friends. Why had he felt so at home in their impoverished cottages and dilapidated villas? The sackcloth on the bare boards at Tuwhare's; the smell of fresh-baked Māori bread, woodsmoke, and sweat. The kitchen at Tony Murray's house where Tony's widowed mother pickled cucumbers, preserved eggs, and boiled peach jam on the coal range. Why had his own home, with its cheap carpet, curtains, and covered lounge suite seemed so barren in comparison? His mother had taught him to excuse himself from the table and say he had had "an ample sufficiency." At Jimmy's and Tony's you "got stuck in" and could leave the table when you felt like it. No censorship was imposed. No manners cultivated. And the paddocks and remnant stands of bush beyond the boundary of the town were their domain, to explore at will.

The last supper was his father's choice: bacon and eggs with hash browns, with a pot of Irish breakfast tea on the side. At home, Gil and his wife ate muesli and fresh fruit, with soy milk rather than cow's milk, and drank fresh-ground coffee. But none of these items were procurable in Moabite, and he had reverted to eating the same meals his mother used to make, day in and day out, so reinforcing his sense of having regressed to a place he had once turned his back on forever. He had also acceded to his father's demand that he take the advertising flyer to Shoprite and buy up supplies of anything that had had its price slashed. "You can save a lot that way," his father said, though he knew his son would ask him what he could possibly do with ten bottles of bleach or a hundred toilet paper rolls.

"That painting you said I could have," Gil said. "I seem to remember you once telling me that your father painted it."

"My father couldn't have painted a house, let alone a picture. That's a work of art. Might even be worth a few bob."

"Then why give it to me, or throw it in the trash?"

"I thought you might like it."

"I sort of do."

"Well then, you can do me a favor and take the bloody thing off my hands." For once, Gil wasn't going to be stonewalled.

"But it did have something to do with your father, didn't it?"

"It belonged to my uncle Fergus, origin'ly. Used to hang in his bungalow at Bulbul."

"Who was Fergus?"

"Like I said, my uncle. Why so many damned questions? It's not yet eight o'clock for Chrissake."

"I'm interested, Dad. I want to know things."

"My father was Jeremiah. He and my mother Mary came out from Ireland in 1920. At least I think it was 1920. But Mary's brother Fergus and his wife, Fiona, left the old country a few years earlier and went to Australia, where they started a ranch in North Queensland."

"Is that where you stayed when you were a kid?"

"Yeah. Me and my sister, Siobhan."

"Was that the house with a dirt floor and the carpet snake in the roof?"

"I wouldn't call it a house."

"What possessed your parents to leave New Zealand and go and stay with your uncle? Wasn't your father a cabinet maker in New Plymouth? Weren't those his smoothing planes and bradawls and chisels we dug out of the garage?"

"Too many fuckin' questions, Gil. If you don't mind, right now I want to finish my breakfast in peace."

A Hidden History

Gil would piece together the story from fragments that Mick grudgingly shared during his weeks in Moabite, and from data gleaned from shipping registers in the National Archives in Wellington, where he spent two frantic days attempting to shed light on the lives of his paternal forebears. But his account was only completed after Mick's death, nine months after Miriam's. Gil did not go back for the funeral, a sin of omission that Megan declared she would never forgive "for as long as I live," so he was surprised to receive a brown paper envelope from her in the mail, containing a quarto-size hardback notebook on which his father had scrawled, "For Gil."

For the first ten pages, Mick's handwriting was controlled and legible, but from August it fell apart, the letters ill formed as if symptomatic of his father's flagging will. Gil remembered what his father had said in saying goodbye: "I can't seem to get up much interest in anything anymore," and he felt guilty that he hadn't tried harder to bring Mick out of his shell. Working with him on his life story might have kept him going.

Megan also sent a copy of their father's will. "Dad wrote the original with an old-fashioned nib pen, in copperplate he'd learned from a book. He kept harping on about giving the will away to someone who'd admire the penmanship, and how he'd given so many things away, and how he wished he'd kept them. I really think you shouldn't have let him chuck all that stuff out when you were here. Some of it might have been important."

Even with his father's few pages of decipherable text and the other material he'd gathered, it was not an entirely factual chronicle Gil compiled, but a narrative fleshed out in his imagination—something that he had never attempted before. But he took heart from a half-remembered comment by his history professor at Auckland University, that what has happened in a certain place at a certain time will always remain a mystery, the solution to which may be inferred or intuited, but the nature of which must remain conjectural—a potentiality for fiction or literature.

At times, he felt that he was writing a biography of himself in a previous incarnation. Growing up, he had dreamed of a future elsewhere, of putting Moabite behind him and being reborn in a more congenial place. Now, however, it was the past that fascinated him, the traits that run in a family, surfacing in one generation only to disappear in the next, by turns oppressive, portentous, and haunting.

The work was painfully slow. It required more time than Gil had at his disposal. So when he received his portion of his father's legacy, he took a semester's leave from the bookshop in order to focus on the writing, each page a rafter, joist, or plank in the many-sided edifice he was building. He told his wife that he felt as if he was working alongside his father in the mill, surrounded by sawdust, offcuts, pine bark, and rejected boards.

"Are you sure you don't mean a millstone?" Maya rejoined, and reminded him of the time they visited Gil's parents, and their two-year-old son Liam went into Mick's bedroom to say good morning.

"How old was he then?" Maya asked.

"Liam?"

"Yes, Liam."

"Must have been three. No, two."

"Whatever. Your father ignored him, right? He was reading his newspaper, or hiding behind it, and Liam asked us why Grandpa wouldn't talk to him."

"I remember."

"And you went and asked him why. And your father said that with small children and animals you had to be careful not to frighten them. That was the excuse he gave for ignoring his grandson."

"So what are you saying? That I don't give Liam enough attention?"

"You work it out."

"Like father, like son. Isn't that what you're saying?"

"I'm not saying anything." But Gil knew that Maya regarded what she referred to as his "time machine fantasy" as a pretext for avoiding the children.

It was an accusation he could not deny, and Paul Auster's chilling words might have been written about him: "Devoid of passion, either for a thing, a person, or an idea, incapable or unwilling to reveal himself under any circumstances, he had managed to keep himself at a distance from life, to avoid immersion in the quick of things. . . . In the deepest, most unalterable sense, he was an invisible man." But this is different, Gil told himself. What I am doing now is very different. This is the Chinese box I have always dreamed of making.

New Lives for Old

Mick's father, Jeremiah O'Docherty, migrated from Ireland to New Zealand in 1921 with his English-born wife, Mary Argyle, whom he had married the previous year. They were both thirty. According to Megan, Jeremiah worked as a carpenter on an Anglo-Irish estate in County Clare, and Mary was a teacher in a nearby village. A single studio photograph survives of her in her twenties, an angelic creature in starched white skirt and semitransparent blouse, posing among aspidistras. Megan imagined that Jeremiah had become so infatuated with Mary that he readily fell prey to the conviction that defending her honor would be synonymous with defending the Protestant purity and feudal power he mistakenly associated with her kind. Whatever the truth of this surmise, not long after the outbreak of the Anglo-Irish War in 1919, Jeremiah enlisted in the Black and Tans and participated in the sacking and burning of a town, and possibly two murders. As the Tans fell into disrepute, Jeremiah began to see that the tide of history was not running in his favor, and he and Mary fled to England in 1920, and thence to New Zealand.

Gil was not altogether satisfied with this account. For one thing, he could not reconcile it with something Mick had said when pressed for details about Jeremiah's origins. "I was only twenty when he died. And he never showed much interest in me, so I repaid the compliment and showed bugger-all interest in him. Anyway, you couldn't even tell whether he was Irish or English, despite his brogue, and the only thing I remember him mentioning about Ireland was that it was a one-sided war, with the rebels doing most of the killing and the police doing most of the dying."

"But the cause was just, wouldn't you agree?"

"What cause?"

"Freedom from British rule."

"Politicians have causes. Ordinary people fight to save their skins. The Poms sent my father to the Western Front as cannon fodder. Odds were that he wouldn't survive. But he did, for all the good it did him. Came home to nothing. No job. No prospects. No family I ever heard of. He probably enlisted with the Black and Tans just to earn a living."

"But that would make him English, not Irish."

"What's the difference? Either way, you're working class, you're on your ass."

After a month of internet searches, Gil found proof that Jeremiah had indeed served with a British regiment on the Western Front and later with the auxiliaries in Ireland. But of his complicity in any atrocities, no direct evidence came to light. Gil's overwhelming impression was how blind the fighting was. Things happened outside of any notion of what was just or unjust. A murder became a killing, political expediency was construed as a virtue, and a victim was a martyr. It wasn't that one was blindly following orders—yours not to reason why, let alone committed to some high ideal; it was more a matter of making things up as you went along, or trying to make sense of events long after they had happened, when even memory withheld the coherence that narrative needs. From the safety of a hedgerow on a country road, an invisible enemy opens fire on your vehicle. No one is hit, but a bullet disables the vehicle, which swerves into a ditch. You jump out, shouting at your men to take cover. You return fire, but are not sure where to aim. Firebombs are thrown. Two of your men lie wounded on the ground, crying out most horribly. Time hangs fire. Five minutes feels like an hour. It is as if you are watching this from afar. It is too haphazard and pitiful for words, one man writhing in pain beneath the car, another bleeding to death in the ditch. Outnumbered, you finally surrender. You throw down your rifles, and the IRA men emerge from a hedgerow. A gun is pointed at your head. Someone rummages through your pockets, strewing the contents on the road. Are you going to be shot? Do you start saying your prayers? An insurgent splashes gasoline over the car and is about to torch it when you plead to be allowed to drag your wounded constable out of harm's way. But as you drag him along the road, you drag a trail of spilled gasoline with him, and when the car is set on fire the flames threaten to engulf you and the wounded man as well.

You quench his burning hair with your bare hands. He dies moments later, without a sound. What has any of this got to do with a cause, with freedom, with Ireland, with something worth dying for? On the Somme you cursed the men who commanded the wholesale slaughter in the name of sacrifice. But here, in Ireland, you are caught up in some criminal exercise initiated by idealists who have only the faintest idea what they are doing, and for whom they are doing it. It is a farce. Ignominious. Base beyond belief. Any day, any night, you might be shot dead taking a walk, or drinking a pint in the pub. Your own people will mistake you for a guerilla, or your uniform will be enough to warrant your murder. And so you drink, on duty and off. You spend most of your pay on the stuff. Gin, brandy, whisky, whatever is available, to dull your sense of the absurdity and incoherence of it all until, inevitably and insidiously, the terror of anticipated ambushes, a random bullet, your lack of intelligence as to who or where the enemy are, and the vilification you suffer at every turn, stones thrown, insults hurled, transform you into a terrorist, though it is not a word you use, not giving a damn what you do or who you do it to, burning and bombing shops, setting fire to hayricks and farmhouses, suffering fits of uncontrollable fury and revenge for what is being done to you.

Was this Jeremiah's life? Gil asks himself, as he reads these moldering records of arbitrary death. I cannot blame my father for leaving unexplored such futile memories of a history through which his father passed like a blindfolded man on a tumbril. Others might feel compelled to weave this tragic trivia into a narrative of plans executed, sacrifices made, ideals achieved, and virtue rewarded, but I will not be a part of it.

Mary Argyle's marriage to a common laborer or mercenary soldier may almost have been her undoing. Once settled in New Zealand she could have been accused of being on the wrong side of history as well as the wrong side of the world, but she was not going to be guilty of living on the wrong side of the tracks. Consumed by an ambition to secure a middle-class place for herself and her family, she took charge. And so, in the years before Mick and his sister Siobhan were born, Jeremiah was goaded into spending his spare time renovating one rundown villa after another so that they might finally have the wherewithal to buy a house in a More Respectable Neighborhood.

Michael Fergal O'Docherty was born on the same day in April 1925 that saw the publication of *The Great Gatsby*. By this time, the family was firmly established in Victoria Road, and O'Docherty's Sash and Door was a successful if not booming business. Thanks to his mother's foresight, the infant Mick was already registered for a place at New Plymouth Boy's High School.

How Mary Argyle-O'Docherty came to conceive the scheme that would achieve the social ascendency she desired and felt she deserved was a mystery her husband may never have fathomed. But it became as obsessive as her earlier vision of a house on Victoria Road. Mick would sell his joinery business in New Plymouth and the family would move to North Queensland in Australia where Mary's brother Fergus had a cattle ranch. In return for helping the hard-pressed Fergus and his wife Fiona make a success of their embattled enterprise, Mary and Mick stood to receive a share in the profit and even, at some future date, inherit the property. Why Jeremiah consented to go along with this scheme that he variously described as "sheer lunacy," "hare-brained," and "the sacrifice of everything we've worked for" was, according to Mick's minimalist memoir, anybody's guess. But in 1935, the effects of the Great Depression were hitting home. Fewer and fewer people could afford handcrafted kitchen cabinets, paneled doors, and casement windows, and Jeremiah was already doing more and more bush carpentry to make ends meet. As for Mary, she feared that their fortunes would fall, and they would lose both their house and their social standing, backsliding into the pit of poverty that she remembered so well from her years in Ireland. If Jeremiah allowed his wife's anxieties to determine their fate, it may have been because of some atavistic deference toward her superior station in life and an endemic distrust in his own ability to read the stars. Perhaps, too, he gave his wife free rein so that, in the event of catastrophe, he would be blameless. Or this was the only way he could save their marriage. In any event, they sailed from New Plymouth in the autumn of 1935, and arrived in Sydney five days later.

Mick was nine years old, and his sister Siobhan was two.

Of those first weeks in Australia, Mick would remember a sluggish estuary, pocked mudstone, and a handful of white birds beating upstream into the setting sun. He would recall an ibis picking its way along the tide line, and his father Jeremiah bemoaning the fact that he did not know the names of the birds. In contrast to the clouded Taranaki skies, he would remember walking up an unpaved road, stars in a coal-black firmament, Scorpion spread out across the east and the smudge of the Milky Way. But he did not know then, any more than his father knew, the names of the constellations or even the name of the place they were going to.

They arrived toward midnight, cramped, confounded, bruised, and sweating on a bullock cart that had brought them from the Bloomfield crossing. While Fergus barked orders at two Aboriginal men, Fiona held aloft an unsteady hurricane lamp and fussed over the newcomers as though they were refugees from a shipwreck. Mick took his little sister's hand, as much to console himself as her.

Then Fiona was bustling up the wooden steps of the bungalow, muttering, "Welcome, welcome," and commiserating with her in-laws on their harrowing journey. Although Fergus expressed pleasure at being reunited with his sister, Jeremiah and his son felt superfluous, and after Fiona and Mary had gone indoors "to put the billy on," they loitered on the veranda, listening to the sheep (or was it goats?) in the darkness, bleating like lost souls.

Fiona came to fetch them in. "What are you two doing out there? Come inside. Tea won't be too long."

"I was wondering about your sheep," Jeremiah said. "I thought you were raising cattle."

Fiona laughed. "They're goats! Always yellin' about something. They're worse than the kids. Now, come on in and make yourselves at home. We can't have you standing around out here."

Jeremiah told his son to go with his aunt. He would stay on the verandah for a while. How could he be expected to feel at home in this Godforsaken place? He was gripped by a feeling of utter desolation, a gnawing in the pit of his stomach like hunger pangs. The surrounding forest, the clay that clung to his boots, the goats, were more than he could bear. He yearned to be back where he belonged, in his workshop, working at his own trade, drinking with his mates at the White Hart, or surf casting for kahawai on Ngamotu Beach.

"How far is the sea?" he later asked his brother-in-law, only to be told it was too far to walk.

"And where will you put us up?" he asked.

"In the cottage," Fergus replied. "It'll need a bit of work. The tin scratchers sometimes doss there on their way up to China Camp. But you're a dab hand with carpentry, Mary tells me. You'll have it homely in no time."

"China Camp?"

"Yeah. That's where you'll find most of the tin scratchers. At least them that still hang on, hoping to strike it rich. Fiona knows most of them. Makes a few bob selling them tucker."

Jeremiah and Mary retired that night to the guest room, but Jeremiah could not sleep. He lay in the darkness, his back turned against his snoring wife, bitterly ruing her ambition and haunted by events in Ireland that he thought he had put behind him. He had joined the Tans, fearing that he would be reviled and ostracized if he did not. He had allowed himself to go along with the burnings and the killings, as he had later acquiesced in his wife's decrees, only to exchange one place of exile for another, too cowardly or unimaginative to decide anything for himself. As he lay there trying to ignore his wife's snores, the door opened and his daughter came to him whimpering. Camp beds had been set up for Siobhan and Mick in the hallway, but she was afraid of the dark and wanted her mother. "Come here, love," Jeremiah said. "Come snuggle in with me." And he helped her up onto the cast iron bed, and held her in his arms until she fell asleep.

Day broke on a scene more desolate than he had imagined. Though the bungalow was substantial enough, with wide verandas running around two sides, the surrounding farmland was little more than scrub. Ancient stands of sandalwood and red cedar had been clear felled and milled, and the timber taken on bullock wagons to the coast, from where it was shipped north to Thursday Island or south to Sydney. Fergus had acquired a deforested "selection" for a song, fenced enough of it singlehanded with crowbar, shovel, and axe to keep his cattle from wandering, only to have his herd decimated by cattle ticks. He tried goats instead, and Fiona began a market garden. They crated the produce and took it down to the coast on a horse-drawn cart. The crates were taken out on longboats to waiting ships and sold on the Cairns market. Fergus occasionally tried his luck sluicing for tin at Roaring Meg Falls, and with this meager addition to their income he had gradually built their bungalow. What Jeremiah saw, however, was not evidence of a wilderness tamed but a chaotic landscape of lantana, cottonwood, and grass, dotted with zamia palms, and a stand of bloodwood trees whose trunks resembled the bars of a cage. As for the cottage, it was something between a humpy and a hut: two windowless rooms, a dirt floor, and a decaying canvas lean-to that sheltered a hearth of river stones and a rusty iron cauldron.

After taking stock of their situation, Jeremiah trudged back to the house, took his wife aside, and declared that there was no way they could survive there. "The cottage is uninhabitable. There's nowhere for Mick to go to school. No chance of help if the children get sick. No way we can make this work."

"Have you forgotten that I will be teaching the children?"

"But what will Mick do for companions, stuck out here in the back of beyond?"

"There'll be plenty of time for friends. What he needs now is a good grounding in the basics."

"What basics? Living in the dirt?"

"You're being defeatist."

"No, I'm being realistic!"

"You're not even prepared to give it a go. 'Tis the same as when we left Ireland. Cold feet. Always finding some excuse for not taking the plunge. There's nothing we can't do if we put our minds to it. We can do up the cottage. Fiona says it'll be months before the rains. We've plenty of time in hand. And she's already offered to go half and half with profits from the garden if I help out."

"But to what end, Mary? A stake in this worthless . . ."

"Don't forget, Jeremiah, you agreed to our plan. It wasn't just my idea."

"Then I agreed to nothing. From what I gather, they don't even own the land. They simply occupied it under some kind of informal agreement with the Queensland government. It's probably not even theirs to pass on, even if it was worth something, which it's not."

"Just leave it to me. I've got a feeling. We just have to bide our time, that's all. Trust me, you'll thank me for this one day, Jeremiah O'Docherty."

"And what about Mick? And Siobhan? Will they thank us for dragging them away from a place they loved?"

"It's parents that count, not places."

"What if their parents don't get along? What if their parents violently disagree about what's best for their children?"

"We're here, and we're going to make the best of it. And you must do your bit, for the children's sake. Fergus says the blacks will give you a hand."

"We don't have the money to hire help."

"You don't have to pay them. You just give them flour, tea, sugar, bacca, and they'll do your bidding. That's what Fiona and Fergus do."

"And that's another thing—isn't this their land?"

"Don't talk tosh, Jeremiah. You're as bad as you were back home, always going on about dispossessing the Māoris of what was rightfully theirs. What have they done with the land? What do these niggers do with theirs? We're the ones who take the initiative. We're the ones who do the work, and make something of ourselves."

"Yes, like the English in Ireland."

"Exactly."

A chippy he'd been in the old country, and a chippy he would be again. No better or worse than the next man. No time to dream of what he had once built, and hoped to build upon. No time to complain. Toil took care of that. With the help of Rufus and Billy, who had been born on this land but seemed not to begrudge the strangers who now occupied it and employed them for a pittance, Jeremiah O'Docherty felled red cedars that had been young enough to be overlooked in the onslaught of a generation ago, and used borrowed horses to haul them to a site not far from the cottage. There, Jeremiah and Billy used a crosscut saw to make a stepped series of posts, which they then wrapped their arms around, lifted, and dropped into deep postholes dug from the stony, root-skeined ground. Once the poles were in place and the earth tamped hard around them, Jeremiah and Billy constructed a roof with smaller poles supporting sheets of corrugated iron brought up on a trading vessel from Cairns. Rather than buy milled boards for the walls, Jeremiah decided to use corrugated iron and perhaps replace it at a future date. The windows were also tin sheets on sapling frames, hinged with leather cut from old boots.

"It's hardly better than the cottage," Mary exclaimed after her first inspection of the house. "You and your blacks could have saved yourself a lot of trouble if you'd just have done the cottage up."

Her husband said nothing. He was weary of arguing, and felt he could only keep his sanity by marking out his own domain, marching to his own drum.

The house had three small bedrooms and a long dining room–cum–kitchen where Mary would teach the children by day and they would sit at night and play board games by the light of a paraffin lamp. The floor was Rufus's idea. Some of his kids took Mick out into the scrub and showed him how to pulverize termite mounds with a stone and lug bags of it back to the building site. There, Rufus made a slurry of ant bed and spread it over the tamped earth. When dry it was as hard and smooth as cement. Rainwater drained from the roof into a galvanized iron water tank that had also been brought up from Cairns.

When the work was done, Jeremiah felt like Robinson Crusoe. He had salvaged from the shipwreck of his life the wherewithal to go on living. But unlike Crusoe he had company. Not two Man Fridays that he could use and abuse at will, as his brother-in-law urged him to do ("They only respect a tough overseer"), but men his own age, and as laconic as he was learning to be, who knew far more than they admitted to and applied themselves with biblical dedication to whatever their hands found to do.

If Mary reprimanded him for letting the children run wild, and reiterated her brother's caution against "letting yourself get too friendly with the blacks," Jeremiah assured her that Mick and Siobhan had not seemed so happy in a long time.

"Happiness isn't everything," she replied.

"Then what is?"

"Keeping your eye on the prize," she said. "That's what matters."

It wouldn't be the last time he lost his temper with her, but he simply could not allow her mercenary ambition to go unchecked.

"If you didn't spend all your time buttering up your sister-in-law and trying to make a few extra pennies in Cairns, perhaps you'd be a better mother."

"What do you call the hours I spend every day on their schooling? The evenings I spend washing and mending their clothes, keeping them nice? And who pray tell me is the one who brings in the extra money we need for furniture and those wretched iron sheets in which you have swaddled our home?"

"You do, Mary."

"Well then, we can at least agree on that."

Almost everyone acquainted with Mary Argyle was struck by the apparent contradiction between her zealous cultivation of respectability and the alacrity with which she would stoop to almost anything in pursuit of her goals. It was as if she had fallen from some high estate, yet embraced her degradation as a punishment for what she had been foolish enough to lose in the first place. As her sister-in-law got to know her story, she formed the impression of a woman who had married beneath her, yet done so in a clear-sighted act of self-mortification. When Mary began riding to the tin miners' camp every Sunday with goat's cheese, butter, eggs, and homemade bread on the pretext that she needed the extra income, Fiona confided her misgivings to Fergus:

"Hobnobbing with that riffraff, is it a few extra bob she's after or their sordid company?"

"How does she get on with Jeremiah?" Fergus asked.

"When they're not bickering, you mean?"

"Or the children?

"They seem to spend more time with their father than with her."

"Search me, Fiona," Fergus said. I'm not a good reader of human minds, even if she is my sister. When we were children she was always dressing up. She liked to pretend she was Cinderella. She had an old tiara she'd picked up somewhere, high heels, long dresses, even rouge and powder. Other girls played with dolls and pretended to be mums. She only wanted to be a lady. Now look at her. Midnight has struck and her coach has gone back to being a pumpkin, and she has to get about in gumboots and dungarees, and hobnob with tin scratchers."

"I can't understand her. She puts on airs when she comes up to the house. One minute she's Lady Muck and the next she's gallivanting around with

Archibald Pound. And what about Jeremiah? How she manages to pull the wool over that poor man's eyes, I'll never know. Does he have any inkling of what's going on? He seems to have a soft spot for the Abos, and they for him. What ya reckon that's all about?"

Though Fiona O'Docherty had her doubts, she did not feel at liberty to ask her husband how long Mary and Jeremiah would be staying, or why they had sold up everything and made the journey from New Zealand to Australia in the first place. She suspected some ulterior motive, even a conspiracy hatched between her husband and his sister, but was prepared to let sleeping dogs lie, at least until Jeremiah had finished his house and could begin the promised work of constructing a post-and-rail fence around the site Fergus had marked out for a stockyard. With Jeremiah's help, Fergus would give cattle raising another go, and rid them of the goats. What with the blacks walking through their property as if they owned the place, the goats bleating night and day, and the kookaburras and currawongs chortling and cackling, she sometimes felt she was in a loony bin.

When Fergus went down to his brother-in-law's house that afternoon, his wife's concerns were on his mind. But he was determined not to pry. On seeing how substantial the house was, he began to wonder. Everything about it proclaimed permanence, from the newly planted hibiscus and bamboo by the front door to the water tank that surpassed his own. His sister, Mary, had spoken of a year-long sojourn, a break from the dank Taranaki weather that was supposedly responsible for Mick's bronchitis and whooping cough. She'd promised they would make themselves useful, but Fergus was now asking himself whether the blessings of being closer to his sister and having a mate around to help with the farm were fast becoming a curse.

"I can see what Mary meant when she told us you were a master carpenter," Fergus said, extending his freckled forearms across the roughhewn dining table before interlacing his fingers and cracking his knuckles.

"I wouldn't call it carpentry," Jeremiah said.

"What would you call it, then?"

"Making the best of things."

"It can't have been easy, pulling up stakes and crossing the Tasman to this place."

"Easier for us than it was for you, I imagine, coming out from the old country and having to start over from scratch."

"I think Fiona and me were too busy surviving to reckon what we were in for."

"That's the beauty of work," Jeremiah said. "It doesn't allow you the luxury of thinking."

"You live day to day, hand to mouth."

"And you're your own boss."

"Yeah, there's that about it."

"And you and Fiona obviously get along."

"That too."

"You ever thought of having kids?"

"We've thought about it. But it hasn't happened. The only kids so far are those blimmin' goats, and they get on Fee's nerves worse than any kiddies would. Other than that, we've got it made, really. It's not paradise, but it's as near to it as I'm going to get."

What would paradise be for me? Jeremiah asked himself. Retracing my steps and doing things differently? Making a go of it here? Seeing that Siobhan and Mick get a chance to make something of themselves?

"I was talking to that bloke Pound the other day," Jeremiah said. "Said he was going to strike it rich, buy a lugger, go pearling, or sail round the world."

"You want to watch that bloke. He spins a good yarn. That's what a good story's all about, isn't it? Stretching the truth. But Archie Pound's got other things on his mind that I'm not so sure about. Give him an inch and he'll take a mile. Camps here at the cottage on his way up to Roaring Meg or back down to the coast. I don't mind him cadging a meal, but he's a braggart and an Englishman, and I distrust his promises. Saying he'll pay me back. Dreaming of a bonanza. They all do, I know. But I'm not sure he knows the difference between daydreaming and facing the facts. The best of the tin's gone, and the deeper you go the poorer it is, and the harder you work the less you get. Those with the money to buy water cannon and build sluice boxes are already sitting pretty. Unlike the scratchers, they can't lose."

Jeremiah tamped tobacco into his pipe with his forefinger, lit up, and changed the subject. "Just the same, it must get lonely up here."

"Like I said, who's got time to do anything but work and sleep?"

"I was thinking of Fiona. Must be a hard life for a woman."

"She's got the garden to bother about. And if there's time in the evening she'll read her *Australian Journal*, or listen to the radio. Which reminds me, I'm s'posed to be feeding the chooks."

Before Jeremiah could say another word, Fergus was on his feet and striding off. "Nice nattering to you, mate. Come up to the house again one evening and we'll play a few hands of five hundred."

As soon as Fergus had gone, Jeremiah went in search of Siobhan and Mick. When building the house, he had found it difficult to keep an eye on them, even though Siobhan had her dolls and the doll's house he had made for her, and Mick had become friends with Billy's two boys. Hours would pass before he checked on them. Mick he could trust, and Billy's kids knew how to identify the death adders that lay in ambush among the dry leaves. He also rejoiced that his son, so frail and fainthearted in New Plymouth, was learning to rough it and even fight with his fists in what Billy called "bama way." As for Siobhan, his heart went out to her as she sat in the clearing, talking to the ants or the processionary caterpillars, or combing the thin hair of her battered doll, apparently lost in some imaginary world or consorting with an imaginary friend. He envied her innocent ability to transport herself far from that place, and not complain when her mother disappeared into the garden after telling her to go with her brother and be good. At first he had blamed Mary for her indifference, but after observing the way in which Billy's kids fended for themselves, foraging in the bush or making a day trip down to the coast to fish, he ceased to be so anxious about his own two. Indeed, there were moments when he felt that he was a child, dependent on Billy and Rufus for help, and grateful every time their kids came to the house with offerings of mullet, mud clams, bush hen eggs, or wild pork.

Nor was it always coldness and quarreling between Jeremiah and Mary. There were nights of dutiful intimacy, their cries stifled in case the children heard, and Sundays when they borrowed Fergus's horse and cart and went down to Weary Bay for a family picnic on the beach. Mick would often meet up with Billy's boys—Toby and Doughboy—and wander off with them to fish at the river mouth. While Mary built a fire and cooked damper, Jeremiah would sit under a tamarind tree, smoking his pipe, and watching the Torres Strait pigeons clamoring in the nearby mangroves.

"Isn't this the life?" Mary would say, handing Siobhan a piece of damper, smeared with raspberry jam, then summoning Jeremiah to join her for a cup of tea.

"Fiona was asking the other day what we were doing for Christmas," Mary said.

"Not spending it with them, I imagine."

"Why shouldn't we? They're family, after all."

"Then why ask me, if it's already arranged?"

"That's just it, there is no arrangement. Everything's up in the air. I hardly know where I stand with Fiona, and Fergus won't say anything."

"Perhaps we'd better do something on our own, then. Spend the day at the beach."

"But if we just go off on our own, and there is something wrong, it'll give entirely the wrong impression."

"If you ask my opinion, Mary, we've been giving the wrong impression ever since we came here."

"Why can't you give me a little support, now and then? You seem determined to make matters worse, to bring things to such a pass that we'll have no option but to leave. And then where will we be?"

"On our way back to where we belong, hopefully."

"My God, Jeremiah. Sometimes I wonder why I married you."

"We fell for each other. Remember?"

Mary said nothing. She poked at the embers of the fire, raking out another charred damper. She called Siobhan to her. But the child was digging a moat around a sand castle at the edge of the sea and did not want to leave off what she was doing lest a wave wash her castle away.

Jeremiah climbed to his feet and padded down to where his daughter was playing. "Come on, love," he said, "let's go and find Mick." Heaving Siobhan up onto his shoulders and calling to his wife that they were going to see what Mick was up to, Jeremiah and his daughter headed off along the beach.

There were Aboriginal families camped among the paper barks, their fan-palm humpies offering Jeremiah a glimpse of a homeliness he had failed to find. He greeted them, and they greeted him in return with peremptory nods of the head.

As Christmas approached, many of the Aboriginal families in the area decamped, abandoning their makeshift shelters on the beach to the mercy of the impending storms, and sauntering in dribs and drabs along the old Aboriginal road that ran north toward Black Mountain and south toward Daintree. Billy and Grace remained, however, fulfilling their duties on the farm and expressing concern for the safety of Jeremiah's family. Rufus also stayed put, appearing out of the bush every morning and ensconcing himself in a rail-backed chair outside the house. Mary, who compared him to a piece of coal, objected to his presence. "What's he doing there all day, staring into the trees?" Jeremiah passed the question on to Rufus, who jutted his jaw toward the mountain. "Might be big wet, boss. Bugger things up."

What did Rufus and Billy know that Jeremiah didn't? How bad could rain get? A veteran of the weather of western Ireland and Taranaki, he could not imagine he or his household were in any danger. And neither Fergus nor

Fiona had mentioned any meteorological phenomena they should guard against. Still, Rufus kept vigil, alert to the slightest veering of the wind, sniffing to divine how much ozone was in it, or whether it carried the scent of dead leaves. Jeremiah watched him from a distance, as if the man was a living barometer, straining his ears for the sound of thunder, sensing what conspiracies the weather was hatching. Billy enlightened him a little, explaining that enemies could send storms to destroy them, but it took only a split second for the Aboriginal man to see the skepticism in the white man's face, and to stop himself from saying anything more.

When Archie Pound came by on horseback, brazenly asking Jeremiah where his wife was, Jeremiah wished he possessed the power of sorcery, and could dispatch a storm to play havoc with the cockney's camp.

"What do you want with my wife?"

"Run outta butter, mate. Thought she might have some put away for me."

"I thought she made deliveries last week."

"Yeah, but I wasn't there, mate. I was up in Cooktown, wasn't I?"

"I'll tell her you came by."

"You do that, mate. Butter, remember. And eggs if she's got any. Can't work without me damper and scrambled eggs, can I?"

On Christmas Day, Billy gave Mick a spear and a hunting boomerang. Siobhan received a woven basket containing wait-a-while berries, walking-stick palm fruit, quandongs, and zamia nuts, presumably from Billy's wife Grace. Mary was irritated by the gifts. "Now they're bound to think we owe them something in return," she said.

"What's wrong with that?" Jeremiah asked.

"I don't like being beholden," his wife said. "That's all."

Whether any manipulation was involved in Mary Argyle's gifts to her son and her daughter is impossible to say, though when Mick opened the inlaid wooden box his mother had bought for him in Cairns and found nothing inside, he could not hide his disappointment, and when the dress Siobhan was given did not fit she confessed she did not much like it anyway, and preferred the mysterious forest fruits and the dillybag in which they had come.

This sense of hopes dashed may have exacerbated the absurdity of celebrating Christmas in such suffocating heat and in defiance of the simmering tensions that had been building for months between Fiona and Mary. When Fergus uncorked two bottles of his celery wine, glasses were poured and emptied with unseemly haste, and Fiona and Mary made no move to complete the cooking they had started together that morning. As the four adults drank, Mick went outside to throw his weapons at tree stumps, and Siobhan sat on the bare floor sorting her multicolored fruits. But in the kitchen, the roast turkey and potatoes shriveled in their greasy moat, and the tomato salad sat undressed on a sideboard.

"I've never known such heat," Mary said, gulping her wine as if it might slake her thirst.

"Gets a lot worse than this," Fergus said unhelpfully.

"You have to wipe your hands every few seconds," Mary said. "And you men, look at your shirts. It's downright disgusting."

"There's more disgusting things than sweating like a pig," Fiona said.

"And what might they be?"

"Other things that make a person perspire."

"Fiona!" Fergus said sharply, "That's enough. There's a child present."

"It's a wonder there's only one."

"If you're trying to say something to me, then say it!" Mary said.

"Penny wise, pound foolish, that's what they say."

"Fiona, enough!" Fergus said.

But the cat was out of the bag, and the scene only grew uglier.

"Spending, that's what I'm saying," Fiona said. "Spending more time in China Camp than in Cairns. More profit in Cairns. But more pleasure in China Camp."

Jeremiah had heard enough. Gathering his daughter up from the floor, and clumsily grabbing her basket of fruit in the same movement, he walked from the room and out into the dismal day.

With Siobhan on his hip he strode about the clearing, calling for Mick to come. He was angry now, his cheeks burning, and the sweat that poured from his forehead blinded him.

"Mick, you little bugger, where are you?" And then, "Mick!" and louder, "Mick! Mick!"

He blundered through the scrub, Siobhan complaining now that he was hurting her. She wanted to get down.

Ignoring her wheedling, he stumbled on toward Billy's camp, certain Mick would be there.

The camp was deserted. Outside Billy's empty *wurun*, the fire-whitened stones and black ash of an earth oven suggested that Billy and his family were long gone, and Jeremiah had no option but to drift back to the scene of his humiliation and sit with his daughter, seething. Mick would return, like a stray animal, for food. Mary would say nothing. Day would suddenly descend into night, nothing resolved.

Billy

Though Billy carried the surname of the whitefella who had fathered him, he had no memory of the man his mother referred to as Roscoe. "Blimmin shot through," Billy said, when Jeremiah asked him if he had another name. Billy's mother raised him for a while, until she moved to Mossman to live with a bama man who refused to have a white man's bastard in his house. So Billy stayed in the bush among the myalls, raised by his grandmother, avoiding the missionaries and troopers who were bent on bringing people into their fold and faith. When Billy married Grace he hoped that his children would not inherit the stigma that the white man called Roscoe left imprinted on his body and mind. But it was as if the deathly pallor could not be diluted, only divided, and so Billy's firstborn was, as the whitefellas liked to say, as black as the ace of spades, while Doughboy, who was born two years later, was paler than Billy, and might have been the incarnation of the father Billy had never known. He did not judge his son for his appearance, and didn't even recognize the irony of the name he gave him. But he knew he would have to be on his guard with whites, even though he preferred working for them to foraging in the bush and moving with the seasons. He knew where he stood with Fergus and Fiona, but Jeremiah confused him. He suspected that this whitefella wanted something from him that he did not have to give. He had helped him build his house. He had shown him how to collect green ant colonies in the mangroves and make a decoction of them for his son to drink, curing him of his cough and runny nose. Toby and Doughboy showed Mick how to dig for mud clams and pipis. If this bloke wanted something else, why didn't he ask? Or did he not know himself what it was?

Rufus teased Billy, saying that Jeremiah was his father, returned from the dead. Billy got fighting mad and Grace had to restrain him. "No way," he shouted. "It's nothing to do with my father. It's all about his wife. She got kura for that Archie bloke, that's what's eating him."

Billy's intuitions were right. Even if Jeremiah was ignorant of the allusion to kura—the grub of the rhynchophorus beetle, known for the tenacity with which it clings to objects, as well as the holes it bores in melaleuca and xanthorrhoea trees—he knew the pain of attachment better than he knew the pain of loss. Perhaps this is why he plied Billy with questions about the bush, learning to make fish poison, roast zamia nuts, use a spear thrower, hunt wild boars, and cook in a ground oven, and persuaded Grace to show Siobhan how to weave a dillybag. It was as if he sought this other life and livelihood as a way of escaping the drudgery of building a cattle yard or having to deal with his wife and her brother. The Aboriginals welcomed him, or at least did not seem to mind his presence. But at the homestead and in his own house he was a stranger. Rufus divined as much, and suggested to his brother-in-law Billy that the spirit of an Aboriginal man must have jumped into the body of this white man, making him crave bama things one day and European things the next, yet never satisfied with either. Like the December weather, raining one day, then fine the next, it was hard to say what season you were in. "Is this the wet?" Jeremiah asked Fergus one drizzling day. "Give it a few more weeks," Fergus said, "and you'll know what the wet is right enough."

The Wet

To the old adage, misfortunes never come singly, one might add that the first of these misfortunes often sets the others in train. In any case, this was Mary Argyle's reasoning when word reached her that Archie Pound was dead. She blamed the tragedy on her own foolishness, then canceled this conjecture almost immediately, and blamed it on Jeremiah, who had courted her because he saw in their alliance an opportunity to improve his lot. Only much later would she blame Archie. And that was only when she had gleaned details of the accident, none of which she could very well solicit herself without revealing the true nature of her interest.

It seemed that Archie's ambition had got the better of him. No longer prepared to waste his life scratching for tin, and increasingly convinced that some deeper vein might be reached in one fell blow, he staked everything on a plan that would redeem the years of thankless toil and isolation. Having bought some plugs of gelignite in Cooktown, he furtively implemented his plan. After drilling six holes in the solid rock, he plugged them with the explosive, calculating that a single shattering blowout would expose the hidden slabs of pure ore that he had dreamed into existence during more nights than he could count. Making the holes airtight with tamped loam and cutting the fuses into varying lengths so that by the time he lit the shortest, the other five would have burned down to the same length, he must have judged that he'd have plenty of time to run for cover before the charges went off. No one knew for sure what went wrong, but the guess was that Archie had, for some reason, lit the last fuse first, and with only three seconds at most to escape, he either failed to extinguish the sizzling fuse or tripped and fell in his panic to get away. He was blown to smithereens, and it would take days before his remains were dragged from under the rockfall that had, in burying him, ironically exposed a lode of tin—insufficient to make a man's fortune, but enough, it was reckoned, to have freed Archibald Pound from his thralldom to the wild north.

The atmosphere was cloying. Clothes clung clammily to the skin. Harnesses became mildewed overnight. Thunder caromed in the hills, presaging storms that did not break. And Mary Argyle nursed her grief, unable to speak of it to anyone. Had Rufus known how wounded she was, he might have concluded that Archie Pound's ghost had jumped into her, making her mourn her sometime lover one day, and England the next.

What broke first was not the rains, or Mary's silence, but a torrent of anguish, torn from the heart of Billy's Grace the night she learned that troopers had kidnapped Doughboy at Rattlesnake Point. Mary woke first to Grace's demented keening, and thought that it was Fiona crying out in distress. After rousing Jeremiah, they dressed, lit the paraffin lantern, and hurried to the bungalow through drizzling rain to find Grace pacing about in the darkness, pummeling her forehead with her fists, then flailing her useless arms. Fiona came down the bungalow steps at the same moment Mary reached the distraught woman. As they tried to calm her and get a word out of her, Jeremiah went in search of Billy. "The police sometimes come for the half-castes," Fiona explained to Mary. "Grace was afraid this would happen . . ."

"They don't sometimes come," Fergus said. "They rarely come. There's very few half-castes taken here."

"Where would they have taken him?" Mary asked.

"Bloomfield Mission, probably, unless the police had other ideas."

"But you can't just take children away from their parents!" Mary protested.

"If that's what happened," Fergus explained, "it's not the end of the world. Billy and Grace'll be able to see him in the weekends. And he might get a bit of an education. Probably more than I got when I was his age."

"But Doughboy's only a child," Mary said.

"By our standards, maybe. But by their standards he's already a young man."

"He's Mick's age!" Mary said, suddenly wondering about her own children, whom she'd left fast asleep and hoped they would stay so.

Fergus was plainly baffled by his sister's sudden interest in the fate of this Aboriginal boy whom, on more than one occasion, she had lumped together with others of his ilk, saying it would be best if they were all rounded up and placed in the custody of the Lutherans. "You've got to take the racial differences into account," Fergus said wearily. "It's not half as bad as you think."

Grace had fallen into the silence of the inconsolable. But as the conversation flagged, she resumed her lamentation, hurling her questions, her complaint, her shattered life into the tear-streaked clearing as if there were someone out there who could hear her and respond.

When Jeremiah returned from Billy's camp he found Mary, Grace, Fergus, and Fiona at the bungalow, sipping mugs of tea. When he announced that he'd failed to locate Billy, Grace began blubbering again as if she'd lost her husband as well as her son. Jeremiah was all for saddling the bay mare and setting off immediately for the Bloomfield Mission, but Fergus said he'd get lost and they'd have more trouble on their hands; he should wait until first light, find Billy, and go with him.

He was thankful he did. The clay was so slippery on the track from the plateau that the mare balked at descending, and Billy gestured that they should dismount, walk the horses to the coast on the old track that skirted the sugarcane fields, and ride the rest of the way to the mission.

They found the German pastor supervising some bama weeding a potato patch. The Lutheran was wearing a grubby soutane, and though he and Jeremiah had not met before, the German appeared to have anticipated the Irishman's arrival. With a nod, Jeremiah bade Billy withdraw with the horses, leaving him to tactfully broach the question of Doughboy's abduction.

Hardly had he begun than the pastor cut him short. "There's been a misunderstanding," the German said. "Some of these children run wild, get neglected, and you feel sorry for them. Sometimes it's all too easy to jump to the conclusion that they have no parents at all."

"They're very independent," Jeremiah said, not really knowing what the Lutheran was driving at.

"That may well be, Mr. O'Docherty, that may well be. But we had the child's best interests at heart."

"So is he here?"

"Safe and sound."

"You make it seem that he wants to be here."

"It happens, Mr. O'Docherty. Sometimes the Lord moves strangely in us, calling us from one path onto another, from one life even. I have seen it often among these poor benighted souls. They will come to us like sleepwalkers, led by the Holy Spirit out of the darkness within them toward the light. Some will flee as quickly as they can, back to the beach or the rain forest, but others want only to stay, to be nourished on God's word, to learn to walk in his ways, to renounce the devilish beliefs they have been forced to embrace. Such souls have already been saved before we spell out for them who has wrought the change in them, who has brought them hence."

Jeremiah had not heard anyone speak this way since his own Catholic childhood in County Clare, and he listened now as if a child again, transfixed, and not at liberty to question any of it.

"But how, if I might ask," he said at last, "did the boy come to be brought here? And who brought him?"

"As I say, Mr. O'Docherty, it was a simple misunderstanding, a minor error on the part of someone who shall remain nameless. It can be corrected at once. All we have to do is ask the child if he wishes to leave or stay."

"But surely it is not for him to say. He is only a child. It is for his father and mother to say. And his father is with me now."

"Then you shall both see the boy, and both ask him what he wishes to do."

Billy reluctantly followed Jeremiah to the dormitory that the pastor had pointed out to them. Doughboy was with a crowd of other children, and if he noticed his father he gave no sign of it, and continued playing.

"Go on," Jeremiah said.

Billy pushed through the knot of children, grabbed his son by the wrist, and hauled him away. When Doughboy uttered no word of protest, Jeremiah was suddenly struck by the thought that the pastor could be right, and that this boy had for some unfathomable reason, spiritual or mercenary, taken it into his head to abandon his parents and come to the mission on his own initiative.

Riding back to Bulbul, Billy and his son sat clumped together on their horse, while Jeremiah followed on his, pondering the choices he had confronted as a young man. Had someone taken him in hand and pointed him in another direction, would he have consented to go or would he, like Doughboy, have played along, already devising a plan of escape, his heart set on a life as different from his parents' and grandparents' as Mick's might prove to be from his? Do we not all come, sooner or later, to a parting of the ways, friends falling out over some trivial difference of opinion, husband and wife watching haplessly as their love dies, or a world of which one dreamed replaced by a world to which one has no choice but to adapt?

The day before the cyclone struck, Toby reported having seen a frilled lizard on a palm frond—an augury of a storm. Rufus also warned the O'Dochertys of something ominous in the wind. But Jeremiah had yet to learn that what he automatically dismissed as mere superstition had a basis in practical experience, and though he had poured scorn on the idea that a thunderstorm could be an agent of retributive justice he was now to discover the painful truth of what Billy and Rufus had been telling him for some time.

It began with a rattle of dry leaves, and the sound of dry leaves falling. Then came the crumpling sound of distant thunder. Suddenly, the rain forest fell uncannily quiet. Even the unrelenting chorus of cicadas ceased, and no bird sang. Then they heard a howling from far off, as if some irate demiurge was tearing through the forest toward them. From their doorway, the family watched in dismay as the forest canopy flattened under the weight of the rising wind and the furious rain that poured out of the sky like a cataract. After shutting the door and jamming a heavy tea chest against it, the O'Dochertys huddled together, listening to the drumming rain, and watching as the wind beat its fists against their tin walls. Jeremiah tried to light his pipe, but his hands were wet and Siobhan was clutching at his trousers in fear. Above the hissing rain, they could hear the wind lacerating the trees. As they quailed, branches began falling on the roof with nerve-shattering bangs.

"We must go the bungalow," Mary said. "We'll be safer there."

"It's too late for that. We'll have to wait it out."

"What if one of those trees comes down on us? It'll crush us to death."

Jeremiah held Siobhan in his arms. Mick had taken refuge under the dining table. Dumb with terror and shivering from the sudden cold, they watched as the tin walls shook, before sheet after sheet was peeled away like newsprint. Through the gaps, the ravening wind roared into the house like a railway train, ransacking and smashing with such fury that the children's cries and screams were drowned out.

They were all under the table now, holding one another as if at any moment the gale would tear them apart and hurl them out into the maelstrom like leaves.

Mary could not stand it any longer. "We must get to the bungalow!" she cried.

"No, we must stay together, here!" Jeremiah shouted.

Lightning lit up the shattered interior, their stricken faces and sodden garments, as if the storm needed to see for itself that justice was being done.

And then, as suddenly as it had come, it appeared to pass.

"Look, it's going away!" Mary exclaimed.

"It's the eye. It's not over," Jeremiah said.

"But we can go now!" Mary said, and before Jeremiah could stop her she was plowing through the debris in the kitchen, and disappeared through the nonexistent doorway.

Jeremiah drew the terrified children closer, trying to shrink into an invincible ball, stunned at what his wife had just done.

Hardly had she stepped outside than the cyclone returned. Bent double against the rising wind, Mary was plucked off her feet and tossed through the air, to land hard amid a tangle of splintered branches. Squinting through the rain, she glimpsed the bungalow, seemingly intact a hundred yards away. Limping, drenched, and whimpering, she picked her way through the writhing buffalo grass toward the bungalow where she threw herself at the door, crying to be let in.

Fergus wrenched the door open, hauled her in, battened the door shut, and cursed her for her folly. Fiona simply looked at the drowned rat with contempt.

Little survived the storm unscathed. The hen house was demolished, and not a hen could be found, dead or alive. Several goats lay among the mangled trees, licking broken limbs, bleating pitifully, or standing stock still as if in shock. As for the house that Billy and Jeremiah had built, it had proved no better able to withstand the onslaught than Siobhan's doll's house. Sheets of buckled tin were lodged in tree forks or scattered across the clearing. The garden that Fiona and Mary had cultivated so diligently had been dashed to pieces. Shredded banana palms, flattened corn and tomato rows, uprooted papaya, lime trees, and taro lay in a rain-soaked and unsalvageable mess. And when Jeremiah and Fergus ventured out into the rain forest they found that the canopy had been stripped away in a long swath that stretched inland as far as they could see.

Most bama had left before the cyclone hit, including Billy and his family. They had taken refuge at the mission, where Doughboy would insist on remaining after his parents drifted back to Bulbul.

As for Mary and Jeremiah, they had little option but to pile their broken possessions and provisions onto a cart and move to Weary Bay.

Fergus half-heartedly implored them to stay. There was room in the house. They could make do. But Mary could not face Fiona, and Fergus, relieved that he did not have to repeat his invitation, watched as the refugees picked their way down the obliterated track and disappeared.

Billy helped them set up camp, though warned that in the event of another cyclone they would be swept from the beach and into the ocean along with everything else that was not deeply rooted there.

"It's not fair," Mary said, sitting among the wreckage. "Everything and everyone has been against us from the start. My brother and his stuck-up wife. This wretched place. Those blacks."

Jeremiah held his tongue. Now was not the time to say "I told you so." In fact, he pitied her. This woman he once loved and lusted after had become nothing more than a disheveled beggar, holding out her hand for a blessing she somehow felt she was owed, from a God she had never acknowledged, a husband she had perhaps never loved. Only her pigheadedness could he admire, her resolve to clear a patch of rain forest near Rattlesnake Point and plant a garden, arguing that they would be closer than Fiona to the *Merinda* when it dropped anchor in the bay, and would be able to get their produce crated and on board before her rival.

"But we have no crates. No wood or nails to make them, no longboat to take them out to the *Merinda*, even if we had fruit or vegetables to sell. We've nothing left, Mary. No savings. No way of surviving here. It's time to cut our losses, and go."

"You go, Jeremiah. Take the children for all I care. I'm not a quitter. I'm staying put."

"Do I have to remind you that the only reason we came here was to inherit Bulbul?"

He assumed it was only a matter of time before she saw sense. Until then, he would rely on Billy to get by.

But Billy was quick to point out the difficulties and dangers. The sea could not be trusted. The area was infested with saltwater crocodiles. Besides, the rains muddied the offshore waters and fish were scarce. They could hunt wild pigs, though without Rufus's dogs that would be dangerous too. They might scrape by on seawater mussels, pipis, and mud clams, but for how long?

Jeremiah was astonished at how rapidly the rain forest recovered from the cyclone. Seedlings sprouted in the clearings. The devastated buffalo grass stood tall again. Amputated bloodwoods put out new shoots, and the battered silky oaks, now attacked by termites, died and disappeared. For the family, however, camped under canvas tarpaulins at Rattlesnake Point, there were no signs of new life. Even the children seemed loath to play or venture out. Mary morosely pottered about, brewing tea, preparing yet another shellfish stew, or foraged for wild yams, while Jeremiah did what he could to shore up their frail shelter against the next torrential downpour. His efforts to build a pit latrine came to nothing; it proved impossible to dig a deep enough hole in the root-entangled sand, and so the family had to dig their individual holes each day, fill them in, and mark them with a stick.

"Things have gone from bad to worse," Jeremiah told Fergus when he visited the beach camp, bringing flour, tea, and plug tobacco as if the refugees on Weary Bay were no better than blackfellas.

"Where's Mary?" Fergus asked.

"She walks to Ayton most days. Mick goes with her. He's got boils, and Mary's trying to get a poultice for them. She'll cadge anything, soap, a bit of goat meat. She has no shame."

"She's a battler, though," Fergus said.

"Aye, she's that."

When Fergus rode off, Jeremiah sat on the tea chest looking out to sea. On the horizon, slabs of falling rain moved slowly south. Siobhan was asleep on a pile of dirty clothes. Unshaven and filthy, his own clothes not washed for days, he forced himself to his feet and dragged the iron cauldron to a hearth of firestones. It was the same rusted try pot he'd taken from the cottage at Bulbul when they first arrived. Now, it was their only means of heating water for bathing and laundry. To fill the cauldron, he carried seawater in a billy, counting his journey to and from the ocean as a penitent might count his steps to a place of pilgrimage and release.

It took thirty journeys before the try pot was full, and another half hour before the fire beneath it had brought the water to the boil.

He now grated slivers of yellow laundry soap into the seething water, and after dumping the dirty clothing into it, stirred it around with a branch he had skinned of its bark.

All this time, Siobhan slept. Not wanting to disturb her, he made no attempt to extract the clothes under her.

He would give the clothes ten minutes, before taking them out—time enough, he reckoned, to set two fishing lines in the vain hope that the incoming tide would deliver a shoal of fish to the famished family.

He had begged Billy to show him where and when to cast his lines, and how to do it. But Billy did not know how to explain what he knew from experience, and played dumb whenever the exasperated Jeremiah repeated his request for a fishing lesson. Day after day, he had watched Billy catch fish, one after the other, from a sea that had conspired to give the white man nothing. And though today would be no different, the routine was imperative, for without it Jeremiah would be reduced to a state of morbid immobility and self-loathing—a bleakness and blackness that swamped his consciousness and that he was powerless to slough off.

After setting his lines, and draping the taut string over forked sticks dug into the sand, Jeremiah turned back toward the camp.

He had hardly gone two paces when he was shocked into running by Siobhan's screams. Such unearthly screams that he had not heard since his time in the trenches, powerless to answer the cries of the dying in no-man's-land. Forcing himself faster across the slowing sand, he stumbled upon a scene that reduced him, for a moment, to insanity. It appeared that Siobhan had woken, discovered that her father was doing the laundry, and attempted to add to the cauldron the soiled garments on which she had been sleeping. In struggling to add them to the try pot she must have tripped, dislodging the pot from its precarious position on the hearthstones, and poured scalding water and clothing over her body.

In desperation he stripped the sodden clothing from his daughter's body. Then, grabbing the billy, he rushed back to the sea. He felt that cold water might cancel the effects of the boiling water, though wondered if saltwater might only make matters worse. Casting the billy aside, he ran up the beach as if there was someone there who might come to his aid, only to turn, crying out to God, his blind and desperate steps faltering as he came back to his screaming child. He could not leave her. What help could he possibly get for her, even if he did go to Ayton or the mission, or sought Fergus or Billy? Suddenly, all thinking ceased as the appalled father watched as the crimson lesions seemed to swell and blister, and what had been his daughter's skin gave way to what lay beneath. Yet she seemed to have passed beyond pain, as if the accident had surprised her and the grisly damage had somehow left her mercifully benumbed. He wanted to wrap her in his arms, yet feared that in touching her he would provoke the pain and do more harm. Only one foot had not been affected, and he held it, squeezed it, mouthing soothing words, as if he might join his consciousness to hers, killing time, or disappearing into a place where only the hushed collapsing of waves on a sandy beach could be heard.

Siobhan was sobbing now. Stunned and trembling despite his attempts to calm her, the child was already somewhere he could not follow her. He waved the flies from her face. When she whimpered, "Daddy," he whispered back, "I love you," but knew his love was as useless as his life had been, the life that had brought her into the world only to bring her to this moment of her death. He prayed that his own life be taken instead of hers, but distant memories of his Catholic childhood came and went like his daughter's labored breathing, ineffectual and broken. He thought of Mary. When would she get back from Ayton? But he could not bring himself to finish the thought.

Aground on the Great Barrier

When Gil told Maya the story of Siobhan's death, he said that writing about this tragedy had left him emotionally devastated. "I keep thinking of Hannah," he said. "How vulnerable our children are."

"But what about your father?" Maya asked. "Wasn't he only a small boy at the time?"

"Nine or ten."

"And his mother abandoning him."

"I can't be sure she did. That's my sister's version of what happened. She said Mick told her things he never told me. Like the note Mary left when she decamped. I know it by heart. 'You are better off without me, and I will be better off without you. I don't have a nurturing bone in my body. I don't think I was meant to marry or have children.'"

Maya gasped. "That's terrible. Does Megan know what became of her?"

"Apparently she went to Cairns and worked as a prostitute serving the seasonal sugarcane workers."

"Your grandmother a prostitute! I thought your father worshipped the ground on which she walked."

"Perhaps that was a fantasy that made it possible for him to live with what happened."

"I think you should write to Megan," Maya said. "This sounds like a cruel and preposterous thing to say, even if the note is genuine."

"Perhaps I should. But what difference would it make? I could never bring myself to include it in what I am writing, even though it might explain a lot of things."

"What things?"

"Her disappearance, and the complete blank I have drawn trying to trace her, not to mention the fact that Mick never saw her again for as long as he lived."

"I suppose it's possible that Mick shared things with Megan he never confided to you."

"I don't think my father shared very much with anyone."

"But surely it's worth trying?"

"I was thinking of sending Megan a copy of what I've written so far. Perhaps it would jog some memories and help me fill in some gaps. It's sweet of you to suggest I do so."

Megan's response to Gil's email was not helpful. She declared that he had opened a Pandora's box that was better left closed. She was also unhappy about the extent to which his narrative relied on conjecture. This would be harmless enough if he was writing purely for himself, but if he was writing a family history that their children would one day read, then it would be the height of irresponsibility to visit this ghastly tale on them.

Gil confided his dilemma to Maya. "Do you think the truth sets us free, or is it better for the skeletons to remain in the closet? Will keeping our children in ignorance of their parents' history make them any happier than if they were free to work out their own relationship with it?"

Maya was against forgetting. Her mother had been sent to stay with relatives in England when she was four, perhaps on the same kinder transport that carried W. G. Sebald's bewildered Austerlitz to Liverpool Street Station and into the care of his Welsh foster parents. Maya's mother would retain no memory of the woman who brought her into the world or the house in Dresden where she spent her earliest years, and her aunt and uncle ensured that she remain in ignorance of the chain of events that led to her parents' deaths in Buchenwald in 1942. It was only in Maya's final high school year that she began the painful process of lifting the veil from her own history. "My mother did not blame her aunt and uncle for keeping her origins from her," she told Gil, not long after they met. "They acted in good faith, with my mother's happiness in mind. But their silence only delayed my mother's grief when it dawned on her that she was not really English and that her aunt was not really her mother. It made her resolve never to hide from the truth, or hide it from anyone she loved, no matter how terrible it was."

Gil pressed on with his research and writing, guesswork though some of it was. The only detail he omitted was the note from Mary, an omission that reflected not his doubts as to its authenticity but his distrust of his sister's motives in sharing it with him when she had shown herself so reluctant to impart anything else.

His attention now turned to other sources. He racked his brains to remember the objects he helped his father clear out from his garage, as if these were clues to a hidden biography he had been, at that time, too obtuse to read. He wondered whether Mick's habit of hoarding was born not of the Great Depression to which Jeremiah returned after their tragic sojourn in Australia, but of a lack of mothering, and whether his father's warning against giving one's heart to a woman was an allusion to Jeremiah's traumatic loss. Indeed, all manner of speculations would wake him in the night and oppress his days. Was Jeremiah's early death at age forty-five, when Mick was twenty, the result of a broken heart or an addiction to whiskey? Was the Mick House an architectural echo of the house at Bulbul, the first wallpapered with copies of Mary's *Australian Journal*, the second with Miriam's *Auckland Weekly*? Was Mick's parsnip wine a throwback to the celery wine Jeremiah's brother-in-law used to make at Bulbul? And was the painting of the brigantine that Mick insisted Gil have a gift from Fergus to Jeremiah in compensation for the legacy that Mary had set her heart on gaining? On this point, it was only when Gil delved deeper that he discovered that the sailing ship was a three-master, therefore not a brigantine but a bark. Further reading revealed uncanny connections between the fate of his paternal forebears at Weary Bay and James Cook's bark, *Endeavour*, that went aground on the Great Barrier Reef a few minutes before 11 p.m. on Monday, June 11, 1770, 166 years to the day before Siobhan O'Docherty met her untimely death. Faced with the real and immediate danger of being cast away with no hope of ever returning home, the panic and anxiety of Cook's crew were not assuaged for two days, by which time the ship's pumps were finally able to bring the leaks under control. On Wednesday, June 13, Cook wrote, with characteristic understatement, this fortunate circumstance gave new life to everyone on board, adding that it was much easier to conceive than to describe the satisfaction felt by everybody on this occasion.

But before the *Endeavour* limped north to sanctuary on the Cook River where it could be careened and repaired, there passed a weary time, and the names Cook gave to various landmarks on the way attest to the prevailing mood: Cape Tribulation, Hope Islands. Weary Bay—an opening that had the appearance of a harbor—sighted on Thursday the fourteenth but on closer inspection proving not to offer enough depth of water for the ship.

As these facts, and the morbid reflections they occasioned, came and went in his waking consciousness, Gil began to wonder if Megan was right and Maya wrong; what good could come of raking over dead coals or conjuring the ghosts of the past? No answers followed the questions. No coherent narrative emerged from the few established facts. No insights came that might help him understand the thoughts that ran through the minds of his forebears, let alone the feelings that afflicted their hearts. He had long been convinced that one's understanding of what happened in history is as plagued by gaps in the record as it is by the bias of the historian. Having now encountered the same shortcomings with genealogy, he realized he needed time out, and retreated to his basement workshop where he hoped the demanding and delicate work of marquetry might restore the peace of mind that writing had destroyed.

Yet writing refused to let him off the hook, and one day in early summer as he was driving Hannah and Liam to Sandfly Bay, it occurred to him that though the lost chapters of his ancestral story could neither be retrieved nor re-created, traces of them might be divined in his own biography. Watching his children scrambling up the great dunes, taking two steps forward only to slide one step back, yet energetically throwing themselves at the shifting sand and clawing their way toward the skyline, he took heart from their exertions and even answered their calls for him to join them on the dune.

Having reached the top of the dune, the children ran into the marram grass. Gil returned to the beach. He had once encountered a sea lion here, and seen yellow-eyed penguins. But apart from a few isolated strollers, the beach was deserted, and Gil was again alone with his thoughts, wondering whether the events that had marked Jeremiah and Mick would have been communicated to him, if not genetically then through some sort of subtle osmosis or karmic echo.

A few days later, waiting to see his dentist, he chanced upon an article in a science magazine, explaining that a group of European researchers had discovered that early life traumatic events can alter a nongenetic mechanism governing gene expression in the sperm cells of adult mice. Gil carefully ripped out the page and later showed it to Maya, who brushed it aside. "Even if it offers an explanation for why we carry the scars of events that occurred long before we were born, it sheds no light on how we live with those wounds or heal them."

So it was that Gil renewed his quest for the black box of his past, focusing now, not on events of one hundred years ago in Ireland, or even the tragedy that had blighted his father's life, but on his own youth.

University

That the events described in the opening chapters of Ivan Sergeyevich Turgenev's *Fathers and Sons* echo certain critical moments in Gilbert O'Docherty's relationship with his father may be explained, not by the uncanny regularity with which art imitates life but by the fact that characters in literature are indirectly drawn from life, despite our disclaimers that any resemblance between them and any real person, living or dead, is purely coincidental.

Within days of completing his university entrance exams in 1979, Gil boarded a train in Moabite bound for Auckland, where he planned to find work over the summer months and save enough money to supplement the government scholarship that covered only his university fees. His parents did not come to the railway station to see their son off, his mother not wanting to make public her grief at his going, and Mick declaring that Gil would be back in Moabite before he could say Jack Robinson. When they shook hands, Gil felt no affection or goodwill in his father's calloused grip, but only the old man's firm resolve, born long ago, not to give in to emotion but to tough life out as if one was embroiled in a battle to the death with some crafty and unidentifiable antagonist. It was not simply that Mick found it impossible to see why a young man would wish to prolong the ignominy of sitting in classrooms and being told what to do when he had a chance of becoming his own man; he felt betrayed, for wasn't his son reneging on a promise he had made several years before, to assist his father in managing the mill, and one day take it over? Gil was selling out, seduced by the very values he had pretended to disdain, and turning his back not only on his father but his own kind. "We may be working class," Mick once told him, "but we have our pride. And it is honest labor that we do. We don't see our fellow men in the light of how we can pick their pockets or pervert their minds. We see them as men like us, no more, no less." Nor were these sentiments solely Mick's. So adamantly did they form the bedrock of Gil's conscience that almost from the moment his train pulled out of Moabite and began its nightlong journey through the Taranaki backblocks he felt that he had signed his father's death warrant. Whatever he gained from the adventure on which he was now embarked, and that he had envisaged for as long as he could remember, those gains would translate into his father's loss.

"We only want what is best for you," Mick had told him that morning, as if finally reconciled to the fact that his son had always been a stranger to him.

"I don't know where we went wrong," his mother said, blaming herself, as she always did.

"But what if my life isn't meant to be the same as yours? Surely your life and Dad's weren't just repetitions of your parents' lives."

It was hopeless. "What's so wrong about our lives?" his mother demanded to know. And she reminded him that they had done everything for him and surely he owed them something in return.

"You will write won't you?"

"Of course I will, Mum."

"You'll keep in touch?"

"Yes, Mum, I'll keep in touch."

During that first lonely summer in Auckland, Gil rented a room in a Mount Eden boardinghouse, and in his spare time began leafing at random through the textbooks assigned for his Pacific history and philosophy courses. His fantasy life was typical of most adolescents: imagined dalliances with mysterious women glimpsed sitting alone in a coffee bar or on a bench in the middle of an art gallery peering intently at a painting in which the infatuated youth could discern no earthly value. But Gil was prone to a less typical daydream whose source he could not fathom at that time, in which some avatar of Abel Magwitch would anonymously bequeath to him a regular stipend that would not only relieve him of having to toil in the wool stores, but open the way to a magical metamorphosis in which his shyness and gaucheness would be shed like an ugly skin.

Gil's dream was partially realized early in his second year when one of his history lecturers took him under his wing. Though Gil was not the only student Professor Levinssohn took a shine to, Gil found himself inducted into a select circle that gathered in Peter and Anna Levinssohn's home every other Saturday evening to sip Rhenish wine, snack on mezze, and talk about a Europe from which the Levinssohns had fled in 1938 in search of a safe haven. Peter's stories of the Germany in which he had come of age and the anti-Semitic shadows that had stolen over his youth, presaging the darkness that would engulf his family and cast him into a moral wilderness that he would never escape, moved the twenty-year-old Gil so profoundly that he began to read with ever-increasing interest everything he could lay his hands on concerning the origins of the Third Reich and the Holocaust. So far did this vicarious journeying take him into a world utterly remote in time and space from the one in which he had grown up that he would often set aside a book or tear his eyes away from a photograph, only to experience complete bewilderment as to his whereabouts. At one point, after reading *The Diary of Anne Frank*, he became obsessed with the thought that he might have somehow saved her life and become her friend.

Years later, when he met Maya Reuter, he innocently told her that she reminded him of Anne Frank, and confided the story of his adolescent infatuation. The confession almost killed their relationship before it had begun. But true to her vow to be honest at all costs, Maya responded to Gil by declaring that she was the reincarnation of no one. "Nor can you hope to relate to me as a Jew. I am a person, as you are. That is the only basis on which we can have a conversation or hope to be friends."

It took Gil a long time to outgrow his desire to be a retrospective hero, or imagine that it might be possible to magically alter the course of events before they actually occurred. But these were the fantasies that drew him to history, attracted him to such fictional works as H. G. Wells's *The Time Machine*, and even at times made him wish that he was Jewish, as if this identity would assimilate him to the tragedy that preoccupied him, and mitigate the deep sorrow whose real origins eluded him.

Another student in Levinssohn's circle of devoted undergraduates recognized Gil's melancholy. "Either you see Professor Levinssohn as a father figure or you are hoping to find in Jewishness an analogue of your own sense of social exclusion," Richard Barrowclough proclaimed one afternoon in the Grand Hotel. "Both options are equally escapist. I think you should learn to see your marginality as a source of strength, and not a wound or a disability. The center cannot hold. Centers are where life reaches its nadir. Centers bleed the vitality out of the world. Centers are where thinking ceases and dogmas are born. It's only at the periphery that you find vitality and freedom."

Gil did not like being told what to think, and resented Richard Barrowclough's articulateness. "Well, then," Gil said, in an effort to outsmart the anarchist, "we're living as far from the center of the world as you can get," and he cited R. A. K. Mason's "Sonnet of Brotherhood"—"here in this far-pitched perilous hostile place / this solitary hard-assaulted spot / fixed at the friendless outer edge of space."

"Mason is a socialist," Barrowclough observed judgmentally, "who would have done himself more justice had he embraced anarchism."

"Like you," Gil sneered.

"Sure, why not?"

Despite himself, Gil felt a deep kinship with Barrowclough, and his reading now included Proudhon and Kropotkin, while his nascent political sensibilities, the seeds of which had been sown when he revolted against the Moabite Masonic Lodge at age fifteen, soon found expression in a zealous participation in protest marches against the 1981 South African rugby union tour. His underground activities made him something of a campus hero— an irony not lost on his fellow conspirator, Richard Barrowclough, who pointed out that Gil might at least pretend to be outraged by apartheid and not just heroically driven to wage a one-man campaign against authority.

Although he had kept up a correspondence with his mother during his first year at university, Gil did not come home for Christmas, explaining that he needed to stay in Auckland to work.

"Your father hoped you would be able to spend the summer with us, and work in the mill," his mother wrote. "Even if you choose to work in the wool stores, Mick wants you to make sure you join the union and keep up your dues. It's a matter of pride for him, as you well know."

Because wages for men under twenty-one were 30 percent less than the wages paid to adult men, Gil had felt hard done by from the start, and was in no mood to join the Storeman's Union, which had rejected his petitions to agitate for equal pay for equal work. When he did return to Moabite at the end of his second year, accompanied by Richard Barrowclough, his non-union status was not the bone of contention between him and his father. It was almost everything that now defined him—his antagonism to the Springbok tour, his friendship with Barrowclough, his disdain for the *Taranaki Herald* (that Mick read daily from cover to cover), and his attempts to persuade his mother to expand her culinary repertoire.

"We not good enough for you, is that it?"

"You're the one who rails against the bourgeoisie, Dad. You're the one who's always going on about the government riding roughshod over the common man, and our bloody conservative press!"

"Watch your language, son!"

"So, it's my language now! The language I learned from you at the mill. One minute you're telling me not to use polysyllabic words; the next you're telling me not to use four-letter ones."

Miriam would struggle to prevent these exchanges from getting out of hand. Or Richard would intervene, with jokes about cooling-off periods and negotiated settlements. Gil would stalk off to the Mick House. Mick would hide behind his *Herald*. And Richard would ask Miriam if he could help her in the kitchen. But in going their separate ways, the four of them seemed only to dwell on their initial confrontation and plot strategy for the next.

When he read *Great Expectations* as a boy, Gil had cast himself in the role of Philip Pirrip, and imagined his father as Joe Gargery, broken fingernails, grimy hands, befuddled in the company of his betters. But Gil had experienced no moments of bucolic intimacy that could be recalled years later, the older man nursing the child back to health, paying his debts, forgiving their estrangement. Instead, a gradual degradation of Mick's soul had created the empty shell of a hermit crab, in which cacophonous echoes of his wife's pleading, his son's broken promises, Jeremiah's drunken rages, and memories of his long-lost sister merged demonically in his dreams. As for Mick's son, there were times when John Lennon's tormented song ran through his head like a river in the night: "Mother you had me but I never had you. I wanted you but you didn't want me. . . . Father you left me but I never left you. I needed you but you didn't need me. . . . Children don't do what I have done. I couldn't walk and I tried to run. . . . Mama don't go. Daddy come home . . ."

To escape the growing tension in the house, Gil took Richard on long walks around Moabite, or into the hills behind the town, showing him scenes from his childhood, and imploring his friend to explain why, when he was away from this place, he would succumb to nostalgic memories of the eccentrics who figured in his childhood and the violent events that haunted its periphery, yet when he returned he felt he was back in prison after a botched parole. "What about you?" he asked. "What's it like when you go home?"

"My father and I could not be any more different. He's a lawyer, and I am outside the law. Yet he funds my misadventures, as he likes to call them, and tolerates my anarcho-individualism as a passing phase. He even says that a misspent youth is the best passport to a profitable career."

"Is your father happy, would you say?"

"Not happily married, but happy after a fashion. A bit like the dormouse at the Mad Hatter's tea party."

"What of my father? What would you say about him?"

"It's not for me to say. He's your father. Like water is water and stone is stone."

"But water can wear stone away, or turn to ice, or steam. If he is to be compared to anything natural, I would say it was stone rather than water."

"I didn't mean anything particularly symbolic in what I said. I meant only that we are what we are."

"And nothing changes."

"If you are destined to change, you will. If you're not, you won't."

"So you're a fatalist."

"A fatalist who believes that we conspire in our own fate."

Gil was not going to be drawn into casuistry.

"If anything was predestined in my life it was that I would leave Moabite. And if anything was predestined for Moabite it was that it would stay the same forever. But because I have changed, I can no longer see it as it was, or still is. You see that hill?" Gil pointed to a conical hill that had been quarried for gravel. "When it was abandoned, it filled with rainwater and became our local tip. My father used to take me foraging there in the weekends. It was the source of nightmare images for me—a bottomless dark green pond, always in shadow, in which the jagged and ominous shapes of rusted car bodies and mangled unidentifiable trash lay submerged. Encroaching on the pond were mounds of smoldering refuse that gave off an acrid smell that made me gag. Yet my father would pick his way through this refuse as if born to the task, dragging a superphosphate sack after him, slowly filling it with his finds. If I lifted my gaze from the rubbish, I would survey the quarry face, take in the pines that ringed it like a coxcomb, then, suddenly dizzy, turn my attention back to my father, now calling me to bring another sack from the truck because he'd found something. God only knows what drew my father to that place, and I can't recall a thing he ever found there."

"Perhaps the whole point was to do something with you."

"What, have me watch him scavenge at a tip every weekend?"

"Having you with him. Doing something with him. Unlike my dad, yours is not a man of many words, Gil. Perhaps doing was his way of saying. Do you want to go there?"

"Where? To the tip?"

"Why not?"

"There's nothing to see. The pond got filled with rubbish. It was bull-dozed over. The town found somewhere else to dump its trash."

Not much was said over the next few days. While Richard lounged in a deck chair under the plum tree reading, Gil spent several hours a day helping his father and Jim Tuwhare at the mill.

The showdown, when it finally did happen, took everyone by surprise, for they had each resolved to keep their opinions to themselves and not say anything that might precipitate any kind of unpleasantness. But one evening, watching the television news, a passing reference to Solidarność's ongoing struggle against the Polish Communist Party compelled Gil to blurt out that the trade union was financed by American capital and was, like so many so-called freedom movements, simply a pawn in the Cold War game. Outraged, Mick demanded that Gil retract his comment. Before Miriam could bring calm to the scene or Richard could persuade his friend to qualify his remark, all hell broke loose and in the ensuing melee Mick cracked his coffee mug over his son's head, drawing such copious amounts of blood that Miriam cried, "My God, Mick, you've killed him!" and immediately rushed to the phone to call 111. Mick stood shell-shocked in the middle of the room, the broken mug's intact handle still hooked on his forefinger, while the stupefied anarchist took it upon himself to apologize for whatever offense he had caused.

"I don't have any quarrel with you," Mick said, not knowing that his son had simply repeated something Richard Barrowclough had told him. "I'm sure you treat your father with more respect than my son shows me."

"I'm sorry just the same," Richard said.

Gil had rushed to the bathroom to wash the blood from his face and inspect the damage. But his probing finger found no deep gash, and when he came back into the sitting room, where the TV was insensitively reciting its nightly litany of fatal car wrecks and criminal assaults, he told his mother to cancel the 111 call and bring him a Band-Aid.

Though Richard reiterated his apologies at breakfast next morning, Miriam's insistence that it was water under the bridge and no use crying over spilled milk forestalled any postmortem. Even if the efforts by Richard and Gil to move beyond face-saving clichés had not been frustrated by Miriam's fluency with hackneyed phrases, they would not have penetrated Mick's stoic armor, his eyes averted, or focused on his bacon and eggs, his comments mere grunts that could have been interpreted as either dissent or assent.

It wasn't until the day of Gil and Richard's departure that Miriam O'Docherty ventured out of the sanctuary that she had spent a lifetime creating for herself and drew her son aside in a last-ditch appeal for his understanding.

"Perhaps, one day it will happen to you, Gil, just as it has happened to your father. You will discover that nothing you have spent your life doing has made any difference to anyone. It's all irrelevant and out of date. No earthly good to man or beast. No one sees your worth. They look on you with pity or contempt. They forget your name. As far as they are concerned you have already passed away."

Gil was confused. Was his mother seeking love for herself or pleading on behalf of her husband?

He took his mother into his arms and held her as she sobbed quietly. "I'll talk to Dad," he said, patting her gently. "Don't worry, Mum, we'll patch things up."

On the train that evening, Barrowclough pretended to read while Gil looked out on a landscape of hills in the gathering dusk. Bringing his face closer to the windowpane, he tried to peer through the reflected furnishings and fittings of the compartment, switching his focus from the shadow of himself to the darkened hills outside. His hard-heartedness oppressed him. His inability to conjure anything more than a clipped goodbye to his crestfallen father. His growing resentment toward Barrowclough. Behind the façade of Richard's political philosophy lay an unforgiving attitude of intellectual disdain. The anarchist seemed to care more for being a provocateur than a person, and there had been moments when Gil preferred his father's stubborn opinions to his friend's condescending cleverness. Though he envied Richard's sophistication and the ease with which he could pick up women, he now wondered whether his own intellectual ineptitude signified a more authentic way of being, despite the shame it caused him. And he reminded himself of Richard's cryptic remark about Peter Levinssohn's marriage. "A match made in hell rather than heaven, wouldn't you say?" He had not challenged Richard. Though aware of his friend's contempt for the women who fawned on him, and his derisive comments about Anna Levinssohn's "intellectual innocence," Gil had never taken Barrowclough to task for his misogyny, fearing that his ability to win an argument on moral grounds would prove as ineffectual as his capacity for logical reasoning.

His disenchantment came to a head at a party during Capping Week. A girl with whom Barrowclough had had a brief affair became drunk and maudlin and, after clumsily attempting to attract the anarchist's attention, passed out. Enlisting the help of a sidekick, Barrowclough dragged the comatose girl from the armchair in which she had collapsed and hauled her around the room by her ankles, pretending to be a horse pulling a wagon. The girl suffered the indignity without protest, her eyes closed, skirt pulled up around her waist, and panties visible. Whooping and hollering, the two horses continued their gallop through the crowded room until, weary of their game, they let the dead weight flop to the floor. Gil did nothing. Though shocked, he said nothing. And it was his immobility that troubled him later, more than the offense itself; the complete disconnect between what he saw and his failure to respond. Not even the memory of Barrowclough's boorishness could extinguish the guilt he felt at his own passivity.

Feeling increasingly isolated, he threw himself into work, determined to complete his degree and shake the dust of Auckland from his shoes. As to what he would do and where he would go, he hadn't the faintest idea. When he confided his confusion to Peter Levinssohn, he was told that he would have to go out into the wilderness of the world, and hope that his destiny would be revealed to him. This was not what Gil had wanted to hear. He had sought a refuge from the elements, only to be told that he would have to submit to them. He had wanted to be shown his path, not have to find it for himself.

Maya

Growing up in the shadows of a sawmill, Gil had acquired a feel for wood, a talent for turning it on a lathe, an eye for its grain and texture, a love of dovetails and joinery. But his social skills lagged far behind his abilities with wood, and people meeting him for the first time often found him as unresponsive as the raw material he sawed, planed, joined, or turned with such aplomb. Gil was well aware of his limitations, especially with women. It troubled him deeply that though he yearned for the warmth of a woman's body he could not believe that any woman would want him. So convinced he was at the hopelessness of his situation that he recoiled from making even the most tentative overture, fearing that it would be rebuffed. It was not simply shyness; it seemed to be something instilled in him, built into his body, and it came down like a portcullis whenever he felt the desire to get close to a woman or talk to her alone.

How can one explain the source of such inhibitions, or uncover the origins of our passions or prejudices? In Gil's case, he would ask himself if his father's misogynistic views and his mother's misery had something to do with his own well-defended, landlocked soul—the still face he carefully cultivated, the unemotional way he responded to displays of affection in his friends. He had the impression that his father was incapable of seeing women as anything other than temptresses and betrayers, and could not recall his parents ever speaking lovingly to each other, or showing affection. Each seemed to hold the other responsible for his or her own unhappiness.

They bickered over money, fussed and fumed over trifles, and often spent days on end in tight-lipped silence.

Yet, when Gil first met Maya Reuter over the counter at the university bookshop and she requested a copy of Hans-Georg Gadamer's *Truth and Method*, his inhibitions fell away despite the fact that his face was aflame and he could scarcely make his way to the philosophy shelves, sensing her behind him.

"I did check," Maya said. "You don't have it." But she followed him anyway and watched as he pretended to search for the book he also knew was not there.

"It is philosophy, isn't it?" he asked, looking up at her. He was racking his brains for some ruse to detain her, or at least not lose touch with her.

"Are you doing philosophy?" he asked.

"Art history actually."

Her smile disarmed him. He was lost for words. But the demon within Gil O'Docherty spoke for him, suggesting that if she left him her name and address he could order the book for her.

"It's all right. I can get a copy from the library."

"But what if it is out to another borrower, or gets recalled? Wouldn't it be better to have your own copy, especially if it's so important for your work?"

She smiled again. She saw right through him. But scribbled her details on the index card he gave her.

When she handed back the card he did not look at what she had written. He was overwhelmed. Her hair dark and close-cropped. That ghost of a smile, as if she not only saw the irony or absurdity of the situation, but enjoyed it.

When she had gone, he inspected the card. She had not bothered to write the title of the book, nor provide her address. She had simply written Maya (03) 477 0237.

Three days later, they met at a Chinese restaurant called the Shangri-La, and over a plate of Szechuan green beans, Maya asked how long he had been working at the bookshop.

If he didn't answer her question, it was because he was already struggling with feelings of inadequacy and shame. "I toyed with the idea of doing graduate work in history, but—"

"What kind of history?"

"I did my degree in Auckland. My favorite professor was German. He encouraged me to go on, but I'm still not sure that's really what I want to do. What about you? Why art history?"

"My background, I suppose."

"In England?"

"Not exactly. My grandparents did not survive the Holocaust, but it wasn't until my final year at high school that I had the time and inclination to find out more about them. I read a lot and pressed my mother for details about how she had come to England. But she was reluctant to satisfy my curiosity. 'The past is another country,' she'd say. 'There's no future in the past.' Cliché after cliché, demarcating the boundary between what could and could not be told. Finally, she gave me the address of an Israeli uncle of hers, and I contacted him. He had some paintings, supposedly done by my grandmother, and he sent me some photographs of them. I had been painting and drawing obsessively from an early age, and was astonished to see my own hand in these watercolors of my grandmother's, even though they'd never been exhibited and may not even have been shared within the family. Certainly, my mother did not know of their existence. When I showed the photographs to her they moved her even more than they had moved me. She said they spoke to her so personally that it was as if they were meant for her, like a love letter across the estranging wastes of time. As for me, I felt as if I was the first person to discover my grandmother's true identity."

"What happened to the paintings?"

"They're still in Israel. Safe, or as safe as anything can be in Israel these days. I like to think that I am their real custodian, that they are safely installed in me, and that my grandmother will have an afterlife in my life. She had eight children. All except my mother were murdered in the Shoah. Ironically her husband was a wealthy entrepreneur, and an avid art collector, though it seems he showed no interest in his wife's watercolors and may not even have known of their existence."

"What kind of things did she paint?"

"Ships at sea. Coastal landscapes. Skies."

"She lived near the sea?"

"No, she came from a small town in Bavaria, surrounded by mountains. It's what makes the imagery so compelling, at least to me. I think the sea symbolized a world she yearned for. A world of open horizons, unparalleled possibilities. The kind of world a woman could not hope to find at that time, especially if she was Jewish. So you can see why I think her paintings explain why I have ended up studying art history, and have become so fascinated by the degenerate art of the Nazis."

"What brought you to New Zealand? Don't tell me it was the prospect of the sea."

"I love the wild coasts around here. But no, I came because there was a job here, and I had given up the hope of finding anything in England."

"No regrets?"

"None yet."

"It's ominous," Gil said, "how the past hangs over us like low cloud over the sea. All those other lives of which we know so little, whose presence we sense. Sometimes I think we do not live our own lives. We live the lives of others."

"It's true. I feel the same."

"I've always been a scavenger. I rummage through litter. I'm intrigued by what other people discard. Kind of like one man's trash being another man's treasure. Some years ago, I was walking past a dumpster and couldn't help noticing that it was filled with personal memorabilia. Probably a deceased's estate. Photos, books, broken furniture, and shoeboxes filled with letters, that sort of thing. I spotted a leather-bound journal among the junk and leafed through it. The entries were all dated between 1933 and 1939, and in German. Out of curiosity I showed it to my professor, who identified it as the journal of a woman who had accompanied her husband from Germany to New Zealand in the 1930s. I didn't want to keep the journal, so gave it to him, but I felt that I had somehow taken custody of this woman's life, and that I was responsible for her. I can't explain this very well. But by taking the journal, I had entered into a relationship with her, and it weighs on my mind, even now, that I owe her something. It's experiences like this that explain why history has always fascinated me, though I sometimes wonder whether my interest in history is a way of avoiding my own."

"That sounds like Nietzsche."

"Does it?"

"How could history be anything else but a mosaic we construct out of the fragmented stories of thousands of individuals whose names remain largely unknown to us?"

"You make history sound depressingly bleak."

"I see it as redemptive. That mosaic we make can be very beautiful. And there can be great beauty in randomness."

"But how can you say such a thing, when so many millions perished in the war, their lives unrealized, their names forgotten?"

"We remember them in the way we live now."

When Maya smiled, Gil was perplexed. Was she serious? Tongue in cheek? He was out of his depth.

"Tell me about your own history, then," Maya said.

"There's not much to tell. Unlike you, I come from a place where no one bothers with the past. My father's parents were Irish, but more than that I do not know. The memories that sifted through the hourglass of my father's mind or that he shared with me were quicksand. I didn't want to get bogged down in them. Dad owned a sawmill. He ran it with a Māori friend who in many ways I was closer to than my own father. Jim used to recite his whakapapa as he worked. . . ."

"His what?"

"His family tree, his family history. When I was small, I thought he was talking to himself, but when I asked him what he was talking about he said it wasn't him that was talking. His ancestors were talking through him, and he was listening. Focused on hearing them. Committing to memory what they said. And everything they said was associated with a place, an event, a story. It was only when I went to university and met Peter Levinssohn that I realized Jim's world wasn't unusual. It was my world that was weird. A world in which people swept the past under the carpet and kept a lid on family scandals, trying to forget where they had come from and why."

"Some of us can never forget. Though we sometimes have to remember to remember."

As the waitress cleared their table, Gil took one of the fortune cookies that had been placed with the bill on the oilskin tablecloth, tore open the cellophane with his teeth, and read, "Embrace this love relationship you have!" His heart pounded.

"What does it say?" Maya asked.

"What does yours say?"

She read it to him. "Life must be lived forward, but can only be understood backward."

Did the word *love* cross his mind that night? He remembers the way she kept tugging her skirt over her knees, a gesture of modesty that both aroused and shamed him. The hands of his mind reach out to touch her dark hair. He drowns in the pools of her dark brown eyes. His fingers describe her eyebrows and move tenderly to her lips. He is aware that every face he sees from this day forth will be ordinary by comparison with hers. He thinks, I may never see her again. He tells himself, She probably sees nothing in me. But something has happened, something has transpired in the space of an hour or two that he cannot put words to. He has been changed utterly, though has no inkling of what this change portends. This uncertainty keeps him from sleep. When at last he does doze off, he wakes with a start as if only a moment has elapsed, and he is dazzled by sunlight pouring into his uncurtained room, surprised that Maya is still in his thoughts, like a guardian angel.

Families

Gil and Maya did not marry until after Liam's birth, and though they intended this event to celebrate and cement the beginning of their family life, it initiated their gradual estrangement. Gil became convinced that Maya's affections had switched from him to their son, and he recoiled from fatherhood. Late one night, holding Liam against his shoulder and wishing he would fall asleep, Gil felt his own life slipping away. We should not have got married, he told himself. We should not have brought a child into this world. Yet, only months before, he had never felt so close to Maya, or so happy.

On the night Maya went into labor, they worked as one, monitoring her contractions, checking that they had packed everything they would need, phoning the birthing unit to say they were on their way. With Maya's contractions becoming more intense, Gil drove through the pitch-dark streets, running red lights, panicking that they would not reach the hospital in time.

At the birthing unit, the midwife on duty seemed more concerned with telling them she was a fill-in, not used to working night shifts, than helping Maya get comfortable. This only increased their sense of isolation, the outside world as indifferent to them as if they had died.

Again and again they returned to their task, Maya shifting her position on the bed, using techniques she'd learned in antenatal classes—all fours, hero pose, pelvic rocking—Gil massaging her lumbar spine or applying hot towels to her back.

Three hours passed. As each new contraction brought screams of agony from Maya, Gil was astonished by her strength and focus.

"Do you want to try the hot tub?" he asked.

"Anything," Maya gasped.

As Gil turned on the taps to fill the tub, the midwife appeared. She was going to find a spare room and catch some sleep. When Gil returned to check on Maya, he became so absorbed in her labor that by the time he remembered leaving the taps running and rushed back to the bathroom, the tub was overflowing. A towel had blocked the floor drain, and the birthing unit was awash. Paddling through water, he unblocked the drain, emptied the tub, and began mopping the floor. All the while, the midwife slumbered and Maya struggled against exhaustion. She would later say she had been in a daze, an emotional vacuum, vaguely aware of what Gil was doing, yet utterly detached.

Gil glanced at the clock on the wall. 4:30. The first sounds of traffic on the street. A world away.

"Fuck! Shit! Oh God, oh God, oh God, oh God," Maya breathed her makeshift mantras until the contraction subsided and she could bury her face in the pillow, change position, mutter something to Gil, before the ferocious waves broke over her again. "I'm going crazy I'm going crazy I'm going crazy. . . . Relax, relax, relax, relax, relax. . . . It'll pass, it'll pass, it'll pass."

At 5:00 a new midwife came on duty. Strong, sensitive, and competent, Shay assured Maya that she was now moving through transition. After monitoring the baby's heartbeat, she urged Maya to get off the bed and sit in a deep squat. Gil was to support her from behind.

Shay positioned a mirror in front of Maya so she could see the baby's head, now bulging along her perineum.

"Only a few more contractions now," Shay said.

Loud cries tore from Maya. Gil's eyes were burning with tears, stirred by the enormity of what Maya was undergoing, observing the yawning opening down which the baby's head was moving.

The head crowned.

Shay massaged Maya's perineum with oil. On the next contraction, the baby's head and body were delivered into Maya's outstretched hands.

Drawing the empurpled bundle of flailing limbs and fierce energy onto her belly, she marveled that he was alive.

The infant howled as the first air invaded its lungs.

As he lay resting on Maya's belly, she gently stroked the blanket that Shay had thrown across him. "He's perfect! I'm so in love with him," she said. And then to the baby: "You're so beautiful!"

"I'm so relieved it's over," Maya said to Gil. "I've never been through such an ordeal in my life. It's so wonderful to have him here finally, after all those months of waiting."

Gil spent the day at the hospital annex, gazing into the face of their son, watching the small hands clutch and claw, the eyelids unsealed, "As if," Gil told Maya, "the lids of the sea slid back and I looked into the depths of the blueblack ocean itself and was seen myself for the very first time."

That night, as Maya slept, he drove to the sea. A full moon rasped its surface with shavings of silver light. He heard the ocean thumping on the rocks. He inhaled the brine-steeped air, and was filled with the bounty of life. But despite his overwhelming love for Maya and his son, he was already oppressed by a sense of loss—though for what he did not know.

What dark seed had been planted in him? Why should his joy be compromised by these forebodings?

With Hannah's birth two years later, the dark ocean claimed him. If he was not in the Captain Cook hotel, drowning his sorrows, he was in the basement of their house, cutting meticulous incisions into his forearms with a marquetry knife.

It was midsummer. The bookshop closed. Maya's teaching year was two months away. They had driven to a river hole for a picnic lunch, and as Gil swam aimlessly in the amber water, Maya waded into the shallows, holding Liam and Hannah by the hand.

Not far from their beach, the river widened enough to be fordable. As they watched, a car lurched down the steep track on the other side of the river and came to a stop near the crossing. A large family clambered from the car, hauling picnic hampers, crates of beer, beach umbrellas, rugs, and folding chairs from the trunk. A small boy that Gil guessed to be six or seven was assigned to carry his father's transistor radio across the river. "And don't get the bloody thing wet," the father bawled as the boy inched his way into the water. It was clear to Gil that the boy would stumble, and stumble he did, but in recovering his balance, the radio touched the surface of the water. The father, who, like Gil, must have been anticipating this mishap, rushed into the river and tore the radio from his son's hand. Without bothering to inspect the damage, he proceeded to cuff the boy about his head. "You stupid cunt, you stupid little cunt, you fuckin' stupid little cunt!" As the father poured scorn on his son, he rained blows down on his head, first from the right, then the left, as the boy cowered, fighting back tears as if he was more afraid to show his distress than to suffer further blows.

The mother now waded into the river to be given an exaggerated account of the incident, whereupon she immediately joined her voice to her husband's. "You useless little shit, you fuckin' bird-brained shit!" And the father again: "You useless cunt, you useless little fuckin' cunt!"

The abuse did not cease. For fully ten minutes, with intervals of brooding silence in which the boy skulked around the beach in search of some tranquil spot where he could lick his wounds, Gil and Maya listened with impotent outrage to the parents' vile invective.

Without a word, Maya took the children back to their car, while Gil gathered their belongings and followed.

Driving back to the city, neither spoke for some time.

"We should have done something," Maya said at last.

"What could we do?" Gil said. "He wasn't our child."

Breaking Point

When Gil first met Maya he could not believe his luck. He compared it to the kind of fortuitous encounter that in fairy tales spells the difference between death and life. But while the new always appears miraculous, and filled with promise, it never entirely extinguishes the banality of the past. Ever since his parents' deaths, and despite his preoccupation with his grandparents' lives, Gil felt the shadows lengthening. Even the house seemed to participate in his loss of passion; books in the living room undusted and sun bleached, curtains fading on the north-facing windows, rugs frayed, varnish on the floorboards worn away, paint on the door frames bearing unsightly scars from the fender of Liam's pedal car. Bedroom conversations atrophied into muttered good nights. Only rarely did he and Maya make love. When they did it was perfunctory and apologetic. They argued daily over money, the division of labor in the home, and Gil's drinking.

His growing intolerance of the children's raised voices and incessant demands made Maya angry and resentful, but she did not voice her feelings for fear of making matters worse. As for Gil, who had reached an impasse with his writing and become indifferent to the unfinished boxes that littered his workbench like miniature coffins, he was loath to share his woes with Maya in case she confided her own, exacerbating his sense of impotence and worthlessness.

Maya had seen his descent into the underworld too many times before. For several years, her career had been on hold. Determined that Liam and

Hannah would want for nothing, she had twice postponed the deadline for submitting her book manuscript to Oxford University Press. Now, with no possibility of a further deferment, she began to panic, imploring Gil to spend more time with the children and help around the house. Rather than rise to the occasion, he resented her inability to cope. Blind to her unhappiness, Gil exhibited the same coldness his father had shown toward his wife.

It was left to Maya to break the ice. "I refuse to get used to this," she said. "I refuse to be like the Germans who said nothing when Hitler came to power, and turned a blind eye to what was happening to the Jews." But Gil disappeared into the basement, and for weeks on end they spoke to each other only to arrange a time for picking up the children from school or taking them to the dentist, the doctor, or a birthday party.

Anzac Day. Three in the afternoon. Maya declares that they should remember the dead.

"Will remembering the dead help the living?" Gil asks.

"It's important," Maya says wearily, though her grandparents are not even a distant memory, and the few photos she has of her mother are photos of a stranger whose voice she has forgotten, whose presence she no longer feels.

"You remember," Gil says. "Your memories can make up for my lack of any."

"Everything I do these days is making up for something you can't do, or refuse to do for yourself."

"What's that supposed to mean?"

"It means that you need help, Gil."

"What! Because I won't remember the dead?"

"Because you won't remember the living, Gil. You show no real awareness of me. You spend more time in the basement than you spend with the children. You're in another world. A world I cannot enter. I have given up wanting to be a part of your life. I want only to regain a sense of my own. I want to remember what it means to be me."

His heart is pounding. He thinks of a cloud coming over the sun on a midsummer day, the landscape filled with foreboding.

"I can't go on like this," Maya says. "I think we should go our separate ways!" She walks out of the room and slams the door behind her.

He goes after her. In the bedroom, she turns her tear-streaked face to him. "I think we should live apart for a while."

"What about the children?" he asks. "Have you thought of them?"

"Of course I have."

"But you say you want to recover your own life without them."

"Without you, Gil, not them. I need to be on my own. To have time to myself . . . to finish my book . . ."

"You mean without the children pestering you?"

"No, Gil. Without having to worry about you. Without having you as an additional burden I have to carry."

"So what do you want to do?"

"It's what I want you to do, Gil. I can manage the children, but I can't mother you. I think you should find a place on your own for a while. It would help me, and it may be a good thing for you, too. I think you need help. Help I can't give you right now—"

"What kind of help?"

"I think you should see a therapist. I think you need to deal with whatever happened when your parents died."

He rents a room on Māori Hill, retreating like a wounded animal to lick his wounds. Yet the world finds a way of breaking through his defenses. Every night around eight he receives a phone call from someone who refuses to identify himself, but waits on the line while Gil feebly asks, "Who's there?" After a long pause, the caller hangs up. At first Gil is bemused, but after three nights of receiving the same anonymous call, he becomes angry. Is it someone like himself, estranged from someone he loves, unable to accept that she is no longer a living presence but a phantom, a memory? Or is it someone finding his loneliness and loss so unbearable that he calls a number every night that has some arcane significance to him, hoping that the person who picks up will offer sympathy and not simply demand to know who's there? He attaches the chain to the front door. It worries him that the dead bolt is broken. He remembers the landlord's description of the previous tenants as "animals." He half expects to be woken by brutal banging on the door, someone looking for the "animals," wanting to settle some score, some unreasoning psychopath who is bent on destroying him. He imagines himself fleeing the house by the fire escape. Will there be time to save his laptop? Why this fear? Because Maya will not agree to see him, will not tell him how she is faring? He calls her, imploring her to meet him. She is teaching all day. But she can find a few minutes around noon on Wednesday. She suggests they meet at the Daily Grind.

He takes a corner table without ordering anything. When she arrives, he asks her what she wants.

"Nothing for me. But you go ahead and order for yourself."

He tells her how much he misses her. She responds icily. She says she now understands why their relationship could never work in the way they once hoped it would. "I remember when we met. You told me that your parents were like strangers. That you had been delivered to them in error, and that your true parents lived elsewhere, and you would have to become a traveler, and go to the ends of the earth to find them. I remember telling you I felt the same way. That my mother was never really there for me, that her thoughts were always elsewhere, dwelling on the past. This is why I was so determined to be a good mother, Gil. But I'm not sure I was cut out to be a good wife."

He knows that if he argues with her, she will walk away. So he asks after Hannah and Liam, even though they will be with him for the weekend.

"I must get back," she says. "I have a meeting."

As she walks out the door he is in love with her. At the very instant that she has become a stranger to him, he realizes that he cannot live without her.

That night there is no phone call to break the silence. A freight train drones in the distance. Cold chills, shuddering, heartache . . . he tries to describe the feelings that overtake him, that make it impossible to sleep. He has flashbacks to Moabite when he was a boy, dreaming of some fabulous elsewhere to which he would one day be transported. He wishes he could go home. But where is home if not with Maya and the children? It does not cross his mind that Maya might be suffering as much as he is. It takes a psychotherapist to enlighten him.

It is suggested to him that he is suffering from delayed mourning. He has sought escape from the devastating loss of his mother and unresolved issues with his father by attempting to write a family history. The therapist speaks of a fantasy in which one imagines one can go back into the past and manipulate events in such a way that a future tragedy is averted. "Unhappiness invariably has a long history," the therapist says. "Like a river, it is impossible to trace all the streams that have fed into it. We can explore the source, to be sure, but we live downstream, in the here and now, and this, ultimately, is where we have to build and rebuild our lives."

It's not as if I am mourning for someone I can name or for something I can put my finger on, Gil thinks. I know something has been lost, that something is missing. I have known this for as long as I can remember knowing anything, from long before my mother and father died. A sense of loss has bled into my life, spread through it like a stain, seeped into me like winter rain.

On his second visit to the therapist, Gil immediately heads upstream. "Why did my father beat me at the slightest provocation? If I did not eat all the food on my plate. If I asked for seconds and did not finish them. If I left my toys out in the rain or did not put them away after playing with them. Why did such trivial things make him so angry? I could never do anything right. Nor could my mother. He hated it if she read a book. He swore at her for spending too much time tending her roses. Why was he so filled with so much rage?"

"Perhaps your father was beaten when he was a child."

"He probably was, because whenever he hit and cursed me he'd slip into an Irish brogue, as if in the heat of the moment he became his own father, who was Irish."

"Perhaps your father did not like himself very much."

"But why did he have to take it out on me and my mother?"

"Anger is a like a chained and starving animal. It craves for release. It is blind to the hurt it causes others in its struggle to be unfettered. Only in retrospect does it feel remorse."

"I don't think my father felt remorse about anything."

"Let's come back to your feelings for a moment. How did you feel when your father beat you?"

"It wasn't the physical pain. It was the unfairness of it. I can't remember ever deserving the punishment he meted out to me. And my mother pandered to him without complaint. But why abuse her? Yet I sensed from an early age that the cause of his rage wasn't anything I'd done, or my mother had failed to do, but something that had been done to him. I think you're right. His father probably treated him the way he treated me. My sister said that our father did not know how to express tenderness. When he felt the need for sex, our mother had to give in to him, whether she felt the need or not. My sister also said that he may have had a brief affair with another woman, but called it off, and resented his family for preventing him from achieving happiness in this other life."

"Do you ever imagine how your life might be happier?"

"Like another period of history that I'd like to have been born in?"

"Or another place. Or with another person."

"Not much. I mean, not obsessively. But my father often accused me of being a changeling. 'I know you're the child of my loins and your mother's womb,' he'd say, 'but I could swear that by some devilish mischief my real son was spirited away and you replaced him.' He'd ramble on about babies getting accidentally exchanged in hospital, and parents getting the wrong baby."

"Doesn't this reveal more about your father than about you?"

When Gil related the story of Siobhan's death at Weary Bay, he suggested that his grandmother had lost her reason when her daughter died, and that Jeremiah, already more deeply attached to his daughter than to his son, never accepted that Mick was alive in place of his sister.

"That's not uncommon," the therapist said.

"So my grandfather transferred his grief to his son, and my father grew up feeling he was the wrong sex, the wrong age, the wrong person, and that the right person could never be brought back to life. He could only fail to fulfill the task of being Siobhan, just like I in turn could only fail to be the child he had never been allowed to become."

"Tell me about your children."

"What do you want to know?"

"Let's begin with their names."

"Hannah and Liam."

"How old is Hannah?"

"She's six."

"And Liam?"

"Nine."

"You mentioned last week that the children spend the weekends with you."

"Yes."

"What do you do together in the weekends?"

"Well, it's not like it was when I was with Maya. I had a workshop then. I set it up in the basement when we bought the house. I like to make the kids toys."

"What kind of toys?"

"Last Christmas I made a wooden fire truck for Liam, and a furnished doll's house for Hannah."

"I imagine they loved those gifts."

"At the time they did. But they lost interest very quickly. The doll's house is back in the basement collecting dust, and Liam's fire truck fell apart."

"How did you feel about that?"

"I was upset. I've always tried to teach the children to look after their things. It upsets me when they treat things so indifferently, things I've spent scores of hours working on, painting—"

"You say you like making things for your children. But what kinds of things do you do together?"

"Well, I admit I'm not much good at the usual father-son things."

"Like?"

"Like playing rugby with Liam in the backyard." Gil remembers a Saturday rugby game, Liam assigned to play first five-eighth, parents on the sideline shouting for their sons to hit hard, to kill . . . "Anyway, Liam's not into sports."

"Perhaps he'd be interested if you were."

"I doubt it."

"What about Hannah? What's she into?"

"She's much more athletic. She's a good swimmer. Loves to swim. And she loves new clothes. Maya's always taking her shopping, buying her new dresses."

"Do you ever take her shopping?"

"No!"

The therapist paused and steepled his fingers. "Do you ever beat your children?"

Gil's cheeks burned. He might have known it would come to this, his own life fused with his father's, tarred with the same brush. He did not want to answer.

"This is not a courtroom, Gil. There's no question of you incriminating yourself. I am not a judge, and nothing you say here will ever leave this room. But if you don't feel secure about broaching this issue, we can come back to it another day. There's no hurry."

"Yes," Gil sighed. "I did."

"You did what?"

"Beat my children. Beat them like my father beat me. Maya said she would leave me if I could not learn to control my temper. She said it was not a sign of strength, but of weakness. A weakness that she and the children could not forgive. And I agreed with her. All I had to do is walk away, or learn to reprimand the children differently. Send Liam to his room to think about what he'd done. Ground him. There were plenty of options, and Maya gave them to me, time and time again—"

"Is that why she wanted you to leave?"

"No, that wasn't the reason. I haven't punished my children in that way for a long time now."

Determined to make more effort to interact with Hannah and Liam, Gil buys a jigsaw puzzle of a clipper ship that he and Hannah complete together that weekend. But when he suggests they all go to Aramoana Beach for a swim, Liam says that he has reached a critical moment in the video game he is playing. "Wait till I've finished this level," he says without lifting his eyes from the console.

"When will that be?"

"I dunno. Just wait, Dad."

He feels like tearing the device from his son's hands and throwing it away. He feels he is being tested, and that Maya is watching him, waiting to see if he passes the test.

"I'll go with Hannah," he says. "You can stay here and finish your game."

"Oh no!" Liam cries. "He got me, he got me! I was almost there and he got me."

"Does that mean you can come with us now? Or are you going to start another game?"

"I'll come with you."

"Then get your gear. Hannah, have you got yours?"

"I left it in your car."

"Liam?"

"I think mine's there too."

Much as he looks forward to seeing the children every weekend, time drags, he becomes quickly bored, and by Sunday afternoon he is counting the minutes until Maya drives by, honks her horn, and the kids race out the door without saying goodbye. He cannot abide their constant quarreling over who got more than whom, snatching at what the other has, needling each other, and ignoring his demands that they behave. He remembers his mother's refrain, "Where did we go wrong," and wonders if the children's fractiousness, like his own irascibility, is evidence of the corrosive effects of their parents' separation.

In his rented room, Gil tinkers with his Australian text, wondering whether to research it further as history or rewrite it as biography. He had hoped that hard work would provide an antidote to the sadness that has immobilized his body and permeated his mind, but he cannot concentrate and comes home in the middle of the afternoon to sit on his porch swing and stare into space.

The only sound is the creaking of the swing as he pushes it back and forth with his heels. He is nostalgic for the ocean. Though he has lived for ten years now in easy reach of the sea, he feels as remote from it as he did as a boy, stuck in an inland town. He yearns for the sea's susurrus in the night, the stench of decaying seaweed and brine, wastes of iron sand fringing a wild confusion of breaking waves. He thinks, Maya has no feeling for the sea. She says she needs time to herself. Time is the last thing I need. It is a millstone around my neck, weighing me down.

Dusk falls. He tells himself that he is learning to live without her, though at any moment, panic will seize him and bring him to his knees. Seeing one of her colleagues in the bookshop, spending time with the few friends that were more his than hers, hearing a new piece of music, finding a new book to read, learning how to cook rather than buy chop suey at the nearby fast-food franchise . . . these things foster in him a nascent sense that there will be a life after marriage. He has convinced himself that Maya befriended and married him out of pity rather than love.

"It falls to you, Gil," his therapist tells him, "to work through the feelings of inferiority that exist not only in you but in the working-class culture into which you were born and the history you are heir to." After letting this sink in, the therapist adds, "People in the past didn't or couldn't tell their story, but you can. This is your project."

He writes these observations in his journal, adding others from books he has read at random, as if these various sources are conspiring to guide him on his way.

For now we see through a glass, darkly; but then face to face: now I know in part; but then shall I know even as also I am known.

"He wanted to start out with the blessings of his family, but they were never given. He quarreled with his parents and his sister. And then, when he was best aware of the risks and knew a hundred reasons against going and had made himself sick with fear, he left home."

"It was quite an eerie feeling to be recognizing traits in myself from a dead man."

On a sweltering February day, Maya phoned Gil to ask if he could take care of the children for a couple of weeks while she flew to London to complete some archival work in the British Library.

"Of course," he said, determined not to show interest, but to appease.

"Are you sure."

"Why wouldn't I be?"

There was a long gap that she refused to fill.

Gil said, "There's actually a favor I wanted to ask of you."

"A favor?"

"When you get back from England, could you take Hannah and allow me to take Liam with me to Australia?"

"Why do you want to go to Australia? And why with Liam?"

"I want to spend some time with him. Real time. Right now he does little else than play video games and live in his imagination. He needs to get out into the world, to experience a bit of real-life adventure."

"What do you mean by real-life adventure?"

"I'd like to take him to North Queensland where my father lived when he was Liam's age."

"So this isn't about Liam having an adventure. It's about you and your father."

"Partly it is. But I want to do something with him, just the two of us. Surely you can understand that."

Maya quailed at the idea. Gil did not seem capable of taking care of himself; how could he look after a nine-year-old boy in the wilds of Australia?

They wrangled for a week before Maya gave in, and signed the legal documents that permitted Gil to take his son out of the country. "If anything happens to him, I will never forgive you," she said, handing him the papers. Then she asked what she should pack to prepare their son for his journey into what Liam was already excitedly calling crocodile country.

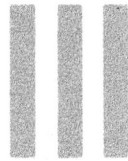

The Unanimous Night

He had dreamed of coming ashore at night, like the obscure man from the south in Jorge Luis Borges's "The Circular Ruins," whose fantasy was to dream another being. Of his own previous life, this man knew nothing. He had even forgotten his own name. All that mattered was this new man, whom he would insert into reality. But reality found its way into him, shouldering aside all thoughts of conjuring the past or discarding his old skin.

Their first night in Cairns, Gil woke to hear Liam whimpering in the darkness. He climbed out of bed, felt his way to the light switch on the far wall, and found his son sitting up in bed, face streaked with tears.

"What is it, Liam?"

"I want Mummy. I want to go home to Mummy."

"But we've only just got here."

"I want my mother."

Gil felt as if he had abducted Liam, torn him from the only person that mattered to him.

"Tell you what, Liam. First thing in the morning, we'll call her. In fact, we'll Skype her, and you can see her and talk to her, just as if she was here in Australia."

"I don't want to Skype her. I want to see her properly. And I want to go home."

As Gil endeavored to console the distraught child and suppress the growing conviction that he had forced his son to play a minor role in a drama he had scripted for his own selfish ends, he was also dimly aware of his own father's suffering at Liam's age, his sister scalded to death, his mother abandoning him, he and his father cast away on a desolate shore. Though Gil no longer believed Megan's story of Mary Argyle's masochistic career as a whore, he'd given up trying to guess what became of her. How much worse for my father, he thought, who must have spent his whole life pondering the fate of the mother who had abandoned him or, worse, lacerating himself with guilt that he might have been responsible for what had befallen the family on Weary Bay.

"Can I read to you? How about a chapter from one of those books we bought at the pier?"

"I don't want to be here. I want to go home."

"Liam, there's nothing we can do right now. It's the middle of the night. Let's sleep and think of our next move in the morning."

"Why don't you and Mummy live together anymore? Why didn't she and Hannah come with us to Australia?"

"We couldn't all come. Besides, this is an adventure for boys. They might have been scared of crocodiles and snakes and Aboriginals."

"Mummy's not scared of anything! She likes snakes."

"I don't think we've any reason to be scared. We're safe and sound here, and before you can say Jack Robinson we'll have finished our little vacation and be winging our way home with lots of fabulous adventure stories to tell Mummy and Hannah. But if we go back tomorrow we'll have nothing to share with them, and they'll be terribly disappointed in us."

"Can you read to me for a while?"

"Sure. Let's see now. 'Late one night, for no particular reason, something stirred in the black mud at the bottom of Berkeley's Creek.'"

Within minutes Liam fell back onto his pillow and closed his eyes. Gil pulled the sheet over him and touched his shoulder. He was moved by his son's vulnerability. He had not reckoned on this, and that searing sense of having done something terribly wrong besieged him again, so when he turned out the light and stumbled back to his bed he lay awake for a long time, staring into the darkness and trying to figure out the right thing to do—head home, press on, resolve his own questions, or respond to Liam's?

The following morning, he rented a four-wheel-drive vehicle, and bought two canvas bed rolls called swags, explaining to Liam that in the old days hobos were called swagmen because they carried their own bedding and clothing with them wherever they went. Then they headed north with Liam's misgivings apparently dispelled by a good night's sleep and the gift of a digital camera.

"Where are we going?" Liam asked.

"To a place called Bulbul. My grandfather lived there. That's your great-grandfather. Wouldn't you like to know something about him and see where he lived?"

"Is it far away?"

"Not too far."

"Are there wild animals there?"

"Crocodiles, maybe. Nothing we have to worry about."

Liam fell silent. Gil was relieved that the stream of unanswerable questions had momentarily dried up, but troubled that so many anxieties filled his son's mind.

"Could I take a photograph of a crocodile?"

"If it was behind a fence you could."

"But what if it wasn't?"

"Then you'd have to be careful. But there's a thousand things you can photograph apart from crocodiles. If I were you I'd be looking out for anything that we haven't got back home, anything you haven't seen before, then, when we get home, you can show Mummy and Hannah."

"What will you get to show them?"

"I'd like to show them what a good time we had, you and I, just the two of us, together."

At first it was easy going. Paved roads, remnant rain forest, glimpses of the sea, and roadside cafés where they could buy hamburgers and cold drinks. But once they had crossed the Daintree River and Liam had seen (and photographed) his first crocodiles on the far bank, the track degenerated, the rain forest closed in around them, and Gil fell prey to a sense of hopelessness, as if the creature that had stirred in the black mud at the bottom of Berkeley's Creek, its monstrous form half imagined and half real, had entered his subconscious, its plaintive cry echoing in his head, What am I? What am I?

When Liam questioned him now, he fobbed him off with "I've no idea," or a grim silence. Although he hated spurning his son, he too felt spurned. The thought that he might have lost Maya was unbearable. The prospect of returning to his job at the bookshop oppressed him. And when, late that afternoon, he reached the Aboriginal settlement where he hoped to find descendants of Billy or Billy's son, he wondered how he could have let himself believe that this godforsaken settlement could be a site of rebirth. As he drove slowly down unsealed streets lined with dull-colored monocrete houses, it occurred to him that when his grandparents came this way in the 1930s this settlement did not even exist.

"Is this where we are going to stay?" Liam asked nervously.

"Not if we can help it."

Forested hills hemmed them in. The windows of many houses were boarded up. A few front yards had been converted into half-hearted gardens. Plastic bags plastered the mesh fences. Radios blared. Men stood around in compact circles swigging beer from cans. A group of women sat clumped together playing cards. A battered car cruised the streets, with a pack of dogs pursuing it.

"Wait here," Gil told Liam as he parked outside the council offices.

Inside, he asked if anyone knew of a man called Billy, or his sons Toby and Doughboy.

"We got lots of Tobys and Doughboys. Which ones you want?"

He could not say. He mentioned Jeremiah and China Camp, the only other names that came to mind.

China Camp rang a bell. He was told to drive north for a couple of miles and look for a turnoff on the left. But it was late in the day, and Gil asked if there was anywhere he and his son could camp.

"That your camper van out there?"

"I'm renting it."

"You might try the beach. That's where whitefellas usually go."

"How do I get to the beach?"

"Drive north, and turn right. You can't miss it."

In the fading light, a pair of big black cockatoos tore and snatched at gum nuts in the bloodwoods, sending twigs and husks showering down on the camper van. "They lord it over us," Gil wrote in his journal, "like carved obsidian kings, their crests sulfurous, the crimson flashing like fire in their black wings." He remembered the unanimous night and the sacred mud, but mostly, that first night at Weary Bay, he felt as if he had been scaled and gutted like a fish.

Liam helped his father gather dry sticks for a fire, saying that they should thank the cockatoos for providing their kindling wood. Stirred by his son's empathy for the raucous birds, Gil suggested that Liam try to take a photo of them. Then he opened a can of baked beans, emptied the contents into a saucepan, and showed Liam how to pierce a slice of bread with a forked stick and hold it over the embers to make toast.

They ate in silence, enervated by their long day on the road, the sea washing listlessly ashore in the darkness.

Beyond the firelight, it was pitch black, so they left their dirty dishes in the grass and took refuge in the camper van, where they unrolled their swags on the tiered bunk beds.

Liam asked his father to read to him.

"Let's see," Gil said as he found the first page in the feeble light. "'What do bunyips look like? it asks anybody who happens to be passing by. Horrible, with webbed feet and horrible feathers, a wallaby tells him, and with horrible fur and horrible tails, adds an emu, and like nothing at all concludes a busy scientist without looking up from his notebook, who then explains, looking right through him: Bunyips simply don't exist.'"

"But it is a bunyip, isn't it?" Liam said.

"Yes, but he doesn't know he's a bunyip yet. He has to wait until another bunyip comes along. It's like us, trying to work out who we are. We can't do it on our own. We need someone else to show us. Someone like us or someone who really likes us."

When Gil went to turn off the light, Liam asked if there were crocodiles out there in the darkness, and whether the sea would rise up in the night and wash them away.

"We've got nothing to worry about," Gil said.

"What about those people you talked to? Is this their beach?"

"I imagine it is. But they were kind enough to let us camp here. Maybe tomorrow we'll go and ask them to tell us more about where we are."

Suddenly, Liam asked, "What things do you worry about, Dad?"

Gil had to think hard. Finally, he said, "Being separated from you and Mummy and Hannah."

"That's what I worry about too. And thunder and lightning."

"Everyone's a bit of afraid of thunder."

"It can be really loud."

Gil assured Liam that it was winter. "There's no chance of thunderstorms. We've nothing to worry about on that score."

As for the fear of separation, he had no panacea, no defense. "When I was your age, my mummy and daddy sent me to stay with my uncle. I was very homesick, just like you were yesterday. But you have at least one of your parents with you. I had nobody. And the house I stayed in was really old and scary, and my uncle was very weird."

"How weird?"

"Well, for one thing, he walked around in the night without any clothes on."

"Why?"

"Maybe he thought he was a bunyip, and he was looking for a mate."

"What else did he do?"

"He didn't eat meat."

"What did he eat?"

"Raw vegetables mostly. Carrot sticks, celery sticks, and lots of peanut butter sandwiches."

"I like peanut butter sandwiches."

"I know you do. What say we drive back to Bulbul tomorrow and buy some bread and peanut butter."

Weary Bay

He had once fancied himself as a historian, yet when it came to his own history he seemed to have lost all sense of historical time. His grandparents had lived here sixty-two years ago, yet it was as if his chronology had been annulled, which is perhaps why he gave the people he spoke to at Bulbul, and later at the mission, the impression that he was laboring under some kind of delusion or was the victim of a practical joke. Not that this was an unusual experience for Aboriginal people, for whom a motley of white misfits and renegades was always seeking sanctuary in their midst, as if displacement from their own world might heal the wounds they had suffered in it.

Gil's attempts to trace the men who worked for his grandfather were also thwarted by the obduracy of almost everyone he spoke to. He would ask a question and be met by a stony silence or laconic, "I dunno." He tried rephrasing his questions, using the simplest English. It made no difference. Was this taciturnity a way of saving face, or a defense against strangers?

At the end of his first day of fruitless inquiry, and with Liam complaining about a rash he had developed on his chest, Gil was about to head back to Weary Bay when a drunken individual with wild eyes and a face as black as anthracite stuck his head through the window of the camper van and asked for a lift. Recoiling from the man's fetid breath, Gil invited him to "Hop in," and asked Liam to move over and make room.

"Where you heading?" Gil asked.

"You goin' to Cooktown, brother?"

"No, I'm heading down to the beach."

"No worries, I'll come with yers."

As the Aboriginal man clambered up into the cab, Liam moved closer to his father.

"I'm Gil. This is my son Liam."

The stranger said nothing.

"Am I going in the right direction?" Gil asked, turning right on to what he supposed to be the beach road.

"Keep goin', brother."

In the gathering dusk, Gil found his way onto a sandy track. Through the open window he could smell the sea.

"You right?" the man said to Liam, who was clearly repelled by the man beside him. "You can call me Quinn."

"I think we'll camp here," Gil said, sensing his son's anxiety and wondering how they could best get rid of their passenger.

"Might be a better camp down there," Quinn said.

"Down where?"

Quinn nodded, as if to suggest Gil go further toward the sea.

Bone-weary and confused, Gil finally reversed into a small clearing among some pandanus palms and switched off the ignition.

Quinn had fallen into a deep sleep and was snoring. As Liam struggled to slide into the driver's seat and extricate himself from the camper van, Gil strolled about, kicking at the ground, looking for somewhere he could kindle a fire and cook their evening meal. He could hear the faint hiss of the ocean, but was disconcerted by the sudden darkness that made it difficult to see anything beyond the headlights of the vehicle.

In the morning Gil found Quinn fishing on the beach. The sky was sullen, waves flopped onto the lackluster sand, and when Gil asked Quinn what kind of fishing gear he used, the Aboriginal man tilted his chin toward the sea as if to intimate that the answer lay out there.

Gil stood awhile and watched. Quinn gently tugged the nylon line to and fro as if feeling for something beneath the surface. His eyes did not stray from the distant horizon where sky blurred into sea.

"I was going to ask if you were related to Toby or Doughboy," Gil said.

"Which Toby?"

"How many are there?"

"Only one. That old Toby."

"Old Toby," Gil echoed. "Do you happen to know Old Toby's father's name?"

"You'd have to ask him."

"My grandfather used to live here. If this is the Toby I am looking for, his father was called Billy and he worked for my grandfather."

"Oh yeah."

Gil was resigned to the interrogation going no further. He trudged back up the shelving beach and joined his son.

"What do you want for breakfast?" he asked Liam.

"Can I have some corn flakes?"

"Corn flakes I didn't get. How about muesli and fruit?"

"But I always have corn flakes."

"I'll buy some when we go to Bulbul."

"And don't forget the peanut butter."

"I won't forget."

Rather than hail Quinn, Gil got in the camper van, switched on the ignition, and waited while Quinn hauled in his line, walked barefoot up the beach, and climbed in beside Liam without a word. Quinn smelled like seawater and charcoal. He appeared to have retreated into his shell, like a hermit crab.

"Does Old Toby live at Bulbul?" Gil ventured, not taking his eyes off the track along which the camper van lurched.

"Might be there, might be down at the river," Quinn said.

"Would you be able to show me his house?"

"You goin' to the store, brother?" Quinn asked.

"I will be, in due course."

"I've run out of smokes."

"You want me to buy you some?"

Gil felt he was getting the hang of things. No direct questions. Cast your thoughts into the wind, then bide your time, waiting for the wind to shift and bring back an answer. Or not, as the case may be.

In this instance, a packet of cigarettes seemed to do the trick, and once back in the camper van Quinn nodded toward the river.

"Down there?" Gil queried.

Quinn simply waved his hand, indicating directions—the gravel road leading to the ford, a track that branched off it and ran parallel to the river.

Only as they neared the water did Gil see the dilapidated jetty, and the shed among the black wattles.

"Where we going?" Liam asked.

"Hopefully to see this Old Toby."

"Might not be here," Quinn said, peering out the window. He had his arm draped over the door panel, and a cigarette smoldered between his stained fingers.

As if Toby's evident absence ended any obligation he had to the white-fellas, Quinn got down from the camper van and wandered off toward the water.

Gil waited, but Quinn clearly wasn't going to help with introductions to the elderly man in a grimy T-shirt and frayed bell-bottoms who hobbled out of the shed, squinting into the sun.

Gil came straight to the point.

"Are you Toby?"

"Who wants to know?"

"My grandfather lived around here many years ago, and a man called Billy worked for him. Billy had a son called Toby. I was wondering if that was you."

"Yeah?"

"I hoped you might be able to show me the place where my grandfather lived."

"That's not 'round here."

"Where then?"

In the same manner as Quinn, Toby pursed his lips, stuck out his lower jaw, and pointed north.

"Could you take me there?"

Toby glanced toward Quinn, standing by the river with his back turned to them.

"What you doin' with that bloke?" he asked Gil.

"He helped me find you."

"Did he now?" Then Toby shouted at the top of his lungs, "Quinn! You fuckin' mongrel. Come 'ere."

Despite the uncouth summons, Quinn sauntered toward them, smoke curling across his face.

"You want to mind your own business, you dopey cunt! Now clear off!"

Quinn's eyes were on the ground. He climbed back into the camper van like a whipped dog, followed by Liam, while a nonplussed Gil thanked Toby for talking to them before driving off.

"What was all that about?" he asked Quinn.

"Bama way, if you go to another fella's camp you got to wait till he asks you to come close. You can't go first. You gotta wait."

"Is that why you went down to the river?"

"You can't be cheeky. You gotta show respect."

"Respect? He wasn't very respectful of you."

Quinn did not answer.

The following day, Gil and Liam drove back to Toby's shed, this time parking some distance off and biding their time in the hope that the old man would come out and greet them.

They waited an hour.

"How does he know we're here?" Liam asked.

"He knows."

"How long do we have to wait?"

"Maybe he's punishing us for our rudeness yesterday. Maybe he wants to show us who's boss."

Gil and Liam were finally invited, albeit grudgingly, into Toby's one-room corrugated iron shed. Soiled sacks covered the dirt floor. There was a narrow cot, a small wooden table, and two rail chairs. Toby did all his cooking under a lean-to outside.

Gil sat with Liam standing warily beside him. Toby sat opposite, deftly rolling a cigarette. Gil wanted to say something, but after yesterday's exchanges he decided on silence.

"That's goin' a long way back," Toby said.

"Yes. My father would have been about the same age as my son back then."

"Longa time back."

"Do you remember Mick? Or his father, Jeremiah?"

"Yeah, I remember."

"My father said you used to play together a lot."

"Where's that Mick now?"

"He died a couple of years ago."

Toby lit his cigarette for the second time, squinted, but said nothing. Gil waited.

"Might be my blimmin' time, comin' up now," Toby said.

"He hadn't been well," Gil said, "after my mother died."

"I last saw 'im, what was it, nineteen—"

"It would have been around 1938–39. Just before the war."

"My dad worked for that old digger. That Jeremiah."

Gil's heart missed a beat. It was as if an old book had fallen open at the right page, yielding an arcane fact he had never dared imagine he might track down.

"That was my grandfather."

"So Mick bin pass away, you say?"

"Yes, a couple of years ago."

Another long pause, but this time, Gil broke the silence, and asked after Toby's brother Doughboy.

"He shot through."

"When was that?"

"Longa time back."

As alcohol had loosened Quinn's tongue, so landscape loosened Toby's. But it took three days before the old man was ready to accompany Gil to Rattlesnake Point, and the best part of two hours for Gil, Liam, and Quinn to accompany him there on foot.

No one spoke. Exhausted waves collapsed on the beach and quickly sank into it. The gray day dragged. Liam scribbled random faces along the tide line with a stick, or erased the pellet-like patterns produced by sand bubbler crabs. He liked the way his bare feet squeaked on the hard sand. Toby stopped often to catch his breath. Quinn, who Gil had discovered was Toby's grandson, scanned the waves for stingrays.

Where the beach came up against the headland, a braided stream trickled across the ribbed sand. Toby said it used to be much deeper and the current much swifter when he was a boy. Bush clearing and tin mining inland had silted up the stream.

"Is this Fritz Creek?" Gil asked, thinking this must have been where Jeremiah and his family drew their drinking water.

"We call 'im Marbaymba."

Gil wondered why no emotions were stirred in him as he stood at the probable spot where Siobhan died. Perhaps it was because no physical trace remained that the event was remembered without any feeling, in the same way that the name of the creek had lost its power to evoke the person who gave it its name.

Gil asked if they could wade across.

Toby shook his head.

"He boss for that place," Quinn explained. "That's his story place, right there."

When Toby wandered off, inspecting the ground for the spoor of animals, Quinn told Gil that when Toby's father Billy was a boy, he'd broken a taboo by catching a stingray near the mouth of the creek. Although it was winter when ordinarily no rain fell, a torrential downpour flooded the hinterland, sweeping away all the bama camps.

Gil shuddered.

"Maybe my grandfather did something wrong by camping here."

"I reckon he didn't know."

"But did Billy know not to catch stingrays here?"

"Maybe he used the wrong bait," Quinn said.

"What kind of wrong bait?"

"You gotta keep freshwater and saltwater things apart. You mix 'em up, you'll get that big flood. Like when you marry wrong way, or you not serious with your in-laws."

Gil looked at the scrub-covered headland that had suddenly become a place to avoid. And he thought of himself as embarked on a pilgrimage à rebours, in which one journeys away from, rather than toward, a potential source of transformative power.

When they turned back along the beach, each with his incommunicable thoughts, Gil did not think, I have come all this way for nothing; rather, I have done what I set out to do and there is nothing more to be done.

As they approached the mangroves that lay parallel to the shore, memory seemed to rejuvenate Toby. No longer limping, he moved rapidly up the sandy slope and disappeared into the swamp.

"Goin' for darkay," Quinn said.

Soon Toby returned, grinning from ear to ear, his arms cradling a dozen mud clams. He indicated to Liam that they were for him.

"Make you strong," Toby exclaimed. "Us kids used to come here," and he enjoined Gil and Liam to follow him to the tide line, where he waded into the sea and proceeded to wash his mud-caked arms and hands and feet. "Mick'd come, too," he said. "Doughboy. All them fellas. All our mob."

Toby also recalled the 1960s, when hundreds of hippies invaded the area. Toby had a boat and outboard in those days, and used to take the hippies from Bulbul, down the river, and along the coast to Cedar Bay where they'd make their camps and smoke weed. One man wanted to go to Rattlesnake Point. Toby warned him away, but the hippie persisted. He wanted to test his mettle. He returned half crazy. "Too much force there," Toby said cryptically. "Even for whitefellas."

Liam was impatient to get back to the camper van and cook the mud clams Toby had given him, but Gil was unaccountably tired, as if he had exchanged his forty-year-old body for Toby's seventy-year-old one. When they finally returned to the vehicle, he could hardly bring himself to show Toby the photos of Weary Bay in the 1920s that he'd acquired from a Brisbane archive. In one, a skiff was riding at anchor off Rattlesnake Point; in another a group of Aboriginals was gathered near the sugar mill, lithe muscular bodies, men, women, and children apparently in their element. Gil asked Toby if he could identify anyone.

Toby took a long hard look, turning the photo this way and that as if he found difficulty in focusing the images.

"This not our mob," he said.

"No one you know?"

"Might be some."

Toby handed the photo back to Gil and turned his head away, looking back along the beach toward Rattlesnake Point. Gil did not trouble him. He'd seen the same reaction with Quinn. As if there were questions that pushed too violently against the doors of memory, or rubbed salt into old wounds, and were best answered with silence.

Bulbul

Two days later, Toby guided Gil up a steep, eroded track and onto the scrub-clad plateau where Jeremiah and Mary Argyle had scratched a living sixty years ago.

This time, Toby held nothing back. As Gil wrestled with the wheel and the camper van skidded from rut to rut, Toby blurted out fragments of Billy's story as if the father's shade was dictating it to his mesmerized son. Unable to take notes, Gil had to find excuses to stop the vehicle and hurry off into the scrub, allegedly for a piss but actually to scribble a surreptitious memo. He would write a cogent version that night, after Liam had fallen asleep, though it would take several days more of checking with Toby before he was confident that he had completed Billy's saga.

Much of what Toby told him corroborated what he already knew. Billy's father was a white man called Roscoe, who had deserted Billy's mother then formed an alliance with an Aboriginal man who beat and abused the boy. Billy sought refuge with his grandmother "out in the bush." When she moved closer to kin camped on the plateau, Billy worked as a roustabout and houseboy with Fergus and Fiona. Following the departure of the O'Dochertys, Billy became the right-hand man to Fergus that Jeremiah was supposed to have been. An indefatigable scrub cutter and stockman, Billy was largely responsible for the success of Fergus's renewed venture into cattle ranching. Doughboy, on the other hand, elected to attach himself to the mission before disappearing one day, never to return to Bulbul. It was rumored that he died of an opium overdose in Cairns.

Sometime in the early 1940s, Billy (now married to Grace) moved to Daintree, hoping to find contract work as a scrub cutter and make some money (Fergus had only recompensed his Aboriginal workers with tea, sugar, and flour). Though the going rate was ten quid an hour, Billy was paid much less, and his ability to move quickly to a new work site was hindered by the police enforcement of the Aboriginals Protection Act, which stipulated that Aboriginals could not freely negotiate work or working conditions with European employers, but had to be assigned. Rather than face arrest, Billy returned to Bulbul and petitioned the Lutheran missionaries to secure an exemption from the act. In 1945 (Toby remembered the date because it coincided with the ending of the Pacific war), Billy acquired title to a small block of land along the Bloomfield River. Despite the opposition of white selectors to Aboriginals owning land, Billy persisted with his plan to grow fruit and vegetables, and, like his erstwhile bosses, sell the produce on the Cairns market. But no one would truck or ship his goods to Cairns, and the mission refused to do business with him. Billy and Grace wound up isolated on a parcel of land that other bama families claimed to be ancestrally theirs.

"My father died of a broken heart," Toby told Gil, who would later interpret the remark in his own way. "Billy tried to ford the river between white and black worlds at its shallowest point," Gil wrote in his journal, "only to be washed into deep water by the flash floods of resentment and prejudice, whether these came from his own kind or from whites. Like my father, except my father had a chance to cross the river, but chose to stay on the other side."

The track was now so deeply rutted that Gil was doubtful the camper van would be capable of getting them to where they wanted to go. He also wondered whether Toby would be able to locate the old homestead. Unkempt grass lashed the door panels of the camper van, saplings whipped against the chassis, and Liam, who had been holding his camera up to his face and surveying the landscape through its lens, cried out as the jolting vehicle rammed the viewfinder into his face. Gil glanced at him. Liam gingerly tested to see if the accident had drawn blood, while Toby stretched out an arm to steady him.

"You right?" Toby asked.

"I'm fine," Liam said.

Gil was surprised by his son's resilience. Since leaving Cairns, he had expressed few qualms at being forced to accompany his father on what Maya had called a wild goose chase, and he had shown no signs of homesickness. Perhaps it is because we are so utterly disconnected from our real lives, Gil thought. As if we have died to all that we were. Perhaps this is why I don't miss Maya, or even Hannah, and have not given a moment's thought to my job. It has all been placed in abeyance, as if this journey to this remote place has corrupted memory and arrested the passage of time.

In the rain forest, however, time had not stood still. No vestige could be found of the homestead, or of the house Jeremiah had built with Billy's help. Regenerating bush covered the clearings where goats had wandered and cattle later grazed. The split-rail fences had disappeared, corrugated iron sheets removed, metal objects buried or rusted away, and packsaddles, hobbles, bridles, and halters reduced to dust. Toby pushed his way through the scrub, inspecting the ground. Lawyer vines snatched at him, and the stench of crushed lantana offended his nostrils. He found the spoor of a snake, wallaby droppings, but no souvenir that he might offer Liam to confirm their affinity. As for Gil, he was not surprised that nature had so completely reclaimed its domain, and instead of disappointment he felt relief and resignation. No ghostly voice summoned him, no filial obligation bound him to this place, no interrupted story cried out for completion, no broken circle demanded to be closed. In fact, he thought, there may come a time when every trace of settler culture will be swept away and the original people of the land find themselves the sole survivors and revert to hunting and gathering, respecting the seasonal taboos that protected certain plants and animals from overexploitation, recovering the ritual usages and entrenched beliefs that enabled them to reach the same kind of truce with their ancestors that he had sought with his.

Toby

Following their return from the plateau, Toby suggested that Gil might want to move from Weary Bay and park his camper van on the river flat near his shed. "I'm easy anyway," he said, as if needing to disavow his own words. "If you stay there or come here, 's all the same to me."

Gil thought it would be a good idea. He could supplement his store-bought food by fishing for river cod and accepting Toby's offer of corn, beans, and Chinese cabbage from his garden; Liam would be able to play with Toby's grandsons. Though Liam asked his father when they'd be going home, he seemed reconciled to staying. As for Gil, he was in a quandary. He knew he wasn't going to find any traces of his grandparents' lives, and could only guess how his father's childhood experiences at Bulbul affected his later life. But Toby intrigued him. Why would he invite two white strangers to share his camp and the resources of his garden? And why did he live outside the pale, as much a stranger to his kith and kin, it seemed, as to the mission? Was it really because he could not stand the drunken raillery and ceaseless fighting, or had he been ostracized?

The old Aboriginal man would spend hours sitting on a log under the mango tree that shaded his shed, gazing at the river or the casuarinas on the opposite bank as if keeping some kind of mandatory vigil. Nor could Gil explain the uncanny sense of sympathy and synchrony that seemed to have developed between Toby and Liam. Even though they seldom sat together, Liam also gave the impression of waiting and watching. As the Aboriginal kids raced about, hurling spears and taunts, or throwing themselves into fist fights, Liam would keep track of them from the steps of the camper van, as if biding his time for the moment when he would join the fray, knowing exactly how to behave. Gil was reminded of the crocodile he had seen at the river mouth. Though inert on the sandbank, it was constantly on the alert, ready to hurl itself forward into the water and seize its prey.

"Liam's a bit shy," Gil explained to Toby, whom he had invited to share a cup of coffee with him in the camper van.

"I used to be too shy," Toby confessed. "Maybe that's why I hit the bottle."

"I don't see you as a drinker."

"Too much blimmin' trouble. That grog'll make you crazy. Make you do bad things."

Gil was well aware of this chaos. Drunks staggering down the night roads like aimless or angry ghosts. Rumors almost every day of a death. A woman who in a drunken rage had killed her husband with a kitchen knife. A young man drowned when he attempted to swim the river after a night's heavy drinking. Another thrown into the police lockup to sleep off the effects of a binge, but going berserk and taking his own life. "Too much shame," Toby said, recalling these deaths. "We got too much shame." In the face of this social mayhem and bitter memories of white violence, Toby appeared to find consolation in the rhythms of the natural world, and would eagerly respond to Gil's curiosity about the numerous correspondences between social and natural phenomena—a death presaged by a kookaburra's early morning cry, the ripening of the parcel apple signifying the best time to catch stingrays (whose flesh is also at its pinkest and tastiest at this time), and storms as vehicles of sorcery.

But it was Liam, not Gil, with whom Toby felt most at home. One afternoon, he called Liam over to where he had kindled a fire. He was heating a piece of ironwood root in the flames, and using his penknife to scrape off the black resin that oozed from the wood. Liam ran back to the camper van and fetched his camera.

Toby filled a Spam tin with water and set it on the fire. When the water came to the boil, he dropped the dark ironwood resin into it. Toby offered no commentary as he took the ball of black tar into the palm of his hand and began kneading it.

Though Gil was curious, and presumed Liam to be too, he held his tongue.

Toby went into his shed, and emerged with a spear and spear-thrower. Squatting by the fire, he began shaping the woomera with his penknife.

"Learned this from my dad," Toby said.

Using the tar, he deftly affixed a small peg to the woomera, and wound lawyer cane around it.

"What other things did your father teach you?" Liam asked.

"How to grow corn. Catch herrings for bait. Catch mullet. Get scrub hen eggs. Dig for mud clams. Too many things."

Gil wondered if Billy had also taught Mick these things, and whether his father's talent for woodwork derived as much from observing Billy as learning from Jeremiah. And once more, he was struck by this strange collapsing of time, this abolition of chronology that rendered the distant past more present than the events of only a few weeks ago.

Yet Toby was in touch with his own father in a way that Gil had never been with Mick. What work do I do that brings me close to him, he asked himself, or brings him to mind? Watching Toby harden his spear tip in the fire, Gil marveled that Toby had not made or used a spear since his father's death. Can mimesis alone explain this recurrence of a skill, this repetition of an action or a thought that is not mediated by conscious deliberation or memory?

Later that afternoon, Toby taught Liam how to throw a spear.

Gil watched as his son acquired the knack. Within an hour he was as accurate as his teacher.

"In those days, we were tough," Toby said, as if remembering a time long before he was born when bama hunted for game in the rain forests and fish in the river, using such spears. "We soft now. Too much whitefella food, too much grog, too much sittin' 'round."

But Toby's idealization of the past was not what it seemed. Gil had noticed the old man's frequent disorientation. Groping for a mug of tea that was clearly within reach. Walking away from his shed instead of toward it. Seeming oblivious to Gil, who was standing a yard away, but responding immediately if Gil spoke.

Toby needed cataract surgery. The diagnosis had been made a year ago, but the old man had refused treatment. Gil discovered this when he took Liam to the local clinic for an ointment to treat the rash that was still bothering him.

"These old men are very pig-headed," the nurse told Gil. "They're too ashamed to admit they can't cut the mustard anymore."

Gil insisted Toby go to Cooktown Hospital to have his cataracts removed. "I'll take you. Liam will come with us."

Toby was afraid that admission to the hospital would be the end of him. Although a recluse, the idea of being cut off from his community rattled him. And though unfazed by the prospect of death, the thought of dying in a hospital terrified him.

"Liam and I will stay close for as long as you need us," Gil said. "You'll be fine."

"Nothin' wrong with my eyesight."

"It's a simple operation," Gil assured him. "You need your eyesight. You need to see clearly."

"I'm not soft."

"No," Gil said. "That's why you can do this hard thing and get your eyes fixed."

Gil might have been talking to his father.

In any event, it was Liam who brought calm to Toby, not Gil. Liam stood beside the old man, who was lying on his back, incongruous in his hospital gown, wearing a stained and battered Stetson that he refused to remove.

When Liam gently lifted the Stetson from Toby's grizzled head and set it down on the bedside table, Toby grinned, touched by the innocence of Liam's gesture or amused by its incongruity. Gil was moved by his son's compassion, and for a split second rebuked himself for never having reached out to his father, never fully realizing that the man who tormented him was himself tormented.

"The child is father to the man," Gil murmured, though neither Toby nor Liam heard him.

Toby drained the tumbler of water that Liam gave him, and turned his gaze on Gil.

"You leave any water outside your camper van?"

"I don't think so."

"Them, whatchamacallem spirits, might come lookin' for a drink, and make trouble."

"What spirits?"

"Might be anyone."

Though perplexed, Gil and Liam were soon ushered from the ward by an irritated matron, and told not to come back until visiting hours tomorrow.

After checking into a guest house on the main street, father and son bought hamburgers and French fries from a local café and sat together on a bench, eating in silence. A young Aboriginal man walked by, with a young woman following him at a safe distance, muttering, "Fuckin' docile, me? Fuckin' docile, me!" The man seemed not to hear her. Raising her voice, she repeated the phrase. The man stopped. Gil anticipated an ugly scene, but as the woman approached the man, he put his arm around her shoulder, and they walked on together. Gil was touched, and imagined himself stopped on a street somewhere and Maya catching up with him and putting her arm around his shoulders.

As he and Liam continued their take-out meal, a white guy in singlet, frayed jeans, and flip-flops sat down next to them. He was soon joined by an Aboriginal girl who had just bought a pack of Winfield cigarettes in the café. "Don't you go givin' any of those cigs away," he ordered. "You get your brothers and sisters to fuckin' buy their own." His girlfriend assured him she would. "I get sick of people comin' up to me saying, 'Heh, you my cousin, you my sister.' I tell 'em, 'I work for my living, you fuckin' well work for yours.'" Gil wondered what kind of work she did, and again he was overwhelmed with a desire to see Maya.

When Liam asked for an ice cream, Gil gave him some money and reminded himself to withdraw more from an ATM. It was only then that he realized why he had been thinking of Maya. He'd promised to phone her. He made a quick calculation. Two p.m. in Cooktown, so it would be 4:00 p.m. in New Zealand. He remembered passing a phone box not far from the hospital. When Liam sauntered out of the café, Gil told him they were going to drive to a phone box and call Maya and Hannah.

"Why can't you use your cell phone?" Liam asked.

"Battery's almost dead."

Gil drove back toward the hospital and found the phone box, but it was out of order, and there was only enough life in his cell phone for a quick call. All he had to do was punch in the numbers. Why was he hesitating?

He dialed, and passed the phone to Liam. "You talk first. Tell mummy we're fine, and we'll call again when we get back to Bulbul."

He listened as his son stumbled over his words, sharing all that he had seen and done since leaving Cairns.

"Tell Mummy the phone's about to die," Gil said.

Liam rambled on, as if trying to press a lifetime of experience into two fading minutes.

When the call was over, Liam gave the phone back to his father.

"What did she say?" he asked.

"She said to take care."

"Anything else? Did she send any message to me?"

"She just told us to take care."

Toby was discharged the following afternoon. He was disappointed not to be able to see clearly, but Gil had spoken to the surgeon and was told it would take several days before Toby would discern any significant improvement in his eyesight. In the meantime, Gil would administer the eye drops they'd been given, and Toby should keep a plastic patch over his eyes and lie low.

Given that Toby had half expected never to leave the hospital alive, he was only too happy to follow Gil's directions, and even to eat some of the food Gil cooked that evening over his Primus stove.

"My sons should be taking care of me," Toby said as he clumsily forked the pasta into his mouth.

Within minutes of finishing his meal and brushing his teeth, Liam turned in, while Gil walked Toby to his shed. The sun was melting into the inland range. He could feel the rivers' stealthy presence, and was strangely comforted by Toby's presence, as if the old man was guiding him through the dying light.

After Gil had rekindled Toby's fire, the two men sat in silence under the lean-to, watching tongues of flame devour the triangle of sticks Gil had built over them. He knew that Toby's sons were dead but had never gone fishing for details. Now, in the intimacy of the fire, Toby confided that his first son, Cedric, had been obsessed with motorbikes. Though no one at Bulbul owned one, whitefellas sometimes came through the settlement, revving their angry machines and doing wheelies in the main street before disappearing down the narrow road to the north. Their black leather and insignias, the collective roar of the machines as they kicked up dust and skidded on the loose gravel, captured Cedric's imagination, and Toby knew it was only a matter time before his son would get a bike in the only way he could—by stealing it. It happened in Mossman. Cedric somehow succeeded in kick-starting the bike, hit the road, and drove straight into an oncoming car. He was killed instantly. "Clarrie went the same way," Toby said. "Only he hit the grog, and got into dope. Most of the time, you never got a word out of 'im. But when the dope ran out he'd go crazy." One night, Clarrie climbed the bell tower at the mission and hanged himself with the studded leather belt he'd inherited from his older brother.

"Did you have other children?" Gil asked.

"Maudie shot through after that."

"Maudie was your wife?"

Toby did not answer. His face was in shadow. Flames from the campfire flickered in the plastic window plastered over his eyes. The river slipped by in the darkness.

When he returned to the camper van, Gil sat at the small folding table, his back turned to his sleeping son, and began writing in his journal. "Driving back from Cooktown, we passed a mountain of granite stones. When I asked Toby about it, he said, 'Kalkajaka,' as if naming it enabled him to put it from his mind. When I pressed him to tell me if it was a story place, he said that the mountain was dangerous. You could get lost there, or fall to your death among the stones."

Gil became haunted by images of petrification. Toby had described people stuck between an irrecoverable past and an inaccessible future. Immobilized in present time, cursed by the empirical present. Grog and dope, the fever pitch of a fistfight, a one-night stand, the transitory high of a poker game, offered only momentary respite. The impact of Toby's story, coupled with the drunken mayhem of Bulbul, the darkness pierced with catcalls and uncouth challenges, the day deceiving calm when people slept off the excesses of the night, or played cards for articles of clothing in lieu of cash, or aimlessly roamed the streets, persuaded Gil that he was witness to the aftermath of a catastrophe that had left its survivors unhinged and dislocated. The dead had become wraiths, vainly attempting to goad the bereaved back to life, though the only semblance of life was what a besotted mind, a broken body might recognize . . . a febrile agitation, a voice heard from across a turbid river, a mysterious light in the darkness, or a violent video flickering on a TV screen as campfires had once flickered in forest clearings or along the coast. The difference between the Holocaust and what had happened here seemed merely a difference in the degree of its organization, the intensity of its collective effort, and the relative smallness of the population that had to be swept from the land in order for the invaders to settle and farm it at will.

One night he walked along the river alone, imagining that the fireflies in the lank grass embodied the souls of the dead, moving fitfully and ineluctably to their final resting place, destined to lodge like engrams in the brain, buried or brought back into the light of day depending on someone's needs in the here and now. But unlike the river, human lives flowed on without beginning or end. Our only awareness is that time passes, and the only truly infallible memories are not the ones we bear in mind, but those that have impressed themselves on our bodies and souls and will in time be impressed on the bodies and souls of those who follow us.

When Gil asked Toby why he had shown such kindness to two white strangers, given that whites had been so callous and cruel to bama in the past, Toby pretended not to understand the question.

"I mean, why should you invite us to camp near your shed, giving us vegetables and fruit from your garden, showing Liam how to catch mullet and river cod—"

"Your dad and me were mates," Toby said. "Your grandfather treated my father fair and square."

"I wish my father could have met you again."

"Your little boy's his spitting image."

Now it was Gil's turn to appear perplexed.

"My grandsons don't want to know anything I can teach 'em. They don't wanna learn. Grow up, get some grog, chuck it in, that's their way."

Yet Liam was spending more and more time with Toby's grandsons, fishing and even fighting with them. Indeed, when Liam belted a boy who'd been bullying him, Toby was filled with pride. "He standing up for 'imself now," he told Gil, whose only concern was that Liam was unscathed and that there would be no repercussions from the bully's parents.

But the danger that lay in wait for Liam was not in Bulbul but the bush.

When a boy called Llewelyn ran breathless into Toby's camp one morning and Toby shouted to Gil to come quick, Gil's first thought was that Liam had got himself into trouble on the river.

It was much worse. Liam had stepped on a death adder as he climbed over a fallen log in a grove of paper barks.

His heart pounding, Gil urged the panting Aboriginal boy to take him to Liam.

Soon, there was no need to follow his befuddled guide. He could hear Liam's screams.

Whether Liam had been paralyzed by fear or venom, Gil did not know. But he did know what to do. Pulling his T-shirt over his head, and for a moment imagining this was happening in some B-grade movie, he tore the shirt into strips and tied a tourniquet around Liam's thigh.

"You'll be fine, you'll be fine."

The pain was so intense that Liam could not speak. He was beginning to foam at the mouth, and had difficulty catching his breath.

"Here, now," Gil said, hoisting Liam onto his shoulders.

Llewelyn watched from a distance as the white man stumbled, recovered his footing, and began trotting back to his grandfather's camp.

Later Gil would ask himself how he managed to carry his son's dead weight that half mile to the camper van, and drive at breakneck speed to the clinic at Bulbul where his frantic calls brought both nurses to his aid.

One of them inspected the wound, while the other telephoned Cooktown for a helicopter ambulance.

"I think it was a death adder," Gil said.

The sister did not need to know. Within minutes she had administered a generic antivenin and swaddled Liam in a blanket.

Gil held Liam's hand, as Liam had held Old Toby's, while his panic-stricken son vomited and sobbed.

Then the helicopter was thudding north along the coast, Rattlesnake Point below them and inland the ominous bulk of Black Mountain.

In his son's ashen face, Gil saw death. Grasping Liam's hand, he willed his own life into him. The paramedic assured him that his son would be all right. The vomiting was a reaction to the neurotoxins.

But when Gil looked into Liam's terrified face, he rejected the assurances.

Time hung fire. Glancing at his watch, Gil was surprised to see that it was past midnight. Having received a second shot of death adder antivenin, Liam now lay sound asleep in intensive care.

Slipping noiselessly from his son's bedside, Gil crept out into a corridor and phoned Maya.

"He's going to be fine," he said, after explaining what had happened.

"What do you mean fine?"

"He's in good hands. It's been a shock. But he's going to be fine."

"I can't believe you let something like this happen."

"I didn't let anything happen."

"Then how did he come to be bitten by a deadly snake?"

"It was an accident."

"Why weren't you with him? Why weren't you watching him?"

"You can't keep your eyes on a nine-year-old boy every minute of the day. He was with some mates, playing in the bush."

"What mates?"

"Some local kids he's gotten to know."

"Aboriginal kids?"

"Maya, he's going to be all right. No one was to blame. You can't even see these snakes. They're disguised as dead leaves. They don't move away when they hear you coming. They're not like other snakes."

There was a long silence. Gil thought Maya had decided not to talk to him, or was preparing another salvo of recriminations.

"When will you come home?"

"As soon as he's out of hospital. A couple of days, they say. But if he's up to it I'd like to take him out on a trip to Great Barrier Reef. It's something I promised him weeks ago."

"Isn't that dangerous? Weren't a young couple left stranded there last year, and drowned?"

"I don't know, Maya. But I promised him. I'm sure it'll be safe. And then we'll come home."

Maya did not ask about his research. But he asked about her writing.

"It's been slow going," she said. "I worry about Liam. But Hannah's been a wonderful companion. I think she realizes how much hangs on this for me."

"That's good to hear."

"Will you call me again when Liam's awake? I'd like to talk to him."

"Of course. He'll want to talk to you, too."

"No matter what time it is, just call. I don't think I'll sleep tonight anyway."

"You know you've got nothing to worry about."

"Easy for you to say that, Gil. But I do worry. Just call me, all right?"

"I'll call you."

When Liam was discharged from the hospital, Gil managed to hitch a ride back to Bulbul with a middle-aged nurse, who was curious to know what Gil and Liam were doing at Bulbul.

"Some relatives of mine used to live there," Gil said.

"And you've been visiting them?"

"No, they used to live there. About sixty years ago."

Nurse Batten found this very odd. But her curiosity was piqued.

"But if they're not living there now, who are you staying with?"

"We've been camping with an Aboriginal man who knew my father."

Though aware that further prying might seem rude, the nurse could not help herself.

"Your father was an Aboriginal?"

In exasperation, Gil said yes.

"Well, if you don't mind me saying so, you don't look like an Aboriginal."

"No, I pass for white."

"But your son—"

"He passes too."

The nurse retreated, her knuckles white on the steering wheel of the Land Cruiser.

"And now you're on your way home?" she sneered.

"More or less."

"Do we have to go home?" Liam asked.

"That's strange, coming from you. I thought you couldn't wait to get home."

"School doesn't start for a month," Liam said. "Can't we stay till then?"

"You want to watch out he doesn't take off and go walkabout," the nurse said.

"We're both going walkabout," Gil said. "We're heading to Port Douglas tomorrow. I've promised to take Liam out to the Great Barrier Reef."

"What reef?" Nurse Batten asked. "Haven't you heard it's dead?"

"I thought only parts were affected."

"You're welcome to go and see, but the coral's bleached to buggery, and the crown-of-thorns starfish is eating whatever the bloody pollutants haven't killed off."

The Reef

Driving south, they stopped at Cape Tribulation where Gil explained to Liam that Cook gave the cape its name as he and his crew struggled north, searching for somewhere to run their ship ashore, then build a smaller vessel from her timbers and sail to the East Indies.

"Why the East Indies?" Liam asked. "Why not England?"

"Because they did not believe they would find a safe harbor where they could repair the *Endeavour*, and they did not know at that point whether the ship could even be repaired."

After letting Liam absorb this grim information, Gil added, "Imagine if we got stranded here and could never go home."

Liam turned his troubled face to his father.

"But we are going home," he said, oppressed by the cane fields through which they now drove, with their narrow-gauge railway tracks, wagons filled with cane stalks in dead-end sidings, and the stench of burned or fermented sugar.

He thought of Toby's lean-to under the black wattles, the Torres Strait pigeons winging their way toward the open sea at dusk, the river slipping by in the night, fireflies like fallen stars in the buffalo grass. It pained him that he would never see Toby again.

That night, with their mud-caked camper van anomalous in the spick-and-span Tropical Breezes holiday park, Gil and Liam got their first sound night's sleep in three days.

But Gil was in for a rude awakening—Destiny's Child on a blaring radio, and the aggressive friendliness of the holiday makers around the breeze-block changing rooms, marked Tarzan and Jane.

Toweling himself dry after a hot shower, he was assailed by a young man in an Australian Drinking Champion T-shirt, who drunkenly challenged Gil to define the difference between truth and belief.

Gil ignored him.

"Nah, fuck everything else, tell the truth. . . . True or wrong. You tell me, mate. I believe what I believe."

"Good on ya," Gil said, summoning the argot he'd learned in his father's mill. Was this idiot showing the effects of a bender last night or had he achieved this state this morning?

"Where you from, then?"

"My son and I have been in Bulbul. You know it?"

"Bull what?"

"Bulbul. It's an Aboriginal settlement up north."

Why is everyone so curious to know where I'm from? Gil wondered. Or is this par for the course, an Aussie way of initiating conversation? It was impossible to know whether one had to submit to being ear-bashed or expected to participate in a conversation.

Out of the blue, the Australian Drinking Champion asked, "Have you ever in your life turned away sex?"

"What?"

"You ever turned down an offer of sex?"

"Sure."

"Yeah?"

As Gil moved to go, his interlocutor felt his way toward an empty shower cubicle.

To what historical source, Gil wondered, could these uncouth phrases be traced? Blacks and whites alike seem to have been so hammered by history that they now seek only to protect themselves against further disaster, talking past each other, withdrawing into their shells, their opinions so final, their judgments so absolute, that they invite no response. How can children endure these walls that shut them out, or break down the walls that shut them in? Gil realized that this was his parents and grandparent's world into which he had been momentarily and accidentally borne, a world from which he now felt liberated.

When he returned to the camper van, Liam was awake, listening to the trilling insects, and the whooping, squeaking, and gulping of birds. Gil asked Liam if he could identify any of the birds by their calls.

"Some I can," Liam said. And he mentioned the bowerbirds, honey-eaters, wagtails, Torres Strait pigeons, and wrens that Toby had told him the names of.

"I've got photos of them, too," Liam said.

"Can I see?"

As Gil scrolled through the camera's store of images, he came across the photos he took of Liam proudly holding up the mullet he'd caught, and was suddenly moved by the memory of that afternoon when he told his son that he had been able to do what he, his father, had never done. Then, as he scrolled on, Gil was astonished to see that he figured in several photos that he had been unaware of Liam taking.

"Am I a bird?" he joked.

"No, Dad. You're a bunyip!"

The trip to the reef was as unsettling as his morning trip to the shower house. Among the last to board the catamaran, Gil and Liam found seats next to a middle-aged couple impatiently waiting for the buffet to open. Both had been drinking heavily, Betty inconspicuously sipping port from a silver goblet, Bill swigging beer from a plastic cup. The young man sitting next to Bill was apparently his son, Matthew.

"Say gidday, Matthew," Bill ordered.

Clearly embarrassed by his parents, Matthew looked toward the distant horizon.

"Whatya reckon?" Bill asked Liam.

"It's pretty cool," Liam said, clicking his camera.

"Look!" Bill shouted. "What's that?"

Gil pretended not to have heard the question.

"I think it's a fishing boat," Liam ventured.

"Betcha there's a few biggies out there, eh, Bill?" Betty said, before realizing her hubby had suddenly dozed off. "Bill, you asleep?" Receiving no response, she turned to Gil. "Silly old duffer. But I love 'im. Yes, believe it or not, I love 'im." Leaning sideways, she smacked an expressive kiss on Bill's washboard temple.

When they reached the reef, the tourists were given flippers and snorkels and ushered into glass-bottomed boats.

Gil might have found satisfaction in seeing that at least one section of the reef was unpolluted and intact, but his mind was on the vastness of the sea.

As if reading his father's thoughts, Liam asked what would happen if the catamaran returned to Port Douglas without them. Before Gil could assure his son that this could not happen, Liam had slipped over the side of the boat. Quickly adjusting his snorkel and face mask, he dived into the translucent depths.

Gil hesitated to follow. Even when Liam surfaced and called for his father to join him, Gil said he would wait for the crowds to disperse. "It's incredible," Liam said. "There's fish everywhere!" And he dived again, so wholly in his element that for as long as he held his breath and remained underwater, his father ceased to exist.

The Return

Far below them in the darkness, Gil makes out the pollen smudges and pallid thumbprints of small towns, stars fallen to earth and splayed on impact, vaguely glowing in the aftermath. Trembling at the thought of seeing Maya, Gil tried to assure himself that he was returning neither to her nor to his old life. Liam was fast asleep, head against his father's shoulder, as Gil again gazed down at the scattered embers of towns and the pitch-black landscape surrounding them.

It was after midnight when the taxi brought them to their destination. Spectral in the streetlight, the house seemed bereft of life. Gil inhaled the warm night air and was aware of the subdued trilling of crickets as Liam ran headlong toward the front door. As the taxi glided away into the night, Gil lugged the first of their suitcases up the steps to where Maya was standing gowned in the doorway like a ghost. He looked on as mother and son became one body, Maya's dark, uncombed hair cascading over the child who was already regaling her with stories of the perils he had survived, the places he had been. Then Maya lifted her head and looked at Liam's father, who was standing on the broken concrete path not knowing what to do or say.

"Thank goodness you're back," Maya said.

Gil dragged the suitcases up the steps as Maya and Liam retreated into the house.

"Where's Hannah?"

"She tried to stay up. She was so excited about seeing you," Maya said, pulling her robe around her. "You must both be hungry."

"We ate on the plane," Liam said.

"And I better be getting back," Gil said.

"Can't you stay?" Liam said.

Gil looked at Maya. "It's good to see you," he said.

"It's good to see you, too."

"How's your writing going?"

"It's gone. I sent it off last week. Now it's fingers crossed."

"I'm happy for you," he said.

"Don't be a stranger, Gil," Maya said, as he turned to go.

"I'll see you tomorrow."

"How will you get back to your place?" she called.

"I'll walk," he said.

"With that suitcase? Why don't you take the car? Bring it back in the morning. Come for breakfast. That way you can see Hannah. And we'll also have a chance to talk."

It is like a single camera shot, sustained for how long he cannot determine. All night or for only a split second, as if in a dream, it pans over a broad river, slipping by in the warm darkness. A fragile jetty suddenly collapses into the stream and is instantly swept away. He glimpses Toby on the sea-slicked sand near Fritz Creek. Then a grove of black wattles. Then the soft scales of a paper bark morphs into the scales of a rock cod. The scales adhere to the backs of his hands and forearms as he cleans and guts the fish. A whiff of woodsmoke. Fingers engrained with ash. Calloused hands. Mist ghosting the surface of the river as he wakes, opens the flimsy door of the camper van, and walks through the dew-drenched grass to where he will relieve himself and tilt his head back, looking for the morning star. Now he is moving like a revenant through the streets of Moabite, that familiar world smaller than he remembers it, at once less monstrous and less momentous, like the first love he hankered for, that stunning beauty destined to go to seed in the fields of time, all that yearning and dreaming withering away like tares on the roadside, or like the guilt he felt at leaving home, as if his departure foreshadowed his mother's death, or began her slow decline. As if in slow motion he inches his way down achingly familiar streets that have not changed, his childhood house behind the holly hedge, the neighbors' rundown cottages, the route he took to school along Kelly Street and across the bridge. He sees the hill where he sledded in winter, the soaped runners so smooth on the wet grass that he could not brake but only throw himself to safety at the last second to avoid the barbed wire, the macrocarpas' scimitars. He floats like a wraith through Trimble's Bush, down Matai Street, past the municipal library whose books he has all read, Trigger's butcher's shop with its blood-stained block that even a wire brush cannot scrub clean, metal hooks through the feet of carcasses, flensed fat, streaky bacon, a pound of mince-meat please, and the Moabite Hotel where the men his father derides mix whiskey and milk and down beer chasers and bet on horses that never come in. Is he really weeping or is this a memory of tears, these images appearing only to disappear, Mick's hoard evacuated from where it has lain for years only to go the way of all flesh, his mother up to her elbows in flour, kneading bread, the road to the mill down which he moves as if invisible, cars slipping by without a sound, the unceasing tide of traffic on the road at night now segueing into the sound of rain on the mill's tin roof, the stench of creosote and damp sawdust, Jim Tuwhare watching him like a hawk. Will Jim say as he said so many times, "You're a chip off the old block, Gil, a chip off the old block"? It is as though he is moved by some ubiquitous and ethereal divin-ity, as indifferent to whether he exists as to the fate of those who have died, not caring whether a building stands for a hundred years or less, not even concerned for the white marble digger on the war memorial plinth, his put-tees like bandages, who looks down at the ground forever, mates drowned in Flanders mud, poppies of blood or body parts trodden underfoot, and the rhododendron that overshadows him shading the last survivors of another war, its branches unable to bear the weight of their loss.

POSTSCRIPT

Fathers and Sons is a creative reworking of a handful of facts that Gil O'Docherty (not his real name) shared with me in the course of a couple of conversations in North Queensland in 2017. Not only does my narrative leave many questions unanswered, such as whether Gil and Maya stayed together and whether the sins of our fathers are ever redeemed in the lives of our sons; it raises vexed ethical and epistemological questions concerning the relationship between fact and fiction.

Because Gil provided me with the skeleton of a story that I would flesh out in my imagination, I might be accused of betraying his trust, in the same way that anthropologists sometimes betray their interlocutors by presuming that their experiences only become intelligible when viewed through some social scientific lens.

It is my hope, however, that Gil and I are collaborators in a single story that interweaves episodes from his life, details from my father's recollections of a year his family spent in the Australian outback in 1913, and ethnographic observations from my fieldwork among the Kuku Yalanji.

The story is one thing. But the story of the story is another, and these metafictional reflections came to preoccupy me in the months after completing my book.

Ours are the afterlives of the dead. We live in the shadows of our forebears, and we risk repeating their mistakes even as we aspire to emulate their virtues. Whether we wish to or not, we often resemble them, mimic their mannerisms, reiterate their prejudices, and bear their burdens. Yet consciously we do everything in our power to give the impression that we are uniquely ourselves, voicing our own thoughts, determining our own destinies, and giving our children chances we never had.

In June 1977, Jacques Derrida is in Oxford, England. He happens on a postcard in the gift shop at the Bodleian Library—a reproduction of a thirteenth-century image from a book of fortune-telling texts, depicting Socrates and Plato with their roles reversed. Plato, whose beautifully written dialogues are our primary source for Socrates's life and thought, appears to be dictating to Socrates. Derrida is stunned. "I stopped dead, with a feeling of hallucination (is [the artist] crazy or what? he has the names mixed up) and of revelation at the same time, an apocalyptic revelation: Socrates writing, writing in front of Plato . . . the one who writes—seated, bent over, a scribe or docile copyist, Plato's secretary, no? He is in front of Plato, no, Plato is behind him, smaller (why smaller?), but standing up. With his outstretched finger he looks like he is indicating something, designating, showing the way or giving an order—or dictating, authoritarian, masterly, imperious."

Not only do certain physical traits run in families, but the preoccupations and ambitions of our forebears recur. Despite their elusive character, they haunt and influence us in more ways than we ever acknowledge. Perhaps this is why we attempt to second-guess our precursors or turn the tables on them by recounting their stories on our own terms, dictating to them rather than being dictated to.

Almost exactly forty years after Derrida's epiphany in the Bodleian, I visited Oxford to give some lectures and ethnographic workshops. The day after my arrival, several graduate students offered to take me on a guided tour of Oxford that would include a visit to the Bodleian. Of all the sights I saw, the one that affected me most was a seventeenth-century pub called the Eagle and Child where, I was told, an Oxford writer's group called the Inklings met from late 1933 throughout the 1940s. Of these writers, C. S. Lewis and J. R. R. Tolkien are the best remembered, and they were, apparently, close friends. Legend has it that the two writers were at loggerheads over the status of myth. Tolkien was a Catholic who, from early childhood, had been entranced by our human capacity for creating "myth-woven" and "elf-patterned" images, and attracted to "heroic legend on the brink of fairy-tale and history." While Lewis was also an aspiring poet, who shared Tolkien's enthusiasm for stories that touched on other worlds and recovered lost forms of human consciousness, he was an atheist.

The story I heard in Oxford about Lewis's conversion to Christianity would undoubtedly appeal to anyone whose conception of history and biography foregrounds life changing and irreversible events, like falling in love, being driven into exile, or suffering bereavement. According to this story,

Tolkien, Lewis, and "Hugo" Dyson were involved in an intense conversation on September 19, 1931, on Addison's Walk in the grounds of Magdalene College. Tolkien and Dyson held the view that though we are fallen creatures, we nevertheless retain from our divine origin a capacity, as "sub-creators," to create truth. Truth combines historical fact and imaginative insight. This thesis found expression in a long poem that Tolkien wrote to Lewis, who, by contrast with his friends, had opined "that myths were lies and therefore worthless, even though breathed through silver."

Within two weeks, Lewis came to believe that the God who had created the world had also entered it as an incarnate human being—in Lewis's words, that "Jesus Christ was the Son of God." For Lewis, this myth was true.

As with all stories, we are consoled that darkness is followed by light, time heals all wounds, losses are made good, sins are forgiven, and error is redeemed by truth. While such outcomes do occur, they rarely occur instantaneously or prove long lasting. A myriad of influences led to the moment of Lewis's conscious embrace of Christianity, including his brother's "conversion" the previous year, his readings of John Bunyan's confession, *Grace Abounding to the Chief of Sinners* (1666), and the Gospel of Saint John. Moreover, he already accepted the existence of God, though was not convinced, until his conversations with Tolkien in the spring of 1931, that a direct relationship between humans and God was possible.

Let me now return to the nature of our relationship with those in whose footsteps we tread. Did Plato create Socrates? Did God create human beings? Did Tolkien convert Lewis? Or did the latter bring the former into being? If history gives birth to myth, and myths to history, who is to say that one is true and the other false? Or that one always precedes the other? In the words of the inimitable Jorge Luis Borges, paraphrasing T. S. Eliot, "The word 'precursor' is indispensable in the vocabulary of criticism, but one should try to purify it from every connotation of polemic or rivalry. The fact is that each writer creates his precursors. His work modifies our conception of the past, as it will modify the future. In this correlation the identity or plurality of men matters not at all."

We like to think that the books under whose spell we fall, like the period of history into which we are born or the people who have the greatest influence over our lives, have an identity that is wholly independent of us, and this gives them power over us. In this view, Plato was simply the mouthpiece of Socrates, translating the master's oracular wisdom into print so that posterity would have the benefit of it. In the same vein, we might conclude that without the poetic arguments of Tolkien, Lewis would not have found his way to Christianity. These perspectives reflect the natural progression of the generations. The past brings the present into being in the same way that parents bring children into the world. But as Sartre observed, "what is important is not what people make of us but what we ourselves make of what they have made us."

There is always a reciprocal movement between the forces that shape our destinies and our responses to those forces. Insofar as we create our precursors, we are not wholly conditioned by them. They may shape us, but we in turn shape them, particularly when they are no longer living and cannot contradict or resist the meanings we assign them. Michael White speaks of this process as re-membering. We imaginatively reorganize the events and persons that have figured most prominently in our lives in much the same way as we reorganize the furniture in our homes to create a more convivial space. By implication, the self is not an autonomous unit, with a distinctive internal character and external appearance, but a part of a collectivity, a member of a family, lineage, or community that includes many other members. Re-membering "evokes the image of a person's life and identity as an association or a club. The membership of this association of life is made up of the significant figures of a person's history, as well as the identities of the person's present circumstances, whose voices are influential with regard to how the person constructs his or her own identity. Re-membering conversations provide[s] an opportunity for people to engage in a revision of the membership of their associations of life, affording an opening for the reconstruction of their identity." I like to think of Gil O'Docherty's marquetry boxes, the chronicles of the Barawa Marah, and my own prose narratives as ways in which the past is reimagined in order to make it bearable, and former lives re-membered so that new lives may be brought into being.

Notes

Preamble

Portions of this chapter previously appeared in *The Palm at the End of the Mind: Relatedness, Religiosity, and the Real* (Durham, NC: Duke University Press, 2009).

1 W. H. R. Rivers, "The Genealogical Method of Anthropological Inquiry," *Sociological Review* 3, no. 1 (1910): 1–12, 1.

2 J. M. Coetzee and Arabella Kurtz, *The Good Story: Exchanges on Truth, Fiction and Psychotherapy* (New York: Viking, 2015), 137; Pablo Neruda, *Memoirs*, trans. Hardie St. Martin (New York: Farrar, Straus and Giroux, 1977), 1.

3 Michael Jackson, *Barawa, and the Ways Birds Fly in the Sky* (Washington, DC: Smithsonian Institution Press, 1986).

4 Robert Desjarlais, *The Blind Man: A Phantasmography* (New York: Fordham University Press, 2019). In this book, a scholar-writer encounters a blind man outside the Sacré-Coeur Basilica in Paris, but is frustrated in his desire to enter into this man's subjective world. Gradually, the writer allows himself to speculate and guess who this man is, and to develop a theory of perception in which a recurring theme is the phantasmic character of human experience and the uncertain nature of intersubjective understanding.

5 David Shields, *Reality Hunger: A Manifesto* (New York: Knopf, 2010).

6 Anand Pandian and Stuart McLean, eds., *Crumpled Paper Boat: Experiments in Ethnographic Writing* (Durham, NC: Duke University Press, 2017), 16.

7 Michel Serres, *The Troubadour of Knowledge* (Anne Arbor: University of Michigan Press, 2003), 65. Cited in Pandian and Stuart, *Crumpled Paper Boat*, 20.

8 William Faulkner once ranked Thomas Wolfe ahead of his contemporaries because he had tried the hardest to do what Miguel de Cervantes and Fyodor Dostoevsky had done, "to put inside the covers of a book the complete turmoil and experience and insight of the human heart . . . to try to put all the experience of the human heart on the head of a pin." He loved best his own masterpiece, *The Sound and the Fury*, for the same reason, "that it was the most splendid failure." Frederick Gwynn, American Fiction class, University of Virginia, February 15, 1957, http://faulkner.lib.virginia.edu/display/wfaudio01_1. Hurt by Faulkner's remarks, Ernest Hemingway nonetheless

echoed them in his 1954 Nobel Prize acceptance speech: "For a true writer each book should be a new beginning where he tries again for something that is beyond attainment. He should always try for something that has never been done or that others have tried and failed." At the Nobel banquet in Stockholm, on December 10, 1954, Hemingway's speech was read by US ambassador John M. Cabot. Ernest Hemingway, "Banquet Speech," accessed September 11, 2020, https://www.nobelprize.org/prizes /literature/1954/hemingway/speech/.

CHRONICLES OF THE BARAWA MAWAH

Being-in-Time

1 Karl Marx, *The Eighteenth Brumaire of Louis Bonaparte* (Moscow: Progressive, 1984).
2 George Eliot, *Middlemarch: A Study of Provincial Life* (Peterborough, ON: Broadview, 2004), 640.
3 In his classic monograph, *The Nuer*, E. E. Evans-Pritchard used the term *structural time* for time measured by reference to the generations or the age-set system, and he coined the term *ecological time* for time measured by environmental or seasonal changes and the associated adjustments of social life to the needs of cattle herds. E. E. Evans-Pritchard, *The Nuer: A Description of the Modes of Livelihood and Political Institutions of a Nilotic People* (Oxford: Clarendon, 1940), 94.
4 Elizabeth Povinelli draws a useful distinction between genealogical and autological imaginaries, the first of which conceives of life as distributed throughout a collectivity, while the second concentrates on the life of an autonomous self. Povinelli, *The Empire of Love: Toward a Theory of Intimacy, Genealogy, and Carnality* (Durham, NC: Duke University Press, 2006).
5 For a complete account of Sewa's history, see Michael Jackson, *The Palm at the End of the Mind: Relatedness, Religiosity, and the Real* (Durham, NC: Duke University Press, 2009), 14–19.
6 Michael Serres with Bruno Latour, *Conversations on Science, Culture, and Time*, trans. Roxanne Lapidus (Ann Arbor: University of Michigan Press, 1995), 64, 70.
7 Bracha Ettinger stresses the maternal root of the word *matrix*, which is cognate with the words *womb, uterus,* and *woman* and also means "source" or "origin." Bracha Lichtenberg Ettinger, "Trans-subjective Transferential Borderspace," in *A Shock to Thought: Expression after Deleuze and Guattari*, ed. Brian Massumi (London: Routledge, 2000), 223.
8 René Devisch, *Weaving the Threads of Life: The Khita Gyn-eco-logical Healing Cult among the Yaka* (Chicago: University of Chicago Press, 1993), 115.
9 Meyer Fortes, *The Web of Kinship among the Tallensi* (London: Oxford University Press, 1949), 239.
10 Claude Lévi-Strauss, *Structural Anthropology*, vol. 1, trans. Claire Jacobson and Brooke Grundfest Schoepf (New York: Basic Books, 1967), 72, 46.

Being of Two Minds

1 Cited by Elizabeth Luther Cary, "Conservative French Art," in *Art and Progress* (Washington, DC: American Federation of Arts, c. 1915), 413–20, 415.

Koinadugu

1 At the very moment when I was coming to terms with this vital interdependency of power and knowledge, Michel Foucault was formulating in Paris what would become one of his seminal contributions to our understanding of the pouvoir-savoir relationship. Michael Foucault, *Surveiller et punir: Naissance de la prison* (Paris: Gallimard, 1975).
2 For a comprehensive account of these mythological connections, see Michael Jackson, "The Migration of a Name: Alexander in Africa," in *Paths toward a Clearing: Radical Empiricism and Ethnographic Inquiry* (Bloomington: Indiana University Press, 1989), 156–69.

Albitaiya

Portions of this chapter previously appeared in *In Sierra Leone* (Durham, NC: Duke University Press, 2004).

1 J. K. Trotter, "An Expedition to the Source of the Niger," *Geographical Journal* 10, no. 3 (September 1897): 237–59, 251.

Primus inter Pares

1 Claude Lévi-Strauss, *Totemism*, trans. Rodney Needham (Boston: Beacon, 1963), 77, 89.
2 Jean-Paul Sartre, *Saint Genet: Actor and Martyr*, trans. Bernard Frechtman (New York: George Braziller, 1963), 49.

Lifelines and Lineages

1 Povinelli, *The Empire of Love*, 4.
2 Laura Bohannan, "Political Aspects of Tiv Social Organization," in *Tribes without Rulers*, ed. John Middleton and David Tait (London: Routledge and Kegan Paul, 1970), 33–66, 37.
3 Bohannan, "Political Aspects of Tiv Social Organization," 38.
4 Michael Jackson, *Allegories of the Wilderness: Ethics and Ambiguity in Kuranko Narratives* (Bloomington: Indiana University Press, 1982), 16–17.
5 Michael Jackson, "Sacrifice and Social Structure among the Kuranko," *Africa* 47, nos. 1–2 (1977): 41–49, 123–39, 132.
6 Michael Jackson, *The Kuranko: Dimensions of Social Reality in a West African Society* (London: Hurst, 1977), 68.

7 Fortes, *The Web of Kinship among the Tallensi*, 10.

8 Evans-Pritchard, *The Nuer*, 202.

9 Cited by John Berger, *Pig Earth* (London: Writers and Readers Publishing Cooperative, 1979), 6.

10 Berger, *Pig Earth*, 9.

Prospero and Caliban

In the chapter title, I allude not to Shakespeare's *The Tempest* but to Octave Mannoni's study of the psychology of the unequal power relationship between colonizer and colonized, and by extension between anthropologist and key informant. Octave Mannoni, *Prospero and Caliban: The Psychology of Colonialization* (Ann Arbor: University of Michigan Press, 1990).

1 Victor Turner, *The Forest of Symbols: Aspects of Ndembu Ritual* (Ithaca, NY: Cornell University Press, 1967), 139, 150.

Tina Komé

Portions of this chapter previously appeared in *In Sierra Leone* (Durham, NC: Duke University Press, 2004).

1 Eliot, *Middlemarch*, epigraph to chapter 4.

2 Ranajit Guha, *Dominance without Hegemony: History and Power in Colonial India* (Cambridge, MA: Harvard University Press, 1997), 20–21.

3 It is customary for personal names to be recycled every other generation, thus preserving the illusion of eternal recurrence. For most Europeans and Americans, individuals who inherit family names are often distinguished by the suffix Senior or Junior, or a number (I, II, III), but in Africa it is not the continuity of a personality but the perpetuity of the lineage that is celebrated. Accordingly, when an individual succeeds in life it will be his family that is praised, since without the blessings of his forebears and the efforts of his parents, he would have achieved little in life.

Abdul's Reminiscences

Portions of this chapter previously appeared in *Life within Limits: Well-Being in a World of Want* (Durham, NC: Duke University Press, 2011).

1 Fortes, *The Web of Kinship among the Tallensi*, 224–27.

2 Abdul may have been thinking of the disastrous fire on January 14, 1986, in which 150 houses in Firawa burned to the ground.

3 Meyer Fortes, "The First Born," in *Religion, Morality and the Person: Essays on Tallensi Religion*, ed. Jack Goody (Cambridge: Cambridge University Press, 1987), 218–46, 234.

4 The principle is beautifully captured in the Tibetan Buddhist notion that "dying does not mean dying; dying means moving" (i.e., a shift or transfer into a new life that

is, however, never an exact repetition or recapitulation of a previous incarnation). Robert Desjarlais, *Sensory Biographies: Lives and Deaths among Nepal's Yolmo Buddhists* (Berkeley: University of California Press, 2003), 275.

5 Children who die before weaning are buried in the rubbish heap area (*sundu kunye ma*) behind the house. Often slivers of stick are inserted under a fingernail so that the child will be recognized if it is reincarnated. And, of course, names are recycled, so that, for example, Tina Komé's firstborn son Kulifa inherited his paternal grandfather's name, which means, literally, leopard slayer.

Limitrophes

1 For a comprehensive study of the leitmotif of lameness and limping in Kuranko stories and comparative myth, see Michael Jackson, "Prevented Successions: A Commentary upon a Kuranko Narrative," in *Fantasy and Symbol: Essays in Honour of George Devereux*, ed. R. H. Hook (London: Academic Press, 1979), 95–131.

Noah's Story

1 These sisters were not children of Sanfan Aisetta but of other wives of Tina Komé, which is why they treated Noah somewhat disdainfully.

2 Jean-Paul Sartre, *Itinerary of a Thought: Between Existentialism and Marxism* (London: Verso, 1983), 42.

3 Jean-Paul Sartre, *The Family Idiot: Gustave Flaubert, 1821–1857*, vol. 2, trans, Carol Cosman (Chicago: University of Chicago Press, 1987), 174.

Taking Stock

1 Simon Nathan, "Conservation: A history: Māori Conservation Traditions," *Te Ara: The Encyclopedia of New Zealand*, July 7, 2020, http://www.TeAra.govt.nz/en/whakapapa/13900/whakapapa.

2 Hannah Arendt, *The Human Condition* (Chicago: University of Chicago Press, 1958), 184.

3 Kenelm Burridge, *Tangu Traditions* (Oxford: Clarendon, 1969), 114; Gregory Bateson, *Naven* (Stanford, CA: Stanford University Press, 1958), 243.

4 Apirana Mahuika's genealogical knowledge is abundantly evident in his published work, notably "Leadership: Inherited and Achieved," in *Te Ao Hurihuri: The World Moves On* (Wellington: Hicks Smith, 1975), 86–113.

5 Ernest Gellner, *Thought and Change* (London: Weidenfeld and Nicolson, 1964), 1.

6 Gil Herdt, *Human Sexuality: Self, Society, and Culture* (New York: McGraw Hill, 1984).

7 The Ashanti "believe that a human being is formed from the blood of the mother and the spirit of the father." K. A. Busia, "The Ashanti," in *African Worlds: Studies in the Cosmological Ideas and Social Values of African Peoples*, ed. Daryll Forde (London: Oxford University Press, 1954), 190–209, 197.

8   On the symbolic contrast and affective contradictions between "blood" and "money" in American kinship, see David M. Schneider, *American Kinship: A Cultural Account* (Chicago: University of Chicago Press, 1968).

9   Jack Goody, *Death, Property, and the Ancestors: A Study of the Mortuary Customs of the LoDagaa of West Africa* (London: Tavistock, 1962).

10 The Māori notion of whakapapa is "the process of laying one thing upon another. If you visualise the foundation ancestors as the first generation, the next and succeeding ancestors are placed on them in ordered layers." Sir Apirana T. Ngata, *Rauru-nui-ā-Toi Lectures and Ngati Kahungunu Origin* (Wellington: Victoria University Press, 1972), 6.

11 This principle is nicely captured in Robert Desjarlais's description of a Yolmo lama called Chabahil Mbeme "who had lived a distinct life, one that would end with his death. That personal life could be portrayed in a 'life story' inscribed on paper—he did this, he said that. But the subject of that biography would himself hold that it would be a mistake to consider his life as an entity unto itself, of a singular duration that began with his body's birth and ended with its death. For one thing, the lama knew his present life to be but one link in a chain of lives. Consequently, he and others understood his existence in terms of a continuity of lives, with the strands of action that coursed through his present life partly the result of karmic deeds enacted in previous lives of his and partly the cause of action in any future lives of his." Desjarlais, *Sensory Biographies*, 53.

12 Meyer Fortes, *Oedipus and Job in West African Religion* (Cambridge: Cambridge University Press, 1959).

13 Annette B. Weiner, *Women of Value, Men of Renown: New Perspectives in Trobriand Exchange* (Austin: University of Texas Press, 1976).

14 Desjarlais, *Sensory Biographies*, 52.

15 A compelling image of genealogical time is provided by the Mormon marriage ceremony known as sealing. Tall parallel mirrors line either side of the sealing room. Because the mirrors are parallel, they reflect off each other, so that when the bride and groom look into either mirror, they look into eternity. The eternity represented by one mirror symbolizes the many ancestors that preceded the Mormon couple, and the eternity represented by the other mirror symbolizes their many descendants. Sealing binds not only wife and husband, but also children and parents. Thus sealings are a way of linking all the human generations together as one. These infinite human generations are represented by the infinities of the two mirrors.

16 On how myths are passed down and owned by families, see Michael W. Young, *Magicians of Manumanua: Living Myth in Kalauna* (Berkeley: University of California Press, 1983).

17 The Nuer "do not present [lineages] the way we figure them . . . as a series of bifurcations of descent, as a tree of descent, or as a series of triangles of ascent, but as a number of lines running at angles from a common point. . . . They see [the system] as actual relations between groups of kinsmen within local communities rather than as a tree of descent, for the persons after whom the lineages are called do not all proceed from a single individual." Evans-Pritchard, *The Nuer*, 202. See also Tim Ingold's illuminating work on genealogical lines; Ingold, *Lines* (London: Routledge, 2016), 107–22.

18 Ernest Young, "The Anglo-Saxon Family Law," in *Essays in Anglo-Saxon Law* (Boston: Little, Brown, 1905), 121–82, 127–30.

19 Piers Vitebsky, *Living without the Dead: Loss and Redemption in a Jungle Cosmos* (Chicago: University of Chicago Press, 2017), 1.

20 The Sora conversion from a focus on the dead to a focus on the (Baptist) Christian God provides a compelling example of the way that vital relationships can be radically reconceptualized for both existential and practical purposes. Vitebsky, *Living without the Dead*, 27–29.

S. B.'s Story

Portions of this chapter previously appeared in *In Sierra Leone* (Durham, NC: Duke University Press, 2004).

1 See Charles Piot's trenchant critique of colonial-era West Africanist anthropology in *Remotely Global: Village Modernity in West Africa* (Chicago: University of Chicago Press, 1990), 1–26.

2 Given S. B.'s notorious relationship with the police, one wonders whether the traumatic childhood event affected him as deeply as a similar incident in Alfred Hitchcock's childhood. When the great director was six, his father decided on a rather severe punishment for a minor offense. The young Hitchcock was sent to the local police station with a note instructing the officer on duty to put the lad in jail. A terrified Hitchcock was locked away for five minutes, though he was not told how long his confinement would last. Later in life he told his biographer that he would go to any length to avoid arrest and confinement.

After the War

Portions of this chapter previously appeared in *In Sierra Leone* (Durham, NC: Duke University Press, 2004).

1 There is a certain poetic irony that I would suffer exactly the same loss of vision as Noah, complete in one eye, partial in the other, though from a different cause.

Within These Four Walls

Portions of this chapter previously appeared in *In Sierra Leone* (Durham, NC: Duke University Press, 2004).

1 Max Gluckman, *Custom and Conflict in Africa* (Oxford: Blackwell, 1955).

Relationship and Relativity

Portions of this chapter previously appeared in *Existential Anthropology: Events, Exigencies and Effects* (New York: Berghahn, 2005).

1 Lawrence Durrell, *Balthazar* (New York: Penguin, 1991), 15.

2 As Hannah Arendt puts it, "The story that an act starts is composed of its conse-
quent deeds and sufferings," and these "are boundless, because action, though it may
proceed from nowhere, so to speak, acts in a medium where every reaction becomes
a chain reaction and where every process is the cause of new processes" (*The Human
Condition*, 190).

3 Regina Thomas, "Frankly Speaking," *Concord Times*, January 8, 2003.

Endings

Portions of this chapter previously appeared in *Life within Limits: Well-being in a World
of Want* (Durham, NC: Duke University Press, 2011).

1 Emmanuel Levinas, "Ethics of the Infinite," in *Debates in Continental Philosophy:
Conversations with Contemporary Thinkers*, ed. Richard Kearney (New York: Fordham
University Press, 2004), 65–84, 75.

2 Michael would remember this sequence rather differently, writing to me in 2018
that he completed his primary education at St. Edward's School in Freetown, then
returned to Bo for his secondary education at King's College, where Kaimah found
him during his first year there and took him back to Freetown, where he completed his
secondary schooling at St. Edward's.

3 A week after Kaimah's death, I received a second email from Kaimah's sister Jeneba
that confirmed many of the suspicions that Kaimah had confided to me in Freetown four years before. "I am sure u know that me and daddy r from the same
mother and father, and we r only two, all the rest r just the same dad, now that
he is gone I am all alone, but I have Michael, so I want to see the best for him, so
that his daddy will be happy where ever he is." As for her half siblings, "I don't
trust them any more," Jeneba wrote, suggesting that clandestine malice had been
responsible for Kaimah's illness and death. She invited me to review Facebook
photos of him, as if these were evidence of the kind of wasting diseases associated
with witchcraft and sorcery. "If u go through my pictures u will see him. I know
what I am talking about, and b4 he died he told Michael not to go to the family
house any more."

Only Connect

1 On money-doubling schemes, see Michael Bürge, "Money Doubling in Sierra Leone,"
Social Anthropology 27, no. 3 (2019); Michael Marah, personal (email) communication,
September 25, 2019.

2 Georg Simmel, *The Philosophy of Money*, 3rd enlarged ed., trans. Tom Bottomore and
David Frisby (London: Routledge, 2004), 128–29.

3 Stan Grant, *On Identity* (Carlton, VIC: Melbourne University Press, 2019), 1, 3.

Transition

1 Kuranko refer to the umbilical cord as *bara yile* (the maternal cord/rope). Only when the umbilical stump has dried is the child said to have passed from the spirit to the earthly world.

2 René Devisch and Claude Brodeur, *The Law of the Lifegivers: The Domestication of Desire* (Amsterdam: Harwood, 1999), 51.

3 Devisch and Brodeur, *The Law of the Lifegivers*, 54.

4 R. B. Onians, *The Origins of European Thought* (Cambridge: Cambridge University Press, 1951), 331.

5 Onians, *The Origins of European Thought*, 336.

6 Onians, *The Origins of European Thought*, 381.

7 Onians, *The Origins of European Thought*, 356.

8 The Latin term *necesse* is related to *necto* and *nexus*, and refers originally to binding or being bound. While there is no obvious relation between necessity and kinship, "both have a natural point of contact in binding which implies not only constraint but also union and proximity." Onians cites, in this regard, the Sanscrit *bándhu-h*, "kinsman," and the widespread idea that kinship ties are given in nature and cannot be changed (*The Origins of European Thought*, 333).

9 George Santayana, *The Life of Reason*, vol. 1 (New York: Scribner's, 1905), ch. 12.

10 Meyer Fortes, *Oedipus and Job in West African Religion* (Cambridge: Cambridge University Press, 1959), 19–26.

11 Shannon Perry, "The Other in Us: Anthropology, Genealogy and Kinship in the 21st Century," in *Anthropologies: A Collaborative Online Project*, April 1, 2012, http://www .anthropologiesproject.org/2012/04/other-in-us-anthropology-genealogy-and.html.

12 Tine M. Gammeltoft, *Haunting Images: A Cultural Account of Selective Reproduction in Vietnam* (Berkeley: University of California Press, 2014), 160, 136.

13 Mette Nordahl Svendsen, "Pursuing Knowledge about a Genetic Risk of Cancer," in *Managing Uncertainty: Ethnographic Studies of Illness, Risk and the Struggle for Control*, ed. Richard Jenkins, Hanne Jensen, and Vibeke Steffen (Copenhagen: Museum Tusculanum Press, 2005), 93–121. On the effects of Agent Orange in Vietnam, see Gammeltoft, *Haunting Images*. See also Adriana Petryna, *Life Exposed: Biological Citizens after Chernobyl* (Princeton, NJ: Princeton University Press, 2013).

14 Sociological explanations are often as fatalistic as biogenetic ones. It could be argued, for instance, that Sierra Leone has never recovered from colonial rule, during which the country's resources were plundered and its people disempowered. Or one might point out that dictators and patrimonial regimes have borrowed so heavily from the International Monetary Fund that the wealth of the country now goes toward servicing this debt rather than providing basic social services, hence the plight of Kaimah and his son, Michael.

15 Edward Fitzgerald, *The Rubáiyát of Omar Khayyam*, trans. Edward Fitzgerald (London, 1859).

16 Thomas Wolfe, *Look Homeward, Angel* (New York: Scribner's, 1957), 5.

I

167 · In the country of the Eastern Kuku-Yalanji—based on Maureen Kozicka, *The Mysteries of Black Mountain* (Cairns, QLD: G. K. Bolton Imprint, 1988), 18–21.

171 · "The chemical necklace of DNA that wraps around the neck"—A. M. Homes, *The Mistress's Daughter* (New York: Penguin, 2007), 7.

176 · "In every departure, deep down and tiny, like a black seed"—Damon Galgut, *In a Strange Room: Three Journeys* (New York: Europa Editions, 2010), 40, 105.

190 · "Devoid of passion, either for a thing, a person, or an idea"—Paul Auster, *The Invention of Solitude* (New York: Penguin, 1988), 7.

191–205 · For insights into and detailed information on tin mining, ranching, and homesteading in North Queensland during the 1930s, I have drawn on the following books: W. Mason and M. Mason, *Kurangee: Cape Tribulation Pioneers* (Mareeba, NQ: Pinevale, 1993); M. Mason, *Living in the Rainforest* (Ingham, NQ: self-published, 1996); and Glenville Pike, *Around the Campfire: An Anthropology* (Mareeba, NQ: Pinevale, 1990).

206 · "Blimmin shot through"—In Australian vernacular, "shot through" implies the abandonment of a spouse or child for whom one was responsible.

207 · "She got kura for that Archie bloke, that's what's eating him"—W. E. Roth, *The Queensland Aborigines*, vol. 2, containing Bulletins 1–8, "North Queensland Ethnography," 1901–1908 (originally published, Brisbane: Government Printer, 1901), republished in a facsimile edition (Carlisle, AU-WA: Hesperian Press, 1984), 23.

208 · It seemed that Archie's ambition had got the better of him—Adapted from Ion Idriess, *The Wild North* (Sydney: Angus and Roberston, 1967), 120–28.

II

249 · For now we see through a glass, darkly—1 Corinthians 13:12.

249 · "He wanted to start out with the blessings of his family"—Saul Bellow, *Seize the Day* (New York: Viking, 1956), 99.

249 · "It was quite an eerie feeling to be recognizing traits in myself from a dead man"—Alan Cumming, *Not My Father's Son: A Memoir* (New York: HarperCollins, 2014), 28.

III

253 · "He had dreamed of coming ashore at night"—Jorge Luis Borges, "The Circular Ruins," trans. James E. Irby, in *Labyrinths* (Harmondsworth, UK: Penguin, 1970), 72–73. The idea of a split between the person who lives and the person who writes intrigued

Borges, who asserted in a brief essay titled "Borges and I" that "I live, let myself go on living, so that Borges may contrive his literature, and this literature justifies me." The last line of the essay states, "I do not know which of us has written this page" (*Labyrinths*, 282–83).

257 · "What do bunyips look like?"—Jenny Wagner, *The Bunyip of Berkeley's Creek* (Sydney: Puffin, 1980).

Postscript

288 · Details from my father's recollections—For a brief account of my father's family's sojourn in a remote outback station in New South Wales, Australia, in 1913–14, see Milton von Damm, *The New Zealand Connection* (Berkeley, CA: Minute Man Press, 2015), 12–14. Also see Eileen Winifrid von Damm (née Jackson), "A Children's Story," in *The New Zealand Connection*, ed. Milton von Damm (Berkeley: Minute Man Press, 2015), 38–45. My own fieldwork among the Kuku Yalanji of southeast Cape York was carried out in 1993–94 and in 1997 in collaboration with Francine Lorimer.

289 · "I stopped dead, with a feeling of hallucination (is [the artist] crazy or what)"—Jacques Derrida, *The Post Card: From Socrates to Freud and Beyond*, trans. Alan Bass (Chicago: University of Chicago Press, 1987), 9–10.

289 · Creating "myth-woven" and "elf-patterned" images—Colin Duriez, *The Oxford Inklings: Lewis, Tolkien and Their Circle* (Oxford: Lion Hudson, 2015), 82.

290 · "Myths were lies and therefore worthless, even though breathed through silver"—C. S. Lewis to J. R. R. Tolkien. In his poem "Mythopoeia," Tolkien creates an imaginary dialogue between Philomythus ("lover of myth," i.e., Tolkien) who attempts to persuade Misomythus ("hater of myth," i.e., Lewis) not to see the world materialistically, but in the light of religion and myth. Duriez, *The Oxford Inklings*, 119.

290 · Within two weeks, Lewis came to believe—Duriez, *The Oxford Inklings*, 120–21.

290 · Paraphrasing T. S. Eliot—T. S. Eliot, *Points of View* (London: Faber and Faber, 1941), 25–26.

290 · "The word 'precursor' is indispensable in the vocabulary of criticism"—Jorge Luis Borges, *Other Inquisitions, 1937–1952*, trans. Ruth L. C. Simms (New York: Simon and Schuster, 1964), 108.

291 · "What is important is not what people make of us"—Jean-Paul Sartre, *Saint Genet: Actor and Martyr*, trans. Bernard Frechtman (New York: Braziller, 1963), 49.

291 · Michael White speaks of this process as re-membering—Michael White, *Maps of Narrative Practice* (New York: Norton, 2007), 136. White is indebted to Barbara Myerhoff for this notion of re-membering as "quite different from the passive, continuous fragmentary flickerings of images and feelings that accompany other activities in the normal flow of consciousness." Barbara Myerhoff, "Life History among the Elderly: Performance, Visibility, and Remembering," in *A Crack in the Mirror: Reflexive Perspective in Anthropology*, ed. J. Ruby (Philadelphia: University of Pennsylvania Press, 1982), 99–117, 111.

Index

Gammeltoft, Tine, 160

Gellner, Ernest, 92

genealogical imaginary, 8

genealogical knowledge, 31, 90–91, 134

genealogical time, 7, 161; affective and psychophysical aspects of living in, 47; ancestors
and, 92; in Global North, 159–60; lineages
and, 8–9, 92; M. N. Marah and, 142; names
and years in, 104; as recurrence of five generations, 92; whakapapa and, 9

genealogy: being-in-the-world and, 9;
being-in-time and, 1; children of Nazis
and, 158–59; continuity over individual
longevity, 150–51; in Firawa, 95; as generation, 30; imagining, 92; indigenous people
and traditional lands, 91; kinship and,
90; Kuranko and, 92; method of, systems
in, 1; modern, business of, 159; ontology,
relationships and, 90, 93; relationships and,
90–93; social order and, 91; theology and,
91, 153; traditional anthropological view, 1;
whakapapa, 9, 89–91

generations: death and, 92; filial and paternal,
69; genealogy as, 30; names and, 296n3; time,
relationships and, 12

Gluckman, Max, 117

God: Allah, 71, 75; as chief, 70–71; Christianity
and, 290; as Dale Mansa, 71; Islamic, 71; M. N.
Marah on, 153; relationships with forebears
and, 94

Godfather, Ibrahim, 145

Goering, Bettina, 159

Grace Abounding to the Chief of Sinners (Bunyan), 290

grandparents and grandchildren, 12

Greene, Graham, 15, 18–19

Guha, Ranajit, 57

Guyan, Alex, 15–17, 19

health and well-being, Yaka on, 11

Hemingway, Ernest, 293n8

hereditary power, 42, 133

Herodotus, 160

hierarchies, 42, 44, 87

history, justice and, 160

Hitchcock, Alfred, 299n2

Hitler, Adolf, 158

Hitler, William Patrick, 158

Hitler's Children (2011; documentary), 158–59

Hoess, Rainer, 159

Homer, 7

hospitality, 26–27

human interconnectedness, 92

Iatmul, 90

identity: difference and, 98; names and, 152;
re-membering, 291

imagination, 4

interconnectedness, 92

interlocutors: anthropologists and, 288; ethnographers and, 35; Kuranko, 2, 157

Internal Security Unit (ISU), 117

intersubjectivity, 2–3, 30, 47, 63, 157

Islam, 37, 69; conversion to, 32; djinn and, 71, 75,
88; Kuranko and, 32, 71, 75, 92; Marah and,
31–32

Jackson, Pauline, 13–22, 25, 41–42, 52, 78, 89, 95,
107, 119

Jalloh, Foday (chief), 142

James, William, 8–9

Johns, Christopher E. F., 127–30

justice, history and, 160

Kabala, 21, 23, 25–26, 35, 41–42; Albitaiya and,
36; British administration in, 57–59; Kaimah
Marah on, 138; S. B. Marah and, 103–5;
poverty of, 138

Kabala election, 2003: interference and violence,
122–32; Johns's report on, 127–30; Ali Marah
and, 123–32; Balansama Marah and, 127,
130–31; S. B. Marah and, 123–32; police and,
124–32

Kabba, Tejan, 111, 127

Kallon, Mohamed, 150

Kamara-Taylor, C. A., 117

Kamato, 33–34

Kandé, Fore, 97

Kawharu, Hugh, 89

kebile, 28–29

Marah, Alhaji Fatmata Balansama, 124, 128

Marah, Ali, 7; Kabala election of 2003, 123–32; Balansama Marah, as father of, 127; N. B. Marah on, 127, 133; S. B. Marah and, 119–20, 123–27, 129–32

Marah, Balansama, 33–35, 61, 127, 130–31

Marah, Bol' Tamba, 36–37, 98

Marah, Damba Lai (chief), 74

Marah, Isata, 137–38

Marah, Jeneba, 138, 141–42, 152–53

Marah, Kaimah: death of, 137–38, 142, 300n3; death of mother, 149; education of, 135–36, 138–41; in Freetown, 136, 146; on Kallon, 150; M. N. Marah and, 139–42, 146, 300nn2–3; N. B. Marah as father of, 135–36, 138–41, 144, 152; S. B. Marah and, 143–44, 149; Tina Komé Marah and, 140–41, 143; on occult powers and witchcraft, 147–48; poem by, 138; on religious practices in Sierra Leone, 144–47; sickness of, 141–42; Sierra Leone and, 136–40, 144–46, 150; Sierra Leone civil war and, 139–40

Marah, Kulifa, 63–66, 68–69, 73, 100, 102–3, 136, 297n5

Marah, Manti Kamara Kulifa, 38–39, 44, 56, 58, 63

Marah, Marin Tamba, 32

Marah, Michael Noah, 137, 159; education of, 142, 152–53; genealogical time and, 142; kinship and, 153; Kaimah Marah and, 139–42, 146, 300nn2–3

Marah, Mohammed Fasilie, 123

Marah, Noah Bockarie, 7, 23–26, 41–42; Albitaiya and, 38; in Bambatuk, 79, 83–84; in Bandakarafaia, 75–76; on Barawa chieftaincy, 30–31; death of, 135, 138; djinn and, 24, 71, 73; education of, 140–41; in Firawa, 72, 95; on *fo' koe*, 47; in Freetown, 52–55, 87, 100, 108–9; on hospitality, 26–27; M. K. Kulifa and, 44; Kuranko and, 23–24, 26, 45, 74, 81–82, 88; life story of, 63; Mammy Kasan and, 79–84; Abdul Marah and, 27–28; Ai Marah, sister of, 81–84; Aisetta Marah, mother of, 73; Ali Marah and, 127, 133; Kaimah Marah, son of, 135–36, 138–41, 144, 152; S. B. Marah and, 64, 79, 85–88, 97, 107–8, 110, 133, 140–41, 150; Tina

Komé Marah, father of, 56–57, 79, 82, 84–85; Marah clan and, 24–25, 29; mother and father of, 29–30; on paranormal gifts, 110; on political office, 88; sense of time and, 45–46; on "Tell Laura I Love Her," 51–52; Yandi and, 80–81, 84

Marah, Pore Bolo, 61, 66, 101

Marah, Sewa (S. B.), 7–9, 27, 32, 37–39, 54–56, 61–65, 95–96; attacks on house of, 125–29, 131; Balacun and, 126–27; Barawa and, 104–5, 111, 143–44; death of, 135; in Firawa, 103, 143–44; on M. Forna, 87, 112, 115; in Freetown, 99–102, 119–21, 123, 126, 132; Freetown police and, 127–28; Johns's report and, 127–29; Kabala and, 103–5; Kabala election of 2003, 123–32; Kuranko and, 101, 105–6, 131, 133; life story, 100–106, 111–17; Ali Marah and, 119–20, 123–27, 129–32; Kaimah Marah and, 143–44, 149; Kulifa Marah and, 100, 102–3, 136; N. B. Marah and, 64, 79, 85–88, 97, 107–8, 110, 133, 140–41, 150; Tina Komé Marah and, 143–44; in Parliament, 104–5, 111, 120–21, 123–24; as political prisoner, 111–17, 157

Marah, Tala Sewa (chief), 26, 29–30, 95–96

Marah, Tina Dondon, 57–58

Marah, Tina Kaima, 56–59, 66, 101

Marah, Tina Komé, 32, 39, 56–69, 100–101; Barawa and, 61–62, 66–68; in Firawa, 64, 66; in Freetown, 57; Kuranko and, 62; literacy of, 66; Abdul Marah on, 66–67, 69–70; Kaimah Marah and, 140–41, 143; Kulifa Marah and, 297n5; N. B. Marah and, 56–57, 79, 82, 84–85; S. B. Marah and, 143–44; Tina Kaima Marah and, 56–59, 66, 101

Marah, Yandi, 80–81, 84

Maran Lai Bockari, 37

Margai, Albert, 86, 117, 132

Margai, Milton, 97

Marx, Karl, 7

Massaquoi, Fatamata (Lango), 139–40, 149

McLean, Stuart, 3–4

Melville, Herman, 19

Mende, 21

Middlemarch (Eliot), 8

migration, 9–10

www.ingramcontent.com/pod-product-compliance
Lightning Source LLC
Chambersburg PA
CBHW071731270326
41928CB00013B/2640